History of Europe
since 1815

the text of this book is printed
on 100% recycled paper

COLLEGE OUTLINE SERIES

History of Europe since 1815

Twenty-first Edition

HENRY W. LITTLEFIELD

BARNES & NOBLE BOOKS

A DIVISION OF HARPER & ROW, PUBLISHERS

New York, Hagerstown, San Francisco, London

The Author

Henry W. Littlefield is President of the University of Bridgeport, Connecticut. He received the degrees of B.S. and M.A. at New York University and the degree of Ph.D. at Yale University. He has honorary doctor's degrees from Bates College, Tufts University, Fairfield University, and Salem College. He has been a visiting professor in the field of social sciences at the University of Maryland and has contributed to the development of programs of higher education in Connecticut, serving on the staff of New Haven College and the Connecticut State Department of Education. Since 1962 he has served as a vice president of the Dana Foundation. He has held many positions of leadership in professional associations and organizations and has served as president of the American Association of Junior Colleges and of the Connecticut Council of Higher Education. He has also been a director of various educational agencies, such as the National Commission on Accrediting, the Learning Resources Institute, and the Museum of Arts, Sciences and Industry. Dr. Littlefield is the author of another College Outline, *History of Europe, 1500-1848*.

Preface

This outline of European history is a tool by which the student can review and coördinate the essential facts, and can construct in his mind a framework into which he can fit the fruits of further study.

Although not intended as a short-cut to, or substitute for, the extensive reading of textbook and collateral material through which alone history can be learned, it is designed to meet a need unfilled either by the detailed textbook or by the skeleton syllabus. In its nineteen previous editions this volume has provided: (a) a convenient manual for daily reference and review, with concisely digested and clearly organized factual material, functional maps, selected bibliographies, a chronological summary, and other essential reference aids; (b) a practical handbook for the multiple-text courses now given so successfully in many universities, courses in which the instructor makes assignments in a wide range of historical literature; (c) an organized compendium of political and social history to accompany histories of Western civilization; (d) an up-to-date supplement to any less recent textbook; and (e) a comprehensive digest for literature courses or any study needing a concise treatment of historical background.

In this, the twenty-first edition, the *History of Europe,* which originally appeared in 1932, has been revised and brought up to the present. The new material in it takes into account the changed perspective of contemporary history following World War II, particularly in regard to global relations. All features which have commended earlier editions to students have been retained. As before, this volume overlaps its companion volume, *History of Europe, 1500-1848,* in order to embrace various beginning periods and be readily adaptable to any of the leading college texts in modern European history.

Throughout the book, stress has been laid on the social and economic undercurrents that relate the nineteenth century so closely to the twentieth.

Acknowledgments

In the preparation of earlier editions of the *New Outline-History of Europe,* the author has been assisted by the helpful criticisms of many college instructors and students who have volunteered valuable suggestions for improving previous editions. Obligations to all of these cannot, for lack of space, be specifically acknowledged here, but for generous aid especial gratitude must be expressed to Mr. John Collins for his original research work and aid in the writing of the entire manuscript. The author is also indebted to Professor Bailey W. Diffie of the College of the City of New York for his painstaking reading and criticism of the galley proofs, and to Miss Ella Wood of the English Department in Hamden, Connecticut, for her minute checking of the manuscript for consistency in punctuation and rhetoric. A special word of appreciation is due to Mr. Edward Fitzgerald, formerly Director of the Art Department of Barnes & Noble, Inc., who contributed materially to the value of earlier editions by his extensive research and skillful execution of the series of excellent functional maps.

Table of Contents

xi

Table of Contents

Maps

Significant Dates

Arkwright's Water Frame . 1769
Whitney's Cotton Gin . . . 1793
Fulton's Steam Boat . . . 1807
Morse's Telegraph 1837
Bell's Telephone 1876
Marconi's Wireless 1896

CHAPTER I.

THE INDUSTRIAL REVOLUTION

The Industrial Revolution, a movement the early phases of which took place in England between 1770 and 1825 and in continental Europe after 1815, changed fundamentally the industrial, commercial, political, and social life of the western world. It consisted mainly in the application of machinery to manufacturing, mining, transportation, communication, and agriculture, and in the changes in economic organization that attended these innovations of methods. The large scale and basic nature of the changes introduced in a period of about sixty years justifies the term "revolution," although the scientific and economic background extends for centuries into the past, and the movement is still going forward at a rate perhaps greater today than ever before.

BACKGROUND OF INDUSTRIAL REVOLUTION

Agriculture. In the middle of the eighteenth century the customs of economic life were little different from those of the Middle Ages. In agriculture the inefficient "open-field" system prevailed. Each peasant cultivated a number of small separated strips of land, into which the large arable fields were divided, and grazed his live stock on the "common" or uncultivated pasture land that was free to all. Fertilization of soil, rotation of crops, and controlled breeding of live stock were unknown. One third of the cultivated land lay fallow every year. Crop yields were poor. The communal organization made innovations of method difficult.

Manufacturing. Etymologically the word "manufacture" means "make by hand." Handicraft was the only method of production. Because it supplied a basic human need, the textile industry dwarfed all others in importance. The making of thread from raw wool and later from cotton (spinning) and the making of cloth from thread (weaving) were the two chief processes of textile manufacture. In the eighteenth century the industry was carried on chiefly in the home with simple hand tools (spinning wheel, hand-loom) requiring little outlay of money. Under this "domestic" system each family was supplied with raw material by a middleman known as a "factor," who also purchased the finished product. Most families carried on a variety of industries—farming in the spring and summer, clothmaking in the winter. Production of goods was essentially production for use, not production for profit in a free market, since the market was small and local and the amount of goods it would absorb was definitely known in advance.

General Economic and Social Conditions. Travel and transportation were difficult and slow. Stagecoaches, sailing vessels, and river barges were the chief means. Little money was in circulation. The rigid class stratification of society and the illiteracy of the mass of the population prevented most men from improving their condition by thrift and enterprise. Government was monarchial (continental Europe) or oligarchic (Great Britain).

CAUSES OF
THE INDUSTRIAL REVOLUTION

Commercial Expansion. The explorations and colonial establishments of the sixteenth and seventeenth centuries led to a great expansion of commerce, to the increased use of a money exchange system, and to the growth of a strong class of business men and capitalists. While the effect of this commercial revolution on technology was not immediate, the en-

largement of the economic horizon showed shrewd men unlimited opportunities for money-making if production could
be increased. The commercial expansion opened up a world
market ripe for exploitation, made available an abundant
supply of raw materials, and implanted a new psychology of
enterprise.

Scientific Progress. For two centuries there had been
steady accumulation of scientific knowledge although little
practical use had been made of it. But the researches in pure
science of such men as Galileo, Newton, Huygens, and Boyle
laid the foundations on which later practical experimenters
were able to build.

Favorable Political Organization. A necessary condition
for the coming of the Industrial Revolution was the
establishment of a considerable degree of political freedom,
and the break-up of the medieval guild system in industry
and of the feudal system of land tenure. This was accomplished in England by the revolutions of the seventeenth
century, and in continental Europe by the French Revolution
and the changes spread abroad by the Napoleonic conquests.

Readiness of England to Take Lead. Conditions in England were particularly favorable for the beginning of the
Industrial Revolution. England had achieved a higher degree of national unity and political stability than other European countries. Though much less populous than France,
England had become, through her successful wars in the
eighteenth century, the leading maritime and colonial power
of the world. She had also advanced further than other
nations in the organization of capitalism; she had a strong
banking system and an abundance of capital seeking profitable investment. England's natural resources, notably an
abundance of coal and iron ore, enabled her to outdistance
her rivals, particularly after the introduction of iron smelting
by coal instead of charcoal (c. 1750), and the widespread use
of steam power (after 1785). The humid climate of England
was ideal for cotton spinning. Finally, the disorder on the
continent attending the French Revolution and the Napoleonic Wars delayed the acceptance of the Industrial Revolution
in France, Germany, and the Low Countries.

Revolution in Agriculture. In the eighteenth century many innovations in agricultural methods and organization brought far-reaching changes that foreshadowed and promoted the Industrial Revolution. Jethro Tull (1674-1741) introduced the machine "drill" which displaced the wasteful method of broadcast seed-sowing. He also pioneered in the use of artificial fertilization. Charles Viscount ("Turnip") Townshend (1674-1738) made experiments with crop rotation. Robert Bakewell (1725-1795) showed that the quality of live stock could be improved by selective breeding. In England, in the late eighteenth century, a large amount of farm land and common was "enclosed"—taken over and consolidated with large estates—sometimes with compensation to the small peasants who had previously cultivated it, often without any compensation. The enclosure movement greatly improved agricultural efficiency and the total crop yield of land but deprived large numbers of small peasants of their livelihoods and forced them to migrate to the cities in search of employment.

INVENTIONS OF
THE INDUSTRIAL REVOLUTION

Textile Industry. A small improvement introduced by John Kay (1733) led to a series of inventions. Kay's "flying shuttle" speeded up the process of weaving and thus increased the demand for thread. James Hargreaves' "spinning jenny" (1767), followed by Richard Arkwright's "water frame" (a water-power operated spinning machine (1769), and Samuel Crompton's "spinning mule" (1779) supplied the demand for thread and created a surplus. Edmund Cartwright's "power loom" (1785) improved weaving methods and thus restored the balance between spinning and weaving. Eli Whitney's "cotton gin" (United States, 1793) made available a large cheap supply of raw cotton for spinning. The net effect of these inventions was to multiply many times the amount of cloth that could be made by a given group of workers.

Steam Power. Fundamental in the new industrial order was the development of a cheap, portable source of power. James Watt's invention of the condenser (1769) and of a practical method of converting the reciprocating motion of the piston into rotary motion (1781) made the steam engine (crude forms of which had been invented earlier by Papin and Newcomen) a practical prime mover for all kinds of machinery. The steam engine soon largely displaced water wheels and windmills. It facilitated and made necessary the production of great quantities of coal and iron. Applications of the steam engine were rapidly discovered. On water Robert Fulton's steam-boat, the *Clermont* (1807), and on land George Stephenson's rail locomotive (1825) were the forerunners of modern transportation. The steam printing press (1814) decreased the cost of printed matter and facilitated the spread of universal education.

Coal, Iron, and Steel. Early in the eighteenth century Abraham Darby and his son made experiments in the substitution of coke (made from coal) for charcoal (from wood) for the reduction of iron ore. In 1760 John Smeaton improved the Darby process by the addition of a water-power driven air blast that improved the quality and yield of coke. About 1784 Henry Cort introduced the "puddling" process for the purification of pig iron made with coke. From this time forward coal and iron went hand in hand with steam as the foundation of industrialization. Later developments of prime importance were the invention (1859) of the "Bessemer process" and of the "open-hearth process" for the large scale manufacture of steel.

Communications. With the development of railways and steam navigation, travel and communication became much more rapid. A penny postal system was introduced in Great Britain in 1840. But the greatest improvement was the practically instantaneous communication by electricity introduced with Morse's telegraph (1837). The development of electrical science late in the nineteenth century led to the invention of Bell's telephone (1876) and Marconi's wireless (1896).

Farming Machinery. The application of machines to farming revolutionized agriculture. A thrashing machine driven by steam was used in England as early as 1803. Later came McCormick's reaper (1834) and steam-driven plows and cultivators (c. 1850).

Machine Manufacture of Machinery. The early textile machines were made of wood and hand-worked iron. One of the important results of the introduction of steam power and large scale iron-making was the application of machinery to the manufacture of machinery. The lathe, the grinder, and the milling cutter for working metals made machines the breeders of more machines and help to explain how the Industrial Revolution expanded with great rapidity after a start had been made. Standardization of parts, which is fundamental in all mass production, was made both necessary and easy by the use of machinery.

Invention after 1830. The early advance of the Industrial Revolution, while rapid compared with previous technological progress, was utterly dwarfed by the flood of invention that came in an ever-increasing tide after 1830. Among hundreds of machines, processes, and scientific principles may be mentioned (1) Faraday's discovery of electromagnetic induction (1831), (2) large scale preservation of food by canning (c. 1845), (3) Daguerre's invention of photography (1839), (4) Ericsson's screw propellor (1836), and (5) Goodyear's rubber vulcanization (1844).

So great was the acceleration of invention in the nineteenth century that some historians speak of a "Second Industrial Revolution," beginning about 1870 and including the enormous development of electrical technology and of industries dependent on internal combustion engines that occurred during the following forty years.

ECONOMIC RESULTS OF THE INDUSTRIAL REVOLUTION

The Factory System. The old method of small production in the home with one's own tools could not meet the competition of machine production, and the cost of machinery was prohibitive to the individual workers. Hence arose the factory system, i.e., large scale production in factories using machines owned by the employer. The factory system stimulated the growth of *division of labor* and of *mass production* through standardization of processes and parts.

Expansion of Industry and Increase of Wealth. Old industries began to produce on a much larger scale than previously. New industries sprang up offering new goods to satisfy man's desires. Particularly significant was the rise of the *producers' goods* industry as distinguished from the *consumers' goods* industry. The increasing productiveness of the machines led to an enormous total increase in wealth, but the surplus was at first concentrated in the hands of a comparatively few rich men. In the long run the total increase in wealth led to a general rise in standards of living.

Rise of Industrial Capitalism. The controllers of the newly created surplus wealth were the industrial capitalists who owned the factories. As the Industrial Revolution proceeded, the power and influence of the industrial capitalists grew ever greater, and it was they who shaped the course of further industrialization by reinvesting their gains in new enterprises rather than distributing the increase to the general population. So great was the productiveness of the machines that in spite of lavish personal expenditures on non-productive display, only a relatively small fraction of the total increase in wealth was immediately consumed. The rapid development (after 1830) of the limited-liability joint-stock corporation greatly facilitated the investment of surplus capital and led to rapid promotion of new industry.

Economic Imperialism. The great problem of the capitalists was the profitable investment of their wealth. The development of multiplied productivity required an ever larger market for the disposal of the product. Hence arose, especially in the later nineteenth century when domestic markets had begun to reach a saturation point, the pressure for imperialistic expansion and "spheres of influence" in the undeveloped parts of the world.

Booms and Depressions. As production for profit in a free market replaced production for use, and as innovations of method upset the balance in established industries, the phenomena of large scale "booms" and "depressions" introduced a new element into economic life.

International Economic Dependence.　The Industrial Revolution enormously accelerated the movement toward international economic dependence that had begun with the Commercial Revolution of the sixteenth and seventeenth centuries. The cotton spindles of England, to take a single instance, depended upon a steady supply of raw cotton from the slave-worked plantations of the United States. As the population of Europe, especially of England, became more and more engaged in urban industry, they raised less food on their farms and became heavy importers of wheat, meat, and tropical food products. In exchange for food, Europe exported manufactured goods. The entire world became a market place. Dislocation of industry in any part of the world often has important repercussions in countries thousands of miles away.

SOCIAL RESULTS OF
THE INDUSTRIAL REVOLUTION

Dependent Proletariat Concentrated in Cities.　With the rise of the factory system came a shifting of population from small agricultural villages to the cities. A vast urban proletariat grew up, propertyless, largely illiterate, and entirely dependent upon wage earning for a living.

Bad Labor and Living Conditions.　The rapid growth of the industrial cities that paid no attention to sanitation or comfort produced foul slums where the masses lived in horrible squalor. With no concern for the welfare of the wage-earner the capitalist and his agents offered small wages in return for long hours in unhealthful factories.

Large Scale Child Labor.　Because little strength or training was required to tend the machines, women and particularly children ranging in ages from six years up were employed in large numbers and mercilessly exploited. Children of pauper parents were farmed out to factory owners on terms that amounted to slavery, unprotected even by the "property interest" that mitigated the rigors of true slavery, and were literally worked to death. These hideous conditions lasted for more than half a century in England but were gradually bettered through the agitation of reformers and the quickening of public conscience.

Insecurity and Mass Unemployment. Because the supply of labor, considered as a commodity, was usually in excess of the demand, and because the workers were without any independent means of subsistence, the fear of loss of the job became a constant specter in the worker's mind. Besides the possibility of discharge for some delinquency there was the danger of large scale shut-downs as a consequence of business depressions. Mass unemployment, new in modern history, became one of the gravest social problems arising from the Industrial Revolution.

Mechanization of Warfare. A far-reaching consequence of the Industrial Revolution was the development of highly efficient mechanized weapons that rendered war immensely more destructive and dangerous to civilized progress.

POLITICAL RESULTS OF THE INDUSTRIAL REVOLUTION

Strengthening of the Bourgeoisie (Middle Class). In England the bourgeoisie attained a large measure of political power through the Reform Bill of 1832, which redistributed seats in Parliament to grant representation to the new industrial centers and to diminish the representation of the so-called "rotten boroughs;" and which gave the right to vote to a large new group of the moderately well-to-do (*ten pound tenants*). It was bourgeoisie sentiment, made politically articulate by the Reform Bill and led by such able men as Richard Cobden, John Bright, and Charles Villiers that brought about the repeal (1846, following a terrible famine in Ireland) of the Corn Laws, that had long subsidized the land-owning aristocracy at the expense of the rest of the people. The bourgeoisie were also successful in putting down the agitation of the Chartists, which was essentially an effort to secure for the lower classes the same political powers as had been obtained by the bourgeoisie through the Reform Bill.

In France the position of the bourgeoisie was strengthened by the Revolution of 1830, which put Louis Philippe on the throne as a constitutional king and provided for effective control of the government by the middle class as in England.

The formation of the *Zollverein*, or Customs Union, in Germany (1834) established a protective tariff, which benefited the bourgeoisie. This offered an example of unification for commercial purposes that was later to foster the political consolidation of Germany.

Rise of Labor as a Political Force. The new proletariat created by the Industrial Revolution, though hampered by poverty, ignorance, and lack of leadership, gradually developed a feeling of common consciousness and sought means to improve their condition by political agitation, combination in Trade Unions, and various types of cooperative action. With the advance of democracy, which was partly favored by the bourgeoisie, the laboring classes grew stronger politically and were finally able to make their influence felt directly in elections and plebiscites. Nevertheless, the slowness of the improvement in the economic condition of the working class and the bitter opposition toward the rise of labor on the part of conservatives in the upper and middle classes gave rise to radical movements among the workers, based on a belief that no reform short of overthrow of the existing capitalistic system could be of much benefit in the long run.

Dependence of Military Superiority on Industrialization. The Industrial Revolution led to a new balance of world powers as it became ever more clear that military strength depended on industrialization. The thoroughness of the Industrial Revolution in England, France, and Germany, and its relative weakness in Russia and Eastern Europe, generally was the most powerful factor contributing to the European dominance by the first three states at the beginning of the twentieth century. The Europeanizing of the world in the nineteenth century carried the Industrial Revolution with it: so Japan, by its sudden acceptance of the Industrial Revolution in the later nineteenth century, became the dominant power of the Orient: so the industrialized Northern United States were able to defeat the South in the American Civil War.

INTELLECTUAL AND CULTURAL RESULTS OF THE INDUSTRIAL REVOLUTION

Adam Smith and Laissez Faire. The social and economic changes made by the Industrial Revolution stimulated the growth of the science of economics or "political economy" as it was usually called. Nineteenth century economic thinking stems chiefly from Adam Smith, whose *Wealth of Nations* (1776) argued forcibly for non-interference by government with business. Smith held that each man is the best judge of his own economic affairs; that the free play of competition and the universal desire for enrichment would result in the maximum increase in total wealth; and that though individuals might be selfish and unconcerned with the common good, their collective activity would automatically, as if guided by an "invisible hand," tend to the economic welfare of all. Smith thus powerfully supported the economic doctrine known in France as laissez faire; government should be merely an omnipresent policeman protecting property and compelling the performance of contracts. This laissez faire doctrine appealed strongly to the new capitalists of the Industrial Revolution.

The Classical Economists. The ideas of Smith were developed and elaborated by the school of "classical economists," the leaders of which were Thomas Malthus, David Ricardo, Nassau Senior, and James Mill. In 1798 Malthus formulated his "principle of population," which asserted that any improvement in the economic condition of the poor would be counterbalanced by an increase in population, since population tends to increase to the limit of the means of subsistence. It therefore followed that grinding poverty and a high death rate from starvation, disease, and war must forever be the lot of the mass of mankind. The only conceivable alternative (which Malthus hardly took seriously) was the limitation of the population by "moral restraint." Ricardo enunciated the celebrated "iron law of wages," which stated that wages must inevitably tend to an amount just capable of maintaining life, much as the coal fed into a steam engine was just capable of maintaining the fire under the boiler.

The Socialists. Against the terrible, if cheerful, pessimism of the individualist economists arose the socialists, who refused to accept as irremediable the bad conditions brought by the Industrial Revolution. Robert Owen's experiment at New Lanark, Scotland, was a cooperative community scheme for improving the condition of the worker. The success of

the New Lanark experiment raised hopes for a rapid ameliora-
tion of social conditions, but later experiments of the same
sort by Owen and others were disappointing. In France,
Saint-Simon, Fourier, and Louis Blanc tried to improve conditions, but their idealistic schemes were not practical. However, they created a public opinion against the system of
laissez faire, which demanded and obtained better working
conditions, a higher standard of living, an increased leisure,
and a greater freedom for women and children.

Rise of Engineering and Research. The Industrial Revolution immensely stimulated scientific investigation. As
manufacturing techniques became more complex, experts
were required to manage and improve them. The profession
of engineering became indispensable to the industrial civilization. Science began to be more and more pursued for its
services to technology. In time, large scale industrial endow-
ment of laboratory research became the accepted way of for-
warding invention. The achievements of the new applied
science appealed powerfully to the imagination of the common man.

Secularization of Interests. The progress of the Industrial Revolution eventually placed an undreamed-of variety
of material goods in the hands of a large part of the population. The mass-circulation newspaper, the automobile,
the motion picture and the radio—all products of the Industrial Revolution—have supplied man with a whole new set of
interests, and far more than the arguments of philosophical
agnosticism have brought about the secularization of view
point and wide-spread religious indifferentism that is characteristic of contemporary life.

Significant Dates

CHAPTER II.

METTERNICHISM

The downfall of Napoleon (1814-1815) resulted in a general resettlement of European affairs at the Congress of Vienna. The period 1815-1830 is often called the "Era of Metternich" because the policies and influence of Prince Clemens Metternich, Austrian Chancellor and Foreign Minister, were dominant in continental Europe, and because the main political and social movement of the times arose from the conflict between the supporters and the opponents of Metternich's ideas. Leading characteristics of Metternichism were (1) support of political absolutism, (2) suppression of nationalistic ambitions, and (3) forcible preservation of the *status quo* as established by the Congress of Vienna. Metternichism may thus be summed up as reaction from the French Revolution and the ideas it had spread abroad. Opposed to Metternichism was the movement known as "liberalism." Liberalism favored greater political, intellectual, and economic freedom for the individual. It also favored nationalistic aspirations. It found its support in two principal groups: (1) the intellectuals, patriots, and romantics who were inspired by the eighteenth century "enlightenment" and by the French Revolution with its doctrines of the "Rights of Man" and of "Liberty, Equality, and Fraternity," and (2) the rising moneyed class or bourgeoisie whom the Industrial Revolution was enriching and who desired political power to increase and consolidate their economic gains. A large part of nineteenth century history is concerned with the growth of this double-rooted liberal movement and its struggle with the forces of conservatism.

THE CONGRESS OF VIENNA

Leaders. Besides Prince Metternich, the important diplomats at Vienna were Talleyrand for France, Hardenberg and von Humboldt for Prussia, Nesselrode and Rasoumoffsky for Russia, and Castlereagh and Wellington for Great Britain. Tsar Alexander I of Russia, Emperor Francis I of Austria, and King Frederick William III of Prussia also attended in person. With the exception of Alexander I, a dreamy idealist easily manipulated by such a master of the diplomatic art as Metternich, all these men were devoted to the *ancien régime*.

"Legitimacy" and "Compensations." The watchwords of the Congress of Vienna were "Legitimacy" and "Compensations." By legitimacy was meant the principle that the dynastic changes introduced by Napoleon were to be undone and Europe restored to its "legitimate" rulers and their descendants as of 1792. The doctrine of legitimacy was a clever invention of the French diplomat Talleyrand, who wished to prevent any partitioning or other diminution of French territory. Legitimacy fell in well with the reactionary policies of Metternich. By pressing the doctrine of legitimacy and by skillfully taking advantage of quarrels among his opponents, Talleyrand was able to get much lighter terms for France than might have been expected from the magnitude of the Napoleonic Wars and the completeness of the French defeat. Even the temporary return of Napoleon (the Hundred Days) did not result in a very vindictive punishment. In the name of legitimacy the monarchs of France, Spain, Holland, and the Italian states were restored to their thrones. Carried to its logical conclusion, the doctrine of legitimacy would have also restored the territorial boundaries exactly as they were before the Revolution, but the Great Powers did not wish to do this. Each desired some of the spoils of victory. Accordingly, under the euphemistic term "compensations," Great Britain retained

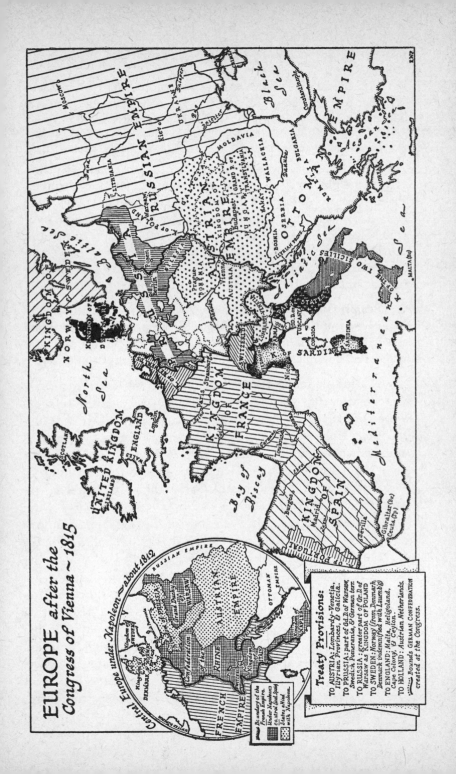

EUROPE *after the*
Congress of Vienna ~ 1815

Central Europe under Napoleon~about 1812

Treaty Provisions:

TO AUSTRIA: Lombardy-Venetia,
Illyrian Provinces, & Galicia.
TO PRUSSIA: part of Gd.D.of Warsaw,
Swedish Pomerania, & German terr.
TO RUSSIA: greater part of Gr.D.of
Warsaw as KINGDOM OF POLAND
TO SWEDEN: Norway (from Denmark,
Denmark indemnified with Lauenbg)
TO ENGLAND: Malta, Heligoland,
Cape Colony, & Ceylon.
TO HOLLAND: Austrian Netherlands.
↳ Bounds GERMAN CONFEDERATION
created at the Congress.

the French and Dutch colonies she had seized, Holland was compensated by being allowed to annex the Austrian Netherlands (present-day Belgium), Austria was compensated by receiving Venetia and Milan in Italy, while Hapsburg rulers were seated on the thrones of Tuscany, Modena, and Parma. The Germanies were reorganized into a loose confederation of thirty-eight states with Austria the outstanding member. Prussia received part of Saxony and some land along the Rhine. Sweden was given Norway in return for Finland, over which Russia had gained control in 1809. Outside the realm of "legitimacy" and "compensations," almost the only constructive reform of the Congress of Vienna was a pious gesture against the African Slave Trade.

Suppression of Nationalistic Ambitions. The total disregard by the Congress of Vienna of the principle of national self-determination made most of its work temporary and provided fuel for many revolutions in the nineteenth century.

Machinery for Enforcing the Vienna Settlement. Immediately after the Congress of Vienna, two alliance systems were formed to preserve the settlement. The first was the so-called Holy Alliance, proposed by the pious Alexander I, and joined by Russia, Austria, and Prussia. The Holy Alliance was intended by the Tsar to give expression in international affairs to the precepts of Christianity—justice, charity, and peace. The Holy Alliance was later joined by most of the other states of Europe. In the hands of the realistic diplomacy of Metternich and others, the Holy Alliance proved to be nothing but the "verbiage" that Metternich called it, but in the minds of the liberals of the time it became a symbol for everything reactionary and suppressive. It was not, however, the Holy Alliance but the Quadruple Alliance—an agreement of Austria, Great Britain, Prussia, and Russia—that actually furnished the teeth of the Vienna settlement. Although deserted a short time later by Great Britain, the Quadruple Alliance, with Metternich as its directing genius, dominated European affairs during most of the period 1815-1830. Under the Quadruple Alliance agreement, a series of international congresses was held (Aix-la-Chapelle, 1818; Troppau, 1820; Laibach,

1821 ; Verona, 1822), which took collective action to crush out liberalism wherever it might appear, even arranging for armed intervention in the internal affairs of friendly states.

TRIUMPH OF REACTION (1815-1830)

France Under Louis XVIII and Charles X. In 1815 Louis XVIII was restored to a fairly prosperous country, for although the wars of Napoleon had cut deeply into national resources material and human, the resilience of the French people and particularly the beneficial land distribution introduced by the Revolution brought about rapid economic recovery. The Charter of 1814 provided a constitutional monarchy somewhat similar to the system in Great Britain, although with greater powers in the hands of the king. But the bitterness of factional spirit prevented this constitutional system from functioning smoothly. On the one hand were the Ultra-Royalists, former émigrés and their children, greedy for revenge and the reëstablishment of their privileges, and contemptuous of the mild liberalism of the Charter; on the other hand were the Republicans and Bonapartists, bitter at the restoration of the king and the defeat of the Revolution. These irreconcilable groups kept politics in an uproar, although it is probable that the majority of the nation was willing to accept any compromise that would preserve quiet.

In the first year of the restoration (1815-1816) the Ultra-Royalists dominated the Chamber of Deputies and instituted a fierce reaction marked by rioting and proscriptions (the White Terror). From 1816 to 1820 a more moderate government, led by the King and Elie Decazes, maintained order and governed in the spirit of the Charter. But in 1820, following the assassination of the King's nephew, the Duke of Berry, a new Ultra-Royalist reaction undid the conciliating work of the preceding four years. The press was muzzled, the civil rights guaranteed by the Charter were suspended, a police espionage was established, and the property qualification for voters was raised. In 1823 a French army, led by the Duke of Angoulême, intervened in Spain to crush the liberal movement in that country. Upon the death of Louis XVIII (1824) his brother, Count of Artois, became king as Charles X. A stanch reactionary, Charles X, with the aid of the Ultra-Royalist Chamber, granted an indemnity ($200,000,000) to the émigrés for the land they had lost. He also allowed the return of the Jesuits and continued the policy of entrusting public education entirely to the clergy. But his policies gradually alienated large groups, and in 1827 the Ultra-Royalists lost their majority in the Chamber of Deputies. Particularly irritating to the bourgeoisie was Charles' device for raising the immense indemnification for the émigrés. He reduced interest payments on the public debt and applied the savings thus made to annuities to the émigrés. This meant that payment was to be made directly from the pockets of government bond-holders, i. e., the bourgeoisie. By 1830 liberal dissatisfaction with the rule of Charles X had reached a boiling point.

Spain and Liberalism. In Spain the liberal Constitution of 1812 was revoked by Ferdinand VII upon his restoration. A thoroughly reactionary policy was substituted. This served to bring about a revolt in 1820 and a short-lived triumph for liberalism (1820-1822). Metternich assembled the Powers of the Quadruple Alliance at Verona (1822) to discuss the Spanish revolt and arrange for its suppression. At this conference, which was attended by France as well as the Powers of the Quadruple Alliance, it was decided that France would intervene in Spain under a general mandate of the Powers. Great Britain refused to support this scheme but did not attempt forcibly to resist it. A French army invaded Spain in 1823 and after much fighting, forced the Liberals out of Madrid into Cadiz, where they fortified themselves with Ferdinand, a prisoner. Ferdinand was released upon promising to establish a moderate government. Once safe, however, Ferdinand repudiated his promises and once more set the wheels in motion to crush liberalism. The reaction of 1824 was much more intense than that of 1814. Even the Duke of Angoulême, the leader of the French invading army, protested against Ferdinand's excesses. Reaction and absolutism, with every refinement of stupid and treacherous cruelty, remained supreme in Spain until Ferdinand's death in 1833, after which a bloody and destructive civil war kept Spain in an uproar for many years.

During the long period of war and disorder (beginning in 1808 with Napoleon's interference in Spanish affairs) the Spanish colonies in South America had been in revolt. By

1823 most of them had succeeded in establishing independent governments. It would have been thoroughly in accord with the policies of Metternich and the Quadruple Alliance for the European Powers to have suppressed the South American revolt, but this could not be done without the active assistance of British sea-power. The leading British statesmen, Castlereagh and (after 1822) Canning, while unsympathetic with revolution, considered that British economic interests would be best served by an independent South America, and accordingly Great Britain refused to coöperate with the Metternich policies. In 1823 James Monroe, President of the United States, having reached an understanding with Canning, proclaimed the famous Monroe Doctrine, which asserted that the United States would consider it an act of aggression for any country to colonize further in, or otherwise to interfere with, the new republics of South America. The Monroe Doctrine, supported by both Britain and the United States, made the extension of Metternichism to the New World quite hopeless.

Portugal and Liberalism. While the Portuguese royal family found refuge from Napoleon in Brazil (1807-1820), Great Britain was virtually in control of the country. The British occupation was resented both by patriotic reactionaries and by Liberals. In 1820, during a temporary absence of the British governor, the Portuguese army, largely inspired by the contemporaneous revolt in Spain, got control of the government and with the help of the Liberals formulated a constitution similar to Spain's. King John VI returned from Brazil in 1822 and accepted the constitution. In that year Brazil broke away from Portugal and made John VI's son, Pedro I, Emperor. Don Miguel, another son, led the reactionaries against the constitutional government. When the French invaded Spain in 1823, John VI revoked the constitution but succeeded only in incensing the Liberals without satisfying the reactionaries. Don Miguel continued his agitation. In 1826 John VI died, and Pedro I of Brazil became Pedro IV of Portugal. Pedro, a man of liberal sympathies, granted a charter providing for parliamentary government. He then abdicated his Portuguese crown in favor of his seven year old daughter Maria, with the understanding that she should marry Don Miguel. Miguel, who had been banished by his father

in 1824, now returned as regent (1828). Disregarding his
solemn promises to support the constitution of Pedro, Miguel
introduced a savage despotism. His excesses continued until
his deposition in 1834.

Great Britain and Liberalism. Great Britain's desire to
curb the commercial expansion of Spain and Portugal and
to cut in on the South American trade had led her to support
the Monroe Doctrine and to refuse to coöperate with Metternich's program of foreign interference to crush liberalism.
But in her domestic policies during the period 1815-1822,
Great Britain was quite as reactionary as Metternich himself.
Throughout the French Revolutionary epoch (1789-1815),
the fear of the spread of radical French ideas was a bugbear
of the British governing classes. Although England had
established a parliamentary monarchy in the seventeenth century and was thus regarded as "liberal" by the philosophers of
the eighteenth century, she had actually made hardly more
progress toward democracy by 1789 than had the absolute
monarchies of the continent. A tight little oligarchy of landed
aristocrats entirely controlled the government, and although
there was a long tradition of civil rights under the law and
of freedom of the press, the British aristocrats were quite as
capable as those of any other country of enacting repressive
measures as soon as their privileges seemed threatened by
popular agitation. In 1815 the Tory cabinet, fresh from its
triumph over Napoleon and the French Revolution, was less
inclined than ever to offer any measures of reform in a liberal
direction. The period 1815-1822 was marked by an extreme
conservatism. King George IV, Castlereagh, and Wellington
championed reaction. The Tory House of Commons passed
legislation favorable to their class interests (increased duties
on the importation of grain; continuing Enclosure Acts;
abolition of the Income Tax), while acute economic distress
among the lower classes went unrelieved.

In 1816 the discontent of the unemployed workingmen
found expression in a formidable series of riots culminating
in the Spafields Riot in London. In 1817, frightened by continuing disturbances, the government suspended the Habeas
Corpus Act, the principal bulwark of English civil liberty.

In 1819 there was renewed agitation, and a great mass-meeting at Manchester was broken up by the soldiers of the government with some bloodshed. This "Manchester Massacre" resulted in the passage of a group of severely repressive measures known as the "Six Acts." In spite of its outward appearance of success, however, the British reaction was being rapidly undermined by a strong liberal movement. The liberal opposition came from (1) intellectual radicals— William Godwin, Thomas Paine, William Cobbett, Jeremy Bentham, Percy Bysshe Shelley, and Lord Byron, (2) Roman Catholics, particularly in Ireland, who were clamoring for the repeal of the laws denying political office to members of their faith, (3) Protestant dissenters, who objected to the preferential treatment accorded to Anglicans in politics, taxation, and higher education, and (4) the rising industrial capitalists, or bourgeoisie. Because the Industrial Revolution was well advanced in England by 1815, these last formed a powerful body whom in the long run it would be impossible to oppose. During the decade 1822-1832 this liberal movement kept gaining weight in spite of the stubborn standpattism of the conservatives. The liberal foreign policy of Canning was the first indication of the changing order. In 1825, through the instigation of Francis Place and William Huskisson, the act prohibiting combinations of workingmen (trade unions) was repealed. In 1828, by the repeal of the Corporation and Test Acts, Protestant dissenters were admitted to political office. In the following year, the Catholic Relief Act removed the civil disabilities of Catholics. A strong movement, now supported by important men in the cabinet, had developed favoring Parliamentary Reform—extension of the franchise to the middle class and redistribution of seats in Parliament to give representation proportioned to population.

Russia under Alexander I. Alexander I of Russia came to the Congress of Vienna with many liberal ideas. He had granted constitutional charters to Finland and to Poland, and he had taken a considerable share in drawing up the Charter of 1814 that Louis XVIII had granted to France. Under the influence of Metternich, however, Alexander gradually became converted to reaction. Of all the great

European countries, Russia was the most backward educationally and industrially and thus the least fitted for democratic reform. These considerations, the discovery of an assassination conspiracy among the officers of his guard, the uprising of 1820 in Spain and Italy, all contributed to Alexander's change of heart. In 1820 Alexander admitted to Metternich that liberalism was both a failure and a source of danger, and from that time on he coöperated vigorously with the Austrian Chancellor's anti-liberal war.

Central Europe Controlled by Metternich. In central Europe, Metternichism was supreme. All the engines of suppression that his ingenuity could devise were set in motion by Metternich against everything that savored of innovation or freedom. Rigid control of the press and of education, and omnipresent police surveillance were the orders of the day. Not only in Austria, but also in the Germanies and in Italy, Metternich watched for any flare-up and then rushed to smother it. Some promises of liberal reform made by the princes in the Germanies were not carried out. Manifestations of the liberal undercurrent broke out in secret societies, the Burschenschaft and the Wartburg Festival (1817). The Carlsbad Decrees (1819) were the government's answer to these subversive movements. In Italy, Metternich's power was felt from Lombardy and Venetia to the Kingdom of the Two Sicilies. On the surface reaction was firmly entrenched, but liberalism, though driven to cover, still lived. Secret societies (the most important known as the *Carbonari*) were supported by many. As they had done in Portugal and Spain, the Liberals rose up in 1820 and were successful in forcing the promise of a constitution from the king. But as a result of Metternich's conferences at Troppau and Laibach, Austrian intervention was sanctioned, the revolution was stamped out by force, and the constitution was abolished.

DECLINE OF METTERNICHISM (1822-1830)

Non-coöperation of Great Britain. One of the major reasons for the decline of Metternichism and its eventual failure was the foreign policy of non-intervention adopted by Great Britain after 1822. Canning and other British leaders were chiefly influenced in withdrawing from the Metternich system by the desire of promoting British commercial interests rather than by philosophical adherence to liberal principles.

The Greek Revolution. A second cause that worked powerfully to undermine Metternichism was the Greek War of Independence against the Turks, which started in 1821 with an uprising in Moldavia. Though personally sympathetic toward the Greek cause and anxious to see a diminution of the dangerous Turkish power, Tsar Alexander was persuaded by Metternich not to intervene. It was supposed that without foreign help the Greeks would be quickly crushed. The Greeks, however, displayed a heroic national spirit, while the barbarous methods employed by the Turks to put down the rebellion created a revulsion of feeling throughout Europe. Intellectuals and romantics (Lord Byron, Victor Hugo, Wilhelm Müller, and others) took up the Greek cause. After the death of Tsar Alexander (1825), Metternich was no longer able to exercise a decisive influence in Russian affairs, while sympathy for the Greeks and hatred of the Turks were growing throughout Russia. In 1827 the new Tsar, Nicholas I, joined with Great Britain and France, and signed the Treaty of London by which it was agreed that these Powers would intervene to force an armistice in Greece to be followed, presumably, by some sort of compromise on the question of independence. The Turks refused to accept an armistice, and the new allies destroyed the Turkish-Egyptian fleet in the Bay of Navarino (1827). The following year Russia declared war on Turkey. For France and Russia to aid a country in throwing off its "legitimate" rulers was a bitter pill for Metternich. In 1829 the Turks were defeated and forced to accept the Treaty of Adrianople, which acknowledged Greek independence.

Revolutions of 1830. By 1830 discontent with reaction and suppression of nationalistic aspirations had reached explosive proportions in many parts of Europe. In France, Charles X published his July Ordinances (1) restricting further the freedom of the press, (2) dissolving the new Chamber to which a liberal majority had been elected, (3) promulgating a new electoral law narrowing the suffrage, and (4) calling for new elections, which would presumably result in the return of a reactionary majority. Secretly financed and directed by the leaders of the bourgeoisie (bankers, factory-owners, and merchants), a revolt broke out in Paris; armed bands of workingmen barricaded the streets and easily defeated the king's soldiers, who were themselves largely in sympathy with the rioters. Charles X abdicated and fled to England. Louis Philippe, Duke of Orleans, was made king under a constitutional system that placed effective control in the hands of the bourgeoisie. The success of this "July Revolution" in France brought immediate repercussions in other parts of Europe. The Belgians revolted from the Dutch and declared their independence in October 1831, an independence recognized by France and Great Britain the following year. In Italy, the Papal states rose against the Pope, and Parma and Modena forced their Hapsburg rulers to flee to Vienna. But Metternich soon crushed these uprisings and restored the old system. Liberalism was not yet strong enough in central Europe to overthrow Metternichism. The Polish revolt in 1831 was severely put down by Nicholas I. The Revolutions of 1830 marked the end of the first phase of the struggle between liberalism and reaction that formed the leading political issue of the nineteenth century. Metternich had retarded liberalism but had failed to eradicate the influence of the French Revolution.

Significant Dates

CHAPTER III.

THE GROWTH OF LIBERALISM

In England and France the period 1830-1848 was pre-eminently the Era of the Bourgeoisie. Commerce and Industry were in the saddle. In central and eastern Europe, where the Industrial Revolution had not yet penetrated deeply, the period was still the Era of Metternichism with its feudal survivals and political absolutism. During the whole period international diplomacy was in the background and internal social problems were of paramount importance. Outstanding features were the sharpening of the division lines between rich and poor, partly as a result of the rise of industrial capitalism and partly as a result of the decreasing docility and ignorance of the working class. What Edwin Markham has called "the long, long patience of the plundered poor" was beginning to wear out. Increasing numbers of men became converted to the ideas of democracy, which had been opposed even by advanced liberals in the period 1815-1830. Yet in most countries, government remained unresponsive, in general, to public opinion, and thus a dangerous dissatisfaction, unable to find vent in peaceful political activity, was gradually building up to the *ultima ratio* of revolution. Three

25

distinct movements contributed to this dissatisfaction: (1) the movement for national self-determination (Italian states, Hungary, Poland, Ireland); (2) the movement for social and economic betterment among the submerged masses (France, England); and (3) the movement toward democracy (France, England) and toward constitutionalism (Austria, German states). In 1848, touched off by the February Revolution at Paris, all Europe exploded like a firecracker. Although the revolutions of 1848 failed to realize a fraction of the hopes of their supporters, they marked the end almost everywhere of the era of stand-pattism and ushered in an era of change.

REFORMS IN GREAT BRITAIN

Growth of Religious Tolerance. Until 1689 England, like most other European countries, attempted to enforce religious uniformity by law. The Corporation Act (1661) and the Test Act (1673) denied public office to all who refused to disavow transubstantiation and to receive the sacrament according to the rites of the Church of England. Other laws of the sixteenth and seventeenth centuries imposed heavy penalties on public worship of Roman Catholics and Protestant dissenters. The Toleration Act (1689) permitted dissenters to worship publicly but continued to exclude them from public office and the universities. In the eighteenth century there was a great growth of the spirit of toleration and even a considerable flourishing of deistic and atheistic opinion, and at the beginning of the nineteenth century the Test and Corporation Acts had become essentially political rather than religious measures. In 1828, yielding to the general agitation for liberalizing reforms, Parliament repealed the disabling acts as far as they related to dissenters. Roman Catholics continued under the ban. In 1829, influenced chiefly by the threatening state of affairs in Ireland, where Daniel O'Connell had become a powerful Catholic leader, the Tory government, led by the Duke of Wellington and Robert Peel, sponsored the Catholic Relief Bill which abolished the ancient Oath of Supremacy and the declaration against transubstantiation and thus allowed Catholics to occupy seats in Parliament and hold most positions in the government. Finally, in 1858, a further reform threw open public office to Jews.

Parliamentary Reform (1832). The demand for the extension of suffrage and for the redistribution of seats in Parliament to conform with the distribution of population (referred to by the specific term, Parliamentary Reform) was a result of the Industrial Revolution and the rise of the industrial middle class. The Whig party championed reform in order to win the support of the middle classes. After much opposition from the House of Lords, which was overborne only by the threat of creating new peers, the Reform Bill was finally passed in 1832. It provided for the disfranchisement of forty-one boroughs of negligible population ("rotten boroughs"), for the partial disfranchisement of thirty more boroughs, and for the allocation of the seats thus released to the large new industrial cities. The property qualification for voting was broadened rather than reduced, i.e., other kinds of property than freeheld land were taken into account as qualification. This extension increased the number of voters from about 3 per cent to about 5 per cent of the whole population. Practically no concession, therefore, was made to democracy. The Reform Bill further stipulated that all voting must be done in two days instead of fifteen. A serious weakness of the Reform Bill was its failure to provide for vote by ballot, so that it remained possible for powerful men to control many votes. The Reform Bill brought about a re-alignment of the old political parties; the Whigs and many of the new capitalists began to call themselves Liberals; and the Tories, giving up many of their old traditions under the leadership of Robert Peel and accepting into their ranks such of the new business men as wished to proceed with change slowly, began to call themselves Conservatives.

Chartism. The reform of 1832 had been vigorously supported by the working class, but they soon discovered that no benefits whatever accrued to them from its passage. Indeed, the new group of bourgeoisie who had secured political power by the Reform Bill were less sensitive to the needs of the lower classes than the land-owning aristocracy that they replaced. They were wedded to the ideas of laissez faire and free competition, and they were quite free from any sentimental nonsense about political and social privileges carrying with them any responsibility except that of growing rich. Disappointed at receiving a stone for bread, the lower classes began to agitate for something more substantial than the right to make contracts freely at starvation wages in unsanitary factories. This lower-class agitation crystallized around a program for political reform known as the "People's Charter." The program demanded (1) universal manhood suffrage, (2) vote by secret ballot, (3) annual Parliaments, (4) equal electoral districts, (5) removal of property qualification for members of Parliament, and (6) salary payment of members of Parliament. All the objectives of the Chartists except the unimportant point (3) have since been attained in Great Britain. They may seem to modern eyes a temperate expression of the minimum requirements for a democratic government, but in 1838, when first proposed, they were regarded as violently revolutionary, and they found very few defenders among educated and "respectable" men. From 1838 to 1848 Chartism was vigorously agitated in England, but no concessions to it were made by the government. It was regarded throughout as a subversive and incendiary movement to be put down by force. The movement finally collapsed in 1848 when a much advertised gigantic mass-meeting on Kennington Common in London was attended by a comparative handful who were easily dispersed by the police. Although it failed to accomplish any immediate results, the Chartist agitation served to focus the attention of many of England's ablest minds on what Thomas Carlyle called "the condition-of-England-question" and so paved the way for far-reaching political reforms in the last half of the century.

Social Legislation (1832-1848). The period 1832-1848 saw the beginning of much social reform legislation in England. Most of it was pushed through an apathetic or hostile Parliament by the ceaseless effort of a small group of humanitarians. From the modern point of view the total accomplishment seems small, but the foundations were laid for more effective reform in the future. In 1833, through the efforts of Michael Sadler and Lord Ashley, the first important Factory Act was passed. The law limited child labor in specified industries. Although no adequate provision was made for its enforcement, the law was a great break with the naked doctrine of laissez faire. It was bitterly opposed by the capitalists, who gloomily predicted the ruin of British industry as a consequence of government interference. More advanced Factory Acts were passed in 1842, 1844, and 1847. A beginning was also made in 1833 of government support of elementary education. Negro slavery was abolished in the colonies by an act providing gradual emancipation with financial compensation to slaveholders. Less humanitarian and more hard-headed was the New Poor Law (1834) abolishing "outdoor relief" of the poor and establishing a system of workhouses where conditions were deliberately made as harsh as possible to discourage malingering.

Foreign Affairs (1830-1848). During most of this period British foreign policy was directed by the energetic and aggressive Lord Palmerston. In 1831 Palmerston supported the independence of Belgium, which had just revolted from the Dutch, and thus prevented that country from being annexed by France. In 1839 the permanent independence and neutrality of Belgium was guaranteed by all the important powers. In Spain from 1833 to 1838 a political struggle, frequently flaring out in civil war, was carried on between the partisans of Isabella, daughter of Ferdinand VII, and those of Don Carlos, Ferdinand's younger brother. Palmerston and Louis Philippe of France attempted to settle this Spanish broil to the advantage of their respective countries, but they frequently worked at cross purposes, and the net result of their schemes and counter-schemes was an estrangement between England and France. More important than Palmerston's Spanish interference was his policy toward affairs in the Near East. In 1832 a war broke out between Mehemet Ali, the Pasha of Egypt, and the Turks. The Turks called upon Russia for help, in return for which they promised to close the strategic Dardanelles to foreign warships whenever the Tsar was at war. Palmerston was ultimately succesful in preventing this agreement from becoming effective, and he thus made the maintainance of the integrity of the Ottoman Empire and the neutralization of the Black Sea straits a cardinal aim of British policy.

FRANCE UNDER LOUIS PHILIPPE

Bourgeois Character of the July Monarchy. The Revolution of 1830 that established the "July Monarchy" of Louis Philippe was not a widespread popular uprising. It was rather a *coup d'état* engineered by a small group of moneyed bourgeoisie who took advantage of the discontent of the Paris workingmen to effect a political, not a social, revolution. The government they established was less democratic than that established in Great Britain by the Reform of 1832 and was to an even greater extent a class interest government by and for business and industry. High property qualifications kept the total number of electors to less than 250,000 in a population of 30,000,000. The government was "parliamentary" and "responsible" as in England, and the original intention was that the king should reign but should not govern. For various reasons, however, chief among which was the absence in France of a long parliamentary tradition, Louis Philippe was able to assume a much more dominating position than that occupied by William IV or Victoria. In practice the constitutional monarchy gradually developed into an absolutism controlled by the King and his able minister Guizot. Setting their faces against all reform or change, Louis Philippe and Guizot were forced to adopt more and more reactionary policies to suppress growing dissatisfaction.

Opposition to Louis Philippe. Numerous groups in France had grievances against the "July Monarchy." The Legitimists still insisted that Charles X, and later the Count of Chambord, was the rightful king. The Republicans, although they had aided Louis Philippe in securing the crown, were angered by his failure to introduce democratic reforms. Social reformers of various creeds denounced the government for failing to ameliorate the condition of the working classes. Patriots were humiliated by Louis Philippe's unaggressive foreign policy, his willingness to truckle to England, and his dismissal of his Foreign Minister, Adolphe Thiers, when that statesman attempted to assert France's interests at the risk of war. The prevalence of graft in the conduct of the government of Guizot furnished opportunities for disaffected journalists to attack the regime and led to reprisals in the form of press censorship, which served only to drive the op-

position underground without appeasing it. Alexis de Tocqueville summed up the various elements of discontent in a
speech in the Chamber of Deputies, January 29, 1848: "See
what is passing in the breasts of the working classes,—who,
I grant, are at present quiet. No doubt they are not disturbed
by political passion, properly so called, to the same extent
that they have been; but can you not see that their passions,
instead of political, have become social? Do you not see that
there are gradually forming in their breasts opinions and
ideas that are destined to upset not only this or that ministry,
law or form of government, but society itself, until it totters
upon the foundations on which it rests today? Do you not
listen to what they say to themselves each day? Do you
not hear them repeating unceasingly that all that is above
them is unworthy and incapable; that the present distribution
of goods throughout the world is unjust; that property rests
on a foundation that is not equitable? And do you not realize
that when such opinions take root, when they spread in an
almost universal manner, when they sink deeply into the
masses, they are bound to bring with them sooner or later,
I know not when or how, a most formidable revolution?"

The February Revolution (1848). Louis Philippe,
Guizot, and the bourgeois Chamber of Deputies could not
see, as de Tocqueville saw, the real drift of affairs. They
persisted in their policy of suppression and no reform. Because censorship of the press made dissemination of political
opinions through ordinary channels impossible, the opponents
of the government had developed a practice of attending
"banquets" where radical views were expressed and plans
for coercing the government were discussed. The chief reform contemplated by these intellectual radicals was democratic extension of the suffrage. In February 1848 the government attempted to prevent one of these banquets. This
proved a signal for the outbreak of rioting in different parts
of Paris, and when Guizot attempted to restore order by the
use of the National Guard, many of the soldiers refused to
obey their officers. In a riot in front of Guizot's home, fifty
demonstrators were killed or wounded, and this bloodshed
further infuriated the revolutionaries. After a futile attempt
to make terms with the rioters, Louis Philippe abdicated and

made his escape to England. Amid great disorder a provisional government, headed by the Catholic liberal and poet, Lamartine, but including almost every shade of political and social opinion, was selected. The provisional government decreed a general election under universal manhood suffrage for members of a National Assembly to draw up a constitution.

The Second Republic and the Socialists. The provisional government remained in control for four months pending the election of the new Assembly. Pressed by the desperate economic necessities of the unemployed proletariat in Paris and led by the socialist theorist Louis Blanc, the government undertook to guarantee the "right to work" and agreed to employ on public works ("national workshops"), at a wage of two francs a day, all who were unemployed. As the government could not immediately organize productive work for the large numbers who applied, the national workshop idea of Louis Blanc actually developed into a simple dole from the public funds. The number of those who drew this dole rose alarmingly, and conservatives all over the country became terrified. In the elections to the National Assembly, the socialists were snowed under, and one of the first acts of the National Assembly (June 1848) was the abolition of the "abominable" national workshop system. The unemployed workingmen, thus suddenly cut off from the government subsidy they had been enjoying, rose in revolt but were mercilessly crushed by the soldiers of the National Asembly under General Cavaignac in the terribly bloody "June Days" (June 24-26, 1848).

The Second Republic and the Bourgeoisie. Having violently suppressed the social revolt of the working class, the new Assembly, controlled by bourgeois Republicans and conservatives from the agricultural districts, adopted a constitution providing for a single chamber legislature and a president to be elected for four years by universal suffrage. Moderate political reforms were adopted. Capital punishment for purely political offenses was abolished. The right of association and public meeting was guaranteed. While the obligation of the government to furnish work for the unemployed was specifically repudiated, a statement was included in the constitution that the government would assist the unemployed "as far as its resources permitted."

ITALY AND THE REVOLUTION OF 1848

Opposition to Austrian Dominion. Throughout the period 1830-1848 a strong undercurrent of opposition was developing in Italy toward the despotism of Austria and the independent Hapsburg rulers. Mazzini's secret society favored a republic; the Clericals agitated for a federation under the Pope; a third group looked to the liberal Charles Albert, King of Sardinia, as the rallying point for an Italian *risorgimento*. In many centers outside Italy, notably Marseilles, groups of political exiles banded together in a formidable society, "Young Italy." Characteristic of the Italian liberal movement were its intense nationalism and its comparative indifference to the social and economic issues that the Industrial Revolution had infused into the liberalism of England and France.

National Uprising (1848). In March 1848 rebellion against the Austrians broke out in Milan. After several days of desperate fighting the Austrian army, under Field-marshal Radetzky, was driven out of the city. The rest of Lombardy and Venetia immediately joined the revolt. Charles Albert, King of Sardinia and Piedmont, now declared war against Austria and came to the aid of the revolutionists with a disciplined army. In the Kingdom of the Two Sicilies (Southern Italy) a constitutional government had been set up, while in the Papal States the liberal Pius IX was definitely sympathetic to the Italian national aspirations. For a short time (May and June 1848) it appeared that the uprising, headed by the Piedmontese army of Charles Albert, would be successful in throwing the Austrians permanently out of the whole peninsula. But on July 25, Radetzky defeated Charles Albert at the decisive battle of Custozza and reoccupied Milan.

Restoration of Austrian Control. The following year (1849) Charles Albert made a further effort, but was defeated by Radetzky at Novara. Charles Albert then abdicated the throne of Sardinia in favor of his son Victor Emmanuel. The Austrians recaptured all the revolted territory, but sowed the seeds of intense hatred by the cruelty with which General Haynau punished the city of Brescia. Although the attempts of the Italian patriots were thus unsuccessful in 1848-1849, an inspiring example had been set, and there remained, as a powerful gathering ground for a future effort, the constitutional monarchy of Sardinia and Piedmont under the able, liberal, and intensely Italian-minded Victor Emmanuel II.

GERMANY AND THE REVOLUTION OF 1848

Underground Liberal Movements (1830-1848). In Germany, as throughout central Europe, Metternichism continued to rule throughout the period 1830-1848. The Industrial Revolution was just beginning its corrosive influence on the social order represented by the old regime. Bourgeoisie and urban workingmen were still not numerous enough to challenge effectively the power of the landed aristocracy. Economic liberalism, therefore, that had been the real motive power behind the Paris revolution of 1830 and the British Reform of 1832, was largely lacking in Germany. But intellectual and political liberalism, the inheritance of the French rather than the Industrial Revolution, gained headway in spite of Metternich and his secret police, in spite of censorship of the press and of education, and in spite of the strict system of passports designed to prevent the infiltration of radical persons and ideas from abroad. The universities, in particular, became dangerous centers of liberal agitation.

The Frankfurt Assembly (1848). When news of the February revolution at Paris reached Germany, there were simultaneous uprisings in many German cities. Most of the German states demanded a constitutional monarchy, a free press, and a strong Germanic federation. In Baden, Bavaria, Saxony, and Hanover, and in the independent Hanse towns the frightened German princes installed liberal ministries and promised to grant constitutions. Serious rioting broke out in Berlin, and Frederick William IV of Prussia was forced to appoint a liberal ministry and convoke a constituent assembly. In May 1848 an assembly representing all the German states convened at Frankfurt with the intention of drawing up a constitution for the entire German confederation. For nearly a year this assembly deliberated and wrangled; finally, in

1849 it completed the drawing up of a constitution providing a limited monarchy and a union of all the German states. The crown of this proposed united German Empire was offered to Frederick William IV of Prussia. But a reaction against liberalism had set in, and although Frederick William was tempted by the dream of a united Germany under Prussian leadership, his hatred of constitutionalism led him to decline the offer. The Frankfurt Assembly then broke up; its more radical leaders fled the country.

Reaction in Prussia. In the fall of 1848 the tide of liberalism was fast ebbing in Prussia and throughout the Germanies. The failure of the liberals to hold their gains arose from the fact that their movement was the work of a minority of enthusiasts; the bulk of the nation remained apathetic if not strongly conservative. Frederick William IV soon felt himself strong enough to dismiss the liberal ministry he had appointed during the March crisis, and he appointed Count Brandenburg, a stanch reactionary, to administer the government. The Berlin populace was easily cowed by a display of military force. A constitution, indeed, was granted as promised, but it was drawn up by Frederick William himself and his own advisers and contained nothing liberal save empty gestures. A similar reaction occurred in the other German states. Scattered efforts of the liberals continued after the dissolution of the Frankfurt Assembly (May 1849), but they were easily suppressed by Prussian troops. Many political refugees emigrated to the United States. Many more were caught and jailed.

REVOLUTION IN THE AUSTRIAN EMPIRE

Vienna. In Vienna, the capital of Metternichism, dissatisfaction had long been brewing. Revolutionary news from France and Italy precipitated violent rioting (March 13-15, 1848). Metternich resigned his ministry and fled for his life. The weak and helpless Ferdinand I immediately offered liberal concessions; the press censorship was revoked and a constitution was promised.

Bohemia and Hungary. The heterogeneous population in the Hapsburg empire greatly complicated the issues of the revolutionary movement of 1848. As soon as they saw that the Vienna government was shaking, nationalist patriots in Bohemia and Hungary began revolts the object of which, like that of the Italian revolt, was national autonomy rather than any liberalization of the Austrian imperial government. Because of this diversification of aims, there was no co-operation among the liberals in Bohemia, Hungary, and Italy. This disunity in the revolting forces enabled the imperial government to deal with them separately. In June 1848 a Pan-Slavic Congress convened at Prague with the intention of drawing up an independent government for the Czechs, Slovaks, and other Slavic peoples within the Austrian Empire. This movement was quickly crushed by the soldiers of Prince Windischgrätz. More serious was the revolt of the Hungarians. Led by the able and patriotic Louis Kossuth, the Hungarians set up an autonomous state with freedom of the press, abolition of privilege, and annual Diets, and extended the franchise to the middle class (owners of property worth about $1000).

Reaction under Francis Joseph. Having successfully put down the revolt at Prague, the army under Prince Windischgrätz marched on Vienna (October 1848), and after several days of fighting succeeded in capturing the city and restoring the authority of the Emperor. An attempt was made by the Hungarians to save the Vienna revolutionaries, but the relieving army was beaten back, and the only result of the effort was that a more severe punishment was meted out by the victorious Windischgrätz. Immediately after the capture of Vienna, the Emperor Ferdinand abdicated in favor of his nephew Francis Joseph. The real power of the re-established imperial government, however, was Prince Felix Schwartzenberg, a man whose methods and ideas, if not his abilities, were nearly indistinguishable from those of Prince Metternich. As the year 1848 came to a close, it was evident that the revolution, so far as it regarded the internal government of Austria, had failed; reaction was again firmly entrenched. It remained to be seen whether the revolting Italians and Hungarians would be able to make good their efforts at independence. In 1849 this question was answered adversely for both revolting nationalities. The Italians were first defeated, and with the troops thus released the Austrians attacked the Hungarians in earnest. The Tsar came to the help of his brother emperor with an army of 80,000 Russians. Against the overwhelming force of their enemies the Hungarians had no chance; after three months of desperate but hopeless resistance they were compelled to surrender. The notorious General Haynau inflicted a savage punishment on the captured leaders. Louis Kossuth and a few others escaped to Turkey. With the collapse of the Hungarian Republic the Austrian revolution of 1848-1849 came to an end; the dominions of the Hapsburgs remained intact; Metternich was gone, but in his place was his replica, Schwartzenberg; practically all the reforms and concessions except the abolition of serfdom were repudiated. Nevertheless, the revolution had shaken the monarchy to its foundation, and even its apparently complete suppression could never reconstruct the reactionary psychology of the heyday of Metternichism.

Significant Dates

Truce of Villafranca 1859
Battle of Sadowa 1866
Ems Dispatch 1870
Battle of Sedan 1870
Formation of German Empire 1871
Third French Republic . . . 1871

CHAPTER IV.

THE TRIUMPH OF NATIONALISM

The revolutionary upheaval of Europe in 1848-1849 was everywhere suppressed. Small indeed was the visible gain of liberalism, nationalism, and democracy. France changed her form of government from monarchial to republican, but the change turned out to be only temporary. In 1850 it must have seemed to most contemporaries that the efforts of the liberals and patriots had been entirely in vain, and reactionaries rejoiced that the final quietus had been given to all the subversive movements that had been rumbling under the surface ever since the Congress of Vienna. The next quarter of a century was to show how superficial this view of things was. Instead of closing an era of liberal-national agitation, the revolutions of 1848 opened the era of liberal-national victories. By 1871 men could look back and see that almost everything fought for in 1848-1849 had been won. Italy had liberated herself from Austria and was united under a constitutional king. Hungary had secured practical autonomy. Germany was united under a government not indeed liberal by the standards of France and Great Britain, but of revolutionary liberalism by the standards of Metternich. France was a republic. Great Britain had taken a great step toward democracy and was clearly on the path of even greater liberalizing change. Even autocratic Russia had caught the fever and had emancipated her serfs and had begun gestures toward administrative reform. In one sense, therefore, the period 1849-1871 may be looked upon as the fulfillment of the agitation and aspiration of the period 1815-1848. Yet no one could fail to see how different was the fulfillment from the dream. The liberalism of 1815-1848 (except in England where its keynote was economic laissez faire) was dominated by the romanticism of the French Revolution; its heroes were poets, idealists, and intellectuals like Byron, Shelley, Mazzini, and Lamartine. The period 1849-1871 was eminently an age of realism in which practical statesmen like Cavour, Bismarck, Palmerston, and Disraeli were directing in action the mass enthusiasms that had been generated by the idealists of an earlier time.

FRANCE—SECOND REPUBLIC AND SECOND EMPIRE

Louis Napoleon (1808-1873). The candidates for the French Presidency in 1848 were Ledru-Rollin, representing the Labor party, General Cavaignac of the Democratic Republicans, the liberal and poet, Lamartine, and Louis Napoleon. Louis Napoleon was a nephew of Napoleon I who, by clever maneuvering, had put himself before the people as an avenue to peace and security. Sick of the turbulence of party strife, fascinated by the "Napoleonic Legend" and its picture of a Napoleon who had served France unselfishly, the French people elected Louis Napoleon President of France by an overwhelming majority.

Louis Napoleon, President of France (1848-1852). During the first three years of his term, Napoleon did everything he could to overthrow the Assembly and make it possible for him to revise the Constitution in order that he might be reëlected in 1852. By a cleverly administered policy, he gained the support of the army and the populace. The Assembly was dissolved in December 1851, and a plebiscite was submitted to the people asking them to give Louis Napoleon the right to revise the Constitution in order that he might save the Republic. With the army to support his desires, it was only natural that the people gave Louis Napoleon the power to revise the

Constitution by a large majority. Louis Napoleon now drew
up a Constitution which lengthened the presidential term to
ten years and centered all authority in the president through
his appointive power. A year of education along imperialistic
lines was followed with another plebiscite which made Louis
Napoleon Emperor of France in 1852.

Louis Napoleon, Emperor of France (1852-1870). The
first part of Napoleon's reign was one of "veiled despotism"
in which many constructive reforms were brought about. The
government was centered in the hands of Napoleon III. He
controlled the law-making body, commanded the army and
navy, declared wars, appointed most officers of the state; in
short, he was the government. Many hundreds of the old republican leaders and sympathizers were arrested, convicted *en
masse* of "having taken part in the recent insurrections," and
deported. A vigorous censorship of all things distasteful to
the Emperor was instituted. To compensate the French people
for the loss of their freedom, Napoleon founded hospitals and
asylums, beautified Paris, and increased commerce by facili-
tating railroad and steamboat transportation. The success of
France in the Crimean War (1856) added greatly to his prestige. After 1858 his meddling in foreign affairs weakened his
position and culminated in the Franco-German War which
drove him from his throne.

THE FOREIGN POLICY OF NAPOLEON III (1859-1870). Although
Napoleon III had none of the military genius and restless
energy that had characterized his uncle, he was intent on
waging an aggressive foreign policy which would increase the
prestige of not only France, but of himself. When the plebiscite that was to elect him Emperor of the French was pending, he had striven to point out to the peace-loving French
people that their fears of war, following the establishment of
the Empire, were groundless. *"L'Empire c'est la paix"*—in this
famous phrase he promised a policy of external peace and internal development. However, his work in Italy, Mexico, and
Germany resulted in the humiliation of France and the end
of Napoleon's Empire.

SITUATION IN ITALY (1849-1859)

Nationalistic Tendencies. During the European revolutions of 1848-1849 Italy made a desperate attempt to shake off the Austrian yoke in the northern provinces of Lombardy and Venetia, and to depose, or extort constitutions from the independent Hapsburg and Bourbon rulers in the small states. This first attempt at revolution was crushed. But it had served to raise the patriotic aspirations of the Italians to the highest pitch, and during the following ten years the whole peninsula seethed with the spirit of resistance. The petty despots on the thrones of the independent duchies, particularly Ferdinand of the Two Sicilies, continued to apply the time-honored methods of suppression through censorship, arbitrary arrests, and cruel punishments of agitators, but these devices only stiffened the national will to resist while they alienated the minds of liberals and humanitarians all over Europe. It became more and more clear that another general uprising of Italy awaited only a favorable moment, and a coalescence of opinion among the various groups of agitators as to the form of national state that should be set up.

A large group of the bourgeoisie looked to the Kingdom of Sardinia and Piedmont as the natural leader of the Italian states. They hoped that the other states would form a constitutional kingdom with Sardinia as the leading force. After 1850 many of the Republicans and Federalists gradually accepted the idea that a constitutional kingdom, with Sardinia at the head, was the best political form for the prospective Italian state. Sardinia had attracted favorable attention among the Italian States because she was the only state that had successfully resisted Austrian control. The granting of a constitution to his subjects in 1848, by Charles Albert, gained the support of the Liberals.

The Sardinian Leaders. Three great leaders of the nationalist movement in Italy were destined to come from this state.

Victor Emmanuel II (1849-1878). Victor Emmanuel II, who succeeded Charles Albert, retained the Constitution of 1848 in spite of Austrian objection. The Liberals realized that here was a man with desirable traits to foster Italian unity.

GIUSEPPE GARIBALDI (1807-1882). Although he desired a republican Italy, Garibaldi was willing to support a constitutional monarchy with Victor Emmanuel at the helm. He realized that the best chance for liberation lay in that direction. Garibaldi had spent his life in aiding suppressed people in South America and Italy. From his island home at Caprera, he awaited an opportunity to aid Italian unification.

COUNT CAMILLO DI CAVOUR (1810-1861). Cavour was the most important leader who made the unification of Italy possible. His liberalism was influenced by his travels in Great Britain. During the reign of Charles Albert he was one of the editors of the well-known paper *Il Risorgimento* which advocated the preparation of Sardinia to lead the Italian states to national unity. Cavour was Victor Emmanuel's Prime Minister from 1852 to 1861, except for a very brief interval.

The Liberal Reforms of Cavour. As Prime Minister, Cavour fostered internal improvements in the fields of transportation, manufacturing, and agriculture. Free trade was put into effect. Education was improved and the budget was readjusted. The power of the Clericals was decreased by suppressing monasteries and forcing Jesuits to leave the country. These activities appear more important when one realizes that all the other Italian states were dominated by Austria and that all of Cavour's relations with these states called for artful diplomacy.

Sardinia and the Crimean War. By joining France and Great Britain against Russia in the Crimean War, Cavour secured a place for Sardinia among the European nations, her recognition as the leading state in Italy, and the friendship of her allies.

The Plombières Agreement (1858). Cavour concentrated his efforts on gaining the support of Napoleon III against Austria (1856-1858). At an "accidental" meeting at Plombières, France, Napoleon III agreed to support Sardinia in forcing the Austrians from Lombardy and Venetia. In return for French aid, Cavour was to give Savoy and Nice to Napoleon III.

LIBERATION AND UNIFICATION
OF ITALY (1859-1871)

Austro-Sardinian War (1859). Cavour provoked a war with Austria by arousing disturbances in Lombardy and Venetia and forcing Austria to demand that Sardinia disarm or accept the consequences. Assured of French support, Cavour rejected the ultimatum, and in the fighting which followed, the French and Sardinians defeated the Austrians at Magenta (June) and Solferino. These victories were the signals for the states of Tuscany, Parma, and Modena to overthrow their Austrian potentates.

The revolutions in Northern Italy and the mobilization of the Prussians along the Rhine made Napoleon III desirous of stopping the conflict. On entering the war he had announced his intention of freeing Italy "from the Alps to the Adriatic," and great was the astonishment of Europe and the rage of the Italian patriots when, without notifying Cavour, he arranged a truce at Villafranca (1859) with Francis Joseph of Austria. Sardinia was to receive Lombardy; Venetia was retained by Austria; the deposed princes were reinstated, and the Pope was to be made president of an Italian confederation. Victor Emmanuel agreed to the terms because he knew it was hopeless to oppose Austria without the help of France. Cavour resigned as Prime Minister because Victor Emmanuel refused to continue the war. The treaty of Zurich (1859) reënforced the truce of Villafranca.

Annexation of Parma, Modena, Romagna, and Tuscany (1860). The northern duchies refused to become a part of an Italian Confederation with the Pope as president, but voted to join Sardinia. Napoleon objected to this annexation, but the wily Cavour returned to the premiership with a solution. In order to gain Napoleon's approval for the annexation of the duchies of Modena, Parma, Romagna, and Tuscany, Cavour offered to give him Savoy and Nice as was provided for in the conversation at Plombières. There was considerable objection to this arrangement. Nevertheless, the treaty of Turin was signed by Napoleon III and Victor Emmanuel II.

Garibaldi and the Annexation of the Two Sicilies (1860). As Cavour had united the states of the North, Garibaldi made it possible for the Two Sicilies to join Sardinia. When the Sicilians revolted, Garibaldi left his island home with one thousand volunteers called "Red Shirts," and with secret assurances from Cavour that he would not interfere. The "Red Shirts" gained control of Sicily in three months in spite of enormous odds. Then Garibaldi crossed over to the mainland, captured Naples (1860), and forced King Francis II to flee to Gaeta. The delicate diplomatic situation created by this illegal filibustering expedition was handled in masterly fashion by Cavour, while Napoleon's indecision resulted in much loss of face. Napoleon was committed to maintaining the independence of Rome under the Pope, and he was not eager to see a successful revolution in the Two Sicilies, especially a revolution led by a republican adventurer. He protested to Cavour and threatened to stop Garibaldi by force. Cavour pretended to be as outraged by Garibaldi's proceedings as any one else, and finally sent an army to southern Italy, ostensibly to put down Garibaldi's republican revolution. Napoleon would have preferred direct intervention, but the fear of complications with other powers, particularly England where a strong force of public opinion supported the Italians, kept him from taking vigorous measures.

Although Garibaldi favored a republic for Italy, he was willing to allow Victor Emmanuel II to set up a constitutional monarchy, since he felt it was the best that could be done at this time. When Victor Emmanuel II arrived in Naples after having defeated a papal army at Castelfidardo (1860) and making possible the addition of Umbria and the Marches, Garibaldi turned his conquests over to him. Plebiscites in Naples, Sicily, the Marches, and Umbria were overwhelmingly in favor of unification. All Italy except Venetia (still under Austria) and a small strip of territory around Rome (the last remnant of the Papal states) was united under Victor Emmanuel.

The Kingdom of Italy (1861). Italy had been united in less than two short years through the nationalistic desires of the Italians, the diplomacy of Cavour, the intervention of Napoleon, and the conquests of Garibaldi. However, the Italians were laying plans for the acquisition of Venetia and Rome. Victor Emmanuel was declared king, and the Parliament met at the new capital, Turin.

Four Italian Leaders weld the Italian States INTO THE

KINGDOM OF ITALY

Dates indicate year of annexation to the Kingdom of Sardinia (after 1861, the Kingdom of Italy.)

Mazzini

Cavour

Garibaldi

Victor Emmanuel

FRANCE

SWITZERLAND

AUSTRIA

SAVOY (to France, 1860)

TYROL

1859 LOMBARDY

1866 VENETIA

To France, 1860, in compensation for French aid in defeating Austria

PIEDMONT

Magenta Milan Solferino

Verona

Venice

ISTRIA

Turin

NICE

Monaco

PARMA 1860

MODENA 1860

ROMAGNA

STATES OF THE CHURCH

MARCHES

KINGDOM OF SARDINIA

TUSCANY 1860

Florence

UMBRIA

Adriatic Sea

CORSICA (to France, 1768)

ELBA

Rome

1870

SARDINIA

Tyrrhenian Sea

Naples

KINGDOM of the TWO SICILIES 1860

CALABRIA

Messina

SICILY

Mediterranean Sea

E.W.F.

Acquisition of Venetia (1866). During the events leading to the unification of Germany, Italy allied herself with Prussia against Austria in the Seven Weeks' War (1866) in order to obtain Venetia. The Italians were not very successful, but the effectiveness of the Prussian campaigns was great enough to make Austria come to an early agreement and to give Venetia to Italy. The Venetian plebiscite was almost unanimously in favor of annexation to Italy.

Rome Becomes Capital of Italy (1871). The Franco-German War (1870-1871) afforded Italy an opportunity to obtain Rome. Napoleon III had to withdraw his French troops from Rome, and the Italians were able to overcome the few papal soldiers and occupy the city. A plebiscite was favorable to annexation, and Rome became the capital of Italy.

"Italia Irredenta" (1870-1918). Unredeemed Italy consisted of Trentino, in the Alps, and Trieste, on the Adriatic. Although these lands were largely inhabited by Italians, they were controlled by Austria. In 1915 Italy joined the Allies against Germany and Austria on the promise that they would give her Trieste and Trentino. Accordingly, at the end of the World War, Italy received Trieste, Trentino, the southern part of Tyrol, and the districts of Istria and Gorizia.

PRUSSIA AND THE UNIFICATION OF GERMANY

Disunited Germany. Early in the nineteenth century several events paved the way for a national state in the Germanies, but unification was hindered by other circumstances.

TENDENCIES TOWARD NATIONALISM. Napoleon Bonaparte abolished the Holy Roman Empire (1806) and made it possible for a central government, with Prussia at the helm, to be substituted for the weak, decentralized form. The number of German states was reduced from over three hundred in 1789 to thirty-eight in 1815. Also, the War of Liberation had united the German states for a time against a common foe. Finally, the formation of the *Zollverein* (1834) by Prussia offered an example of economic coöperation which could be used as an argument for political solidification.

FORCES OPPOSING CENTRALIZATION. The organization of the Germanic Confederation (1815) was too loose a union to satisfy the Nationalists and would inevitably be superseded by a stronger force. It was obvious that either Prussia or Austria would be the leader, and any union that provided for a partnership between these powers would not be satisfactory. A new government for Germany would have to effect some kind

The Growth of
PRUSSIA
1807 — 1815

☐ Prussia, 1807-1813
▥ Regained, 1815
■ Acquisitions, 1815
⸬ Bounds German
Confederation

of an agreement with the various German princes before they would support a national state. Finally, the reactionary Conservatives would have to be won over to the side of nationalism.

Rise of Prussia. Prussia was the natural leader in the Germanies for many reasons. Prussia was made up of a more purely German population than was Austria. Her state had long been recognized by European powers because of her activities in the War of Austrian Succession, the Partitions of

Poland, and the Napoleonic Wars. In 1850, Prussia granted to her people a constitution which served to satisfy the Liberal forces.

WILLIAM I (1861-1888). William I of the Hohenzollern dynasty brought with him to the throne the qualities that were necessary to foster unification. He was an industrious worker, a good judge of leaders, and he placed great faith in a strong military machine. With the aid of Albrecht von Roon (War Minister) and Helmuth von Moltke (Chief of the General Staff), William I started to reorganize the army and lay the basis for Prussian supremacy. But Parliament opposed William's militarism and refused to give him the necessary funds.

OTTO VON BISMARCK (1815-1898). Bismarck had not had a long diplomatic career when William I called him to curb Parliament. His college days had been spent in various forms of dissipation, and it was not until after 1847 that he began to take any active part in Prussian politics. He became the champion of the Conservatives and backed German unification under Prussian leadership. While he was a representative to the Diet of the Germanic Confederation, he acquired a definite dislike for Austria (1851-1859). Short sojourns in Russia and France as an ambassador acquainted him with the Tsar and Napoleon III.

BISMARCK AND THE UNIFICATION OF GERMANY

Bismarck tried several methods to persuade Parliament to give him sufficient funds for carrying out the military reforms, but the Progressives would not give him the necessary support. With the permission of William I, Bismarck proceeded to rule as a dictator and to lay and collect his own revenue. The guiding principle of Bismarck was "not by speeches and majority resolutions are the great questions of the day to be decided—but by blood and iron." The army reforms were carried out, and Bismarck was ready to challenge Austria for German leadership, to foment nationalism, and to curb political liberalism.

The Danish War (1864). The Schleswig-Holstein affair offered Bismarck the necessary opening for a quarrel with

Austria. These territories, while inhabited by Germans, were controlled by the King of Denmark in a personal type of union. The desire of the Danish people for a closer union was strongly opposed by the nationalistic tendencies in Germany. When Christian IX accepted a constitution which incorporated these duchies into Denmark, the Prussians and Austrians, in a bid for German leadership, voiced their disapproval. Christian IX ignored the German threats, because he mistakenly believed that Great Britain would come to his assistance if he were attacked.

The Danes never had a chance against the combined forces of the Austrians and Prussians. They accepted the Treaty of Vienna (1864) by which Christian renounced all claim to Schleswig, Holstein, and Lauenburg. The duchies were turned over to the joint administration of Austria and Prussia. The quarrel between these two powers over the newly acquired territories led directly to the Seven Weeks' War.

The Seven Weeks' War (1866). The Seven Weeks' War left Prussia the dominant force in the Germanies and excluded Austria from the future German nation.

THE CAUSE OF THE WAR. Bismarck had anticipated that Prussia and Austria would not be able to reach an agreement as to the disposition of the spoils of the Schleswig-Holstein conquest. An Austro-Prussian war was temporarily averted by the Convention of Gastein (1865), which provided that (1) Prussia would receive Lauenburg for a money settlement, (2) Austria was to control Holstein, and (3) Prussia was to administer Schleswig. Bismarck had no intention of allowing this temporary settlement to become permanent. He cynically planned to use the conflict of interests in Schleswig-Holstein as a lever for fomenting an Austro-Prussian war.

ISOLATION OF AUSTRIA. Bismarck knew that any conflict which would oust Austria from the Germanies would destroy the Germanic Confederation which had been created by the Congress of Vienna. Before tearing down the works of the Congress, Bismarck set about to isolate Austria from European aid.

Great Britain was not expected to interfere, because of the concessions granted British commerce under the *Zollverein* and the Teutonic traditions of both groups.

French neutrality was assured by a glib promise from Bismarck at Biarritz. He gave Napoleon III to understand that if Napoleon allowed Prussia to make war upon Austria, Bismarck would see to it that France received some "compensations" (territorial).

Italy was guaranteed Venetia if she would oppose Austria in the South while Prussia was attacking her in the North.

Russia was indebted to Prussia for aid in the Polish Insurrection (1863), and although the Tsar did not favor German unity, he could not very well oppose the Prussians in 1866.

ALLIES OF AUSTRIA.   Many of the lesser German states favored Austria in the coming clash because they did not want to give up their power to a central government. They opposed Prussian militarism, preferring Austria, which was Catholic like themselves. But Bismarck knew they could render no real assistance. He counted on a decisive victory through the superiority of the Prussian military machine, and he knew that there is nothing like military victory to inspire national unity.

THE COURSE OF THE WAR (1866).   Bismarck's secret interference in Holstein provoked a crisis and caused Austria to bring the situation before the Diet of the Germanic Confederation. Prussia claimed this violated the Gastein Convention, and Bismarck dispatched troops into Holstein. The whole affair was arranged in such a way as to make it appear that Prussia was on the defensive. The Prussian military machine was able to subjugate the lesser German states in two weeks, and the battle of Sadowa (1866) completely humiliated the Austrians.

TREATY OF PRAGUE (1866).   The Treaty of Prague (1866) was extremely lenient with Austria, as Bismarck could see a future need for her friendship. Austria lost no territory except Venetia to Italy, and Holstein to Prussia. The Germanic Confederation was dissolved, Prussian leadership acknowledged, and only a small indemnity was demanded. Bismarck's main purpose in waging the war was to get rid of Austrian pretentions to German leadership.

OTHER RESULTS OF THE WAR.   There were several other events resulting from this war, which indirectly led to German nationalism.

Prussia became the undisputed owner of Schleswig, Lauenburg, and Holstein. This afforded her a strong naval base (Kiel) and an invaluable ship canal from the North Sea to the Baltic.

The lesser German states of Hanover, Hesse-Cassel, Nassau, and the free city of Frankfurt-on-Main were annexed and gave Prussia a prepossessing kingdom within the Germanies.

Prussia had all the German states in the North join her in a North German Confederation (1867). The king of Prussia was the hereditary president. The legislature consisted of two houses—a Bundesrat (representative of the princes of the states) and a Reichstag (elected by universal manhood suffrage).

The Southern German states of Bavaria, Württemberg, Baden, and Darmstadt were not forced to join the Confederation, but Bismarck tried to win them over to German unity by respecting them, by the *Zollverein*, by secret agreements, and by warning them of French aggression. Bismarck felt that an armed conflict with France would bring these states into Germany and complete the unification.

The National Liberal Party was formed after the war with Austria. Bismarck began to place confidence in the Liberals, and they no longer distrusted his motives. The Diet was restored to power, and an apology for usurping power was accepted by that body from Bismarck. The new party supported Bismarck, opposed the Clericals, and favored a strong centralized government, militarism, and free trade.

SIGNIFICANCE OF THE SEVEN WEEKS' WAR TO AUSTRIA.   The war with Prussia marked the end of an era in Austria.

Metternichism received its final defeat at Sadowa. Most of the reactionary policies of the Hapsburgs had failed. To the external failure was added the domestic demands for a more democratic government and national status for not only Germans and Italians but also for Slavs and Magyars.

After 1866 Austria had been forced to give up her right to interfere in both Germany and Italy.

The Liberals in Austria profited by the Austrian defeats because they were able to force the Emperor, Francis Joseph, to grant them certain rights. In 1861 a constitution provided for a Diet composed of Hungarians and Austrians which would sit at Vienna.

Due to the activities of the Magyars, the Austrians were forced to grant Francis Déak's demand for a dual monarchy in which the two sections—Austria and Hungary—would each manage its own internal affairs but would be united by a common sovereign, army, and foreign policy. The Ausgleich, which provided for this arrangement, was agreed to in 1867 as a reward for the loyalty of Hungary in the Seven Weeks' War.

INFLUENCE OF THE SEVEN WEEKS' WAR ON FRANCE. The short duration of the war and its result augured ill for Napoleon III. With his attention and energies dissipated in far away schemes—Mexico, Algeria, and Rome—his control over conflicting political parties at home weakened by the contradictions and changes of front that had characterized his recent policy, Napoleon was in no position to challenge the latest steps in German unification. At the outset of war between Prussia and Austria, Napoleon hoped that the war would be long and exhausting for both sides, and that both powers would be glad to accept his mediation. When Prussia won the war so speedily and decisively, it was obvious that Napoleon's proud position as "arbiter of Europe" was gone, and he sought desperately for some sort of "compensation" to save his face before the French people. Bismarck had made vague promises before the war, and Napoleon now vainly tried to get them fulfilled.

The request for the Rhenish Palatinate served only to strengthen Bismarck's alliance with Bavaria, who refused to give up this territory which belonged to her. Napoleon III next tried to secure Belgium and Luxemburg, but Bismarck merely evaded the issue. Napoleon's attempts to get land gave

Bismarck an opportunity to reveal the ambitions of the French Emperor to the European monarchs. It gradually became clear that Napoleon was going to get nothing from Bismarck without going to war for it. This was exactly what Bismarck wanted.

The Franco-German War (1870-1871). The Franco-German war was the final step in the creation of the new Germany and the end of the imperialistic career of Napoleon III. After 1859 the attempts of Napoleon III to appease both the French Clericals and Liberals served only to increase the dissatisfaction and criticism for his inconsistent Italian policy. Liberals and Clericals were united in their opposition to the Emperor.

FOREIGN POLICY OF NAPOLEON III (1860-1871). In order to detract the attention of his subjects from the domestic situation, Napoleon fostered an ambitious foreign policy, but never carried out his schemes with real vigor. The Polish Insurrection (1863) offered an opportunity to satisfy both the Clericals and the Liberals. As Poland was a Catholic country, its liberation from the Tsar was urged by the Clericals. The Liberals in France desired Napoleon to aid Poland, as it would be another conquest for them. Finally, Napoleon III could once more pose as the friend of an oppressed nationality. Although he might have wished to interfere, Napoleon III was afraid that Austria and Prussia would support Russia, and so he only sent a protest to the Tsar. The Poles were unable to oppose Russia without foreign help, and the revolt was cruelly suppressed.

The creation of a French Empire in Mexico was the great plan through which Napoleon III hoped to win the support of the Clericals and Liberals, despite their disappointment over his actions in the Polish Insurrection. The Civil War in the United States and the internal trouble in Mexico made this intervention possible. Great Britain, Spain, and France occupied Mexico (1862) with the understanding that when a satisfactory financial arrangement was made for the Mexican debt, they would withdraw. The necessary agreements were reached, Spain and Great Britain withdrew, but France remained and with 30,000 reenforcements captured Mexico City (1863). The Archduke Maximilian of Austria was made Emperor of Mexico (1864) and was supported by French troops. Napoleon III had hoped to satisfy (1) Austria for his interference in Italy by making Maximilian Emperor of Mexico, (2) the French Clericals by having Maximilian relieve the persecution of the Catholic Church which had been going on under the Jaurez government, and (3) the Liberals by giving them trade concessions in the new land. However, Napoleon's plan went for naught. The Civil War in the United States came to an end (1865), and that country reasserted, in no in-

The Growth of
PRUSSIA
1815～1871

‖‖‖ Prussia, 1815-1865*
‖‖‖ Prussian Acquisitions, 1866
*L-Lichtenberg (to Prussia, 1834).
*H-Hohenzollern (to Prussia, 1849).
xxxxx Bounds NORTH GERMAN CONFED-
FEDERATION, (1866 - 1871)
—Bounds GERMAN EMPIRE (1871-1918)

decisive tone, the Monroe Doctrine; while in Mexico, nationalism was aroused against foreign interference. Rather than face these conditions, Napoleon III withdrew his French troops (1867). Maximilian refused to leave Mexico, and was captured and shot.

OPPOSITION TO NAPOLEON AFTER THE MAXIMILIAN INCIDENT. The failure of the Maximilian Empire served to unite the opposition to Napoleon III on all sides. His foreign policy had been a failure and greatly reduced his prestige. The concessions to the Clericals had been ineffective and they openly opposed the Emporer. In 1869 Napoleon III tried to appease the Liberals by inaugurating a few democratic governmental reforms, but the rise of the Republicans and Socialists more than offset any gains in this direction.

PREPARATION FOR THE FRANCO-GERMAN WAR. Napoleon III decided to risk everything in a last attempt for a successful foreign war. He realized that Bismarck was aiming at such a conflict and that the Seven Weeks' War was only a fore-runner to a war with France. While Napoleon sought allies, Bismarck tried to isolate France. Russia was still grateful to Bismarck for his help in the Polish insurrection, whereas Napoleon had opposed her both at that time' and in the Crimean War. The Italians had not forgotten Napoleon's de-sertion after Villafranca nor the aid of Prussia in obtaining Venetia. The lenient peace of 1866 served to preserve Aus-trian neutrality. Great Britain, under the leadership of the pacific Gladstone, and glad to see the humiliation of Napoleon, was not likely to interfere.

THE EMS DISPATCH (1870). In 1869 the Spanish crown, which had been made vacant by the expulsion of Isabella II, was offered to Leopold of Hohenzollern-Sigmaringen. Bis-marck persuaded Leopold to accept the crown because he knew that Napoleon III would object to any candidate who would tend to unite the German and Spanish thrones. As an-ticipated, Napoleon III protested to William I, and Leopold agreed to give up the throne. The French Emperor then had his ambassador in Prussia demand that the throne would never be held by a Hohenzollern. William I refused to grant this request and sent a message to Bismarck from Ems telling him of the developments. Bismarck reworded the dispatch in such a way as to arouse the French against Prussia and the Prussians against France. France declared war on Germany. The Southern German states immediately joined Prussia against France.

THE COURSE OF THE WAR (1870-1871). The efficiency of Bismarck's government, which was made all the more impos-ing when compared with the corrupt Napoleonic regime, made possible the decisive victories at Sedan and Metz (1870) and the capture of Napoleon III and his Marshal, MacMahon. With the news that Napoleon III was a prisoner, the Republicans under Léon Gambetta, proclaimed the establishment of the Third French Republic. Desirous of obtaining a complete capitulation, Bismarck did not conclude a peace with the Republicans at this time but concentrated on capturing Paris, which finally surrendered after a siege that lasted from September 1870 to January 1871. The surrender of Paris and the fall of Strasbourg ended the fighting.

TREATY OF FRANKFURT (1871). A newly elected French Assembly ratified the preliminary terms of peace which had been drawn up at Versailles, and the final treaty was signed at Frankfurt. The treaty provided that (1) France must give up Alsace-Lorraine with Metz and Strasbourg to Germany, (2) France must pay an indemnity of one billion dollars, and (3) German troops would remain in France until the indemnity was paid.

The German Empire (1871). The most important result of the Franco-German War was the establishment of the German Empire. The war allied the southern states with Prussia, and the victory was partly theirs. As a result, the increased feeling of nationalism was great enough to overcome the ambitions of princes, and the North German Confederation added the states of Bavaria, Württemberg, Baden, and Hesse-Darmstadt, one by one. On January 18, 1871 the king of Prussia became the Emperor of Germany in the palace of Louis XIV at Versailles, and Bismarck saw his efforts rewarded with success.

Significance of the Franco-German War to Europe. The War of 1870 was important to other European powers as well as to Germany. The Treaty of Frankfurt conclusively ended the Second French Empire and brought into being a third republic which attempted to revive the revolutionary watch words of liberty, equality, and fraternity. For the next forty years, the French were to concentrate on wiping out the humiliation of 1870 and on regaining "the lost provinces."

When Napoleon withdrew his French garrison from Rome, the Italians concentrated on capturing that city. Pope

Pius and his papal army were not able to deter the Italian troops, and Victor Emmanuel II held Rome in September 1870.

With Napoleon out of the way, Russia repudiated the terms of the Treaty of Paris (1856) which limited naval strength in the Black Sea, and the Tsar resumed his aggression in the Ottoman Empire and the Balkan States.

Nationalism and Democracy (1830-1871). The period from 1830-1871 was one in which great strides were made in both nationalism and democracy. The countries of France, Italy, Germany, and Hungary all profited by a new patriotism which undid the work of the Congress of Vienna and Metternichism.

The cause of democracy was furthered during this period by events in Italy, France, Austria-Hungary, Germany, Great Britain, Russia, and Spain. Constitutions were granted, the franchise extended, serfdom abolished, and parliamentary governments inaugurated. The years after 1871 were to extend still further the ideas and principles of democracy.

CHAPTER V.

INTELLECTUAL AND SOCIAL MOVEMENTS

In the intellectual and social sphere, the second half of the nineteenth century and the opening years of the twentieth century were a time of the greatest ferment of ideas and revolution in attitudes since the close of the middle ages. Three aspects of this intellectual revolution stand out prominently; (1) the great advance of experimental science and the rise in all departments of thought of the scientific method and the scientific attitude; (2) the conflict between science and the philosophies founded on science, and traditional thinking and traditional religion; and (3) the widespread discussion of the problems of society under the new conditions of the Industrial Revolution.

Science and the Scientific Method. The second half of the nineteenth century was an age of unprecedented discovery in all the sciences—in physics, chemistry, geology, astronomy, biology, and medicine. Not only was a magnificent structure erected on the foundations laid earlier by such men as Galileo, Newton, Boyle, Lavoisier, and Cuvier, but many new sciences were created and new fundamental generalizations were established. The most important achievements of nineteenth century science were the laws of thermodynamics, the theory of electromagnetic waves, the discovery of the relation of micro-organisms to disease and to the consequent development of the aseptic surgical technique and of preventive innoculation, and, most significant of all, in its philosophical implications, the theory of biological evolution. The practical application of scientific discoveries so accelerated the Industrial Revolution as to produce a veritable "Second Industrial Revolution" in the last quarter of the century. But the impact of science on traditional ways of thinking was as remarkable as its effect on industrial technology. The brilliant success of science in its own field captured all imaginations. To many, the way to the ultimate truths of philosophy and religion seemed to be open at last. For the "endless disputing without ever coming to a conclusion" that had characterized the older metaphysics, science seemed to offer a universe of law and order, verifiable by the senses, free from contradiction, and capable of being more and more thoroughly understood as scientific knowledge accumulated. The "scientific method"—collection and classification of facts and the formulation of general laws to account for or "explain" the facts—began to penetrate all branches of thought: historical scholarship and criticism, economic and social theory, philosophy, and finally even the very citadel of intellectual conservatism, religion.

The Conflict of Science and Religion. The conflict between the new scientific spirit and traditional religion produced a great uproar in the second half of the nineteenth century. The conflict had been brewing for a long time, and the publication, in 1859, of Darwin's *Origin of Species* set off a battle that even in our own day has not entirely died out. The scientific assault on traditional religion came from four main sources: (1) the application of historical criticism or "higher criticism" to the Bible, (2) the rise of materialistic and mechanistic philosophies appealing to physical science for evidence, (3) the evidence amassed by geology for the great antiquity of the earth and of life, and (4) the theory of biological evolution. Pressed on all sides by the increasing prestige and popularity of the new science-inspired views, the supporters of traditional religion came to the defense of their threatened ideals with a flood of argument, dogmatism, and refurbished philosophy. The defense was in general of two sorts. Some conservatives tried to meet the scientists on their own ground. They denied the validity of the new scientific discoveries or "reconciled," in one way or another, the traditional religious account with such facts of science as could not be disputed. This line of defense proved, in the long run, quite hopeless. Just as the theologians had been inclined to accept Copernican astronomy in the eighteenth century after nearly 200 years of opposition, so they were inclined, in the nineteenth and twentieth, to accept the facts of geology, the results of historical criticism, and finally (in some cases with reservations) the doctrine of biological evolution. On the facts of science the theologians proved no match for the scientists. But there was a second line of defense for religion that proved able to stand its ground. This was the line of reinterpretation of the field of knowledge covered by religious dogma and of the function of religion in the intellectual and moral life of man. This reinterpretation resulted in the movement known as "modernism" in Protestant Christianity. It involved an abandonment of supernaturalism in religion and an eager acceptance of the findings of science while asserting the claim of religion in moral and spiritual matters.

In a somewhat different way the Roman Catholic Church successfully met the scientific onslaught. Although many Catholic theologians waged a war *à outrance* on the new theories, the Church itself was careful to avoid any official commitment on matters of pure science. It adopted an attitude of acceptance of the findings of science as a valuable description of the phenomenal world, while continuing to assert without compromise its ancient dogma as the ultimate truth divinely revealed. Increasing numbers of men, both Catholic and Protestant, took the point of view that science and religion are different things and that there cannot, properly speaking, be any conflict between them. Any apparent conflict arises because one side or the other attempts to include matters outside its proper field. Down to the middle of the nineteenth century religion had claimed jurisdiction over a large field of thought properly the concern of science. Science claimed its rightful field. The result was an intellectual revolution.

The Rise of Socialism. "The attempt to conceive imaginatively a better ordering of human society than the destructive and cruel chaos in which mankind has hitherto existed"[1]—so Bertrand Russell speaks of the motivating force of socialism, anarchism, and other social philosophies in which the latter part of the nineteenth century was particularly rich. What distinguished the thinking of the nineteenth century from the attempts of such men as Plato and Thomas More to "conceive imaginatively" a better society was the effectiveness of nineteenth century thinking in starting important political and social movements to bring such an ideal society into actual existence. At the beginning of the twentieth century socialism was no longer a philosopher's dream, but was a force in the lives of millions of men. The Industrial Revolution, the spread of rudimentary education, the decline of the power of the traditional conservative forces of religion and feudal loyalty, and the advance of democracy in government all helped to stir up the masses to a realization of their power and their class interests. In all countries of Europe, the ideas of the socialists, while condemned as dangerous and revolutionary by the bourgeois leaders of society, gradually made their influence felt in legislation. The largest and most influential school of socialists—the Marxists—did not, indeed, believe in the possibility of the slow socialization of the state through the democratic legislative process. They held that no real improvement could come without a complete change in the economic system, and that such a change would never be acquiesced in by the bourgeoisie without a violent struggle. While they were not opposed to participation in politics for the sake of gaining control of the state with a view to revolutionizing it, they put no faith in the palliative social reform measures offered, as they thought, as a tub thrown to the proletariat whale by the bourgeoisie to purchase the latter's security and continuance in power. As long as the capitalist system existed, they argued, the state, be it ever so democratic and enlightened, could not be essentially anything but "a committee for managing the affairs of the bourgeoisie."

---

1 From *Proposed Roads to Freedom* by Bertrand Russell. Published by Henry Holt & Co.

EVOLUTIONISTS AND PHILOSOPHICAL SCIENTISTS

The intellectual revolution of the nineteenth century was the work of hundreds of scientists and scholars in all countries. The few names that follow are selected for their representative character and for their influence in popularizing scientific views that most directly conflicted with traditional ideas.

Alexander Von Humboldt (1769-1859), The Naturalist. About 1850, Humboldt published the first volume of his *Kosmos*, a synthesis of the scientific developments of the eighteenth and the first half of the nineteenth centuries. His conception of the universe did not provide for any power beyond nature.

Sir Charles Lyell (1797-1875), The Geologist. Lyell's *Principles of Geology* (1830-1833) set forth his uniformitarian theory which attempted an explanation of the physical formation of the earth. *The Geological Evidences of the Antiquity of Man* (1863) presented a mass of proof, based upon the new geology, that human life had existed on the earth for at least 100,000 years. This was absolutely and positively opposed to the Biblical story of the creation. In this same work, Lyell accepted a theory of evolution that applied to all forms of life.

Auguste Comte (1798-1857), The Positivist. An impressive attempt to create a systematic philosophy from the materials of the new science was that of Auguste Comte. In his *Positive Philosophy* (1842) and *Positive Polity* (1854) he abandoned as "theological" and "metaphysical" all efforts to "explain" phenomena, and preached the "positive" stage of knowledge in which phenomena are only to be observed, classified, and described by the methods of science. The physical sciences, thought Comte, were models of the positive stage of knowledge, and he sought to create a science of man and society, or "sociology" as the crowning achievement of the scientific method. For the old religion Comte substituted a "religion of humanity."

Charles Darwin (1809-1882), The Evolutionist. Darwin's early life was spent in traveling, in the course of which he studied various species of animals of different ages and environment. He pondered the question of the reason for the diversity of animal species, seeking an explanation in some natural mechanism rather than the theory of special *ad hoc* creation. The work of Lyell, who had shown the great antiquity of the earth and of man, and of Malthus, who had vividly described the struggle for existence with the consequent dying off of the less gifted and less fortunate men in economic competition, influenced the trend of his thinking. As early as 1842 he had worked out the main features of his new theory of biological evolution, basing the development of species on the mechanism of natural selection. He did not announce the theory, however, as he wished to perfect details by more extensive observation. Before Darwin had published his results, an unknown naturalist, who had traveled extensively in South America and the East Indies, prompted by Malthus' principles, reached the same conclusions as Darwin. This naturalist, Alfred Wallace (1823-1913), was to share with Darwin the credit for the new theory of life.

Darwinism received its greatest impetus with the publication of the books *On the Origin of Species by Means of Natural Selection* (1859) and *Descent of Man and Selection in Relation to Sex* (1871). In these works, Darwin claims that all life has a common source and that changes due to environment and the selective killing off of less advantaged individual animals in the struggle for life have produced differences which eventually result in new species. Wallace, who had worked out the new hypothesis at the same time as Darwin, helped to place it before the scientists in his work *Contributions to the Theory of Natural Selection* (1871).

Herbert Spencer (1820-1903), The Philosopher. Spencer spent his later years (1860-1903) in popularizing Darwinism. His *Synthetic Philosophy* expanded the idea of evolution into the fields of ethics, philosophy, psychology, and sociology.

Thomas Huxley (1825-1895), The Agnostic. Definitely opposed to the theology of Christianity, Huxley, in his *Man's Place in Nature* (1863), reveals man as but a transitional stage in the evolutionary process. Huxley attacked the authority of Christian morality and substituted fatalism as a guide for conduct. To describe his attitude toward the question of the existence of God, Huxley coined the word "agnostic" or "not knowing," and argued that no man had a right to hold beliefs that could not be justified by the evidence of the senses.

Ernest Renan (1823-1892), The Skeptic. Ernest Renan was the most influential of the scholars who attacked the inspiration and authenticity of the Bible on grounds of historical and philological criticism. His conclusion was that the Bible recorded a primitive fable which had been developed through the ages. In his book *Life of Jesus* (1863) he presented Jesus as a human rather than a supernatural being, and rejected as superstition the miraculous element in the Gospel account.

THE CATHOLIC CHURCH

Traditionalism and Reaction. In addition to the scientific and philosophical assault on its dogmas, the Catholic Church in the nineteenth century was confronted with a strong political opposition. As many intellectual leaders lost faith in religion they began to see in the Church a dangerous reactionary and obscurantist force, and they became anxious to eradicate Church influence in education and politics. This anti-clerical movement was of less importance in Protestant countries because the Protestant Church lacked the unity and international organization of the Catholic Church.

THE CHURCH DOGMA. The Catholic Church, holding itself to be the custodian and dispenser of divinely revealed, unchangeable truth, could not compromise with the new ideas. Protestantism, on the other hand, admitted of individual interpretation, and could allow restatements of doctrine to satisfy those who accepted the scientific philosophy.

CATHOLIC OPPOSITION TO THE PRINCIPLES OF THE FRENCH REVOLUTION. The curbing of the Catholic clergy and the resulting loss of its power and property during the French Revolution, aroused the Church against the principles of liberty, equality, and fraternity. The bourgeoisie, who made up the Liberal Catholics, tried to heal the wound by persuading the Church to forego its claim to temporal authority and confine its attention to spiritual benefactions.

Pius IX (1846-1878). The revolutions of 1848 stifled the liberal leanings of Pius IX and he concentrated his efforts on opposing the principles of 1789. In many European countries, Pius IX was successful in strengthening the position of the Church. The encyclical *Quanta Cura* (1864) reaffirmed the temporal power of the Church and his *Syllabus of Errors* (1864) was a condemnation of not only religious but also political practices. All groups that opposed the old *status quo* of the Church were severely criticized.

OPPOSITION TO THE CATHOLIC CHURCH. The Anti-Clericals emphatically opposed the encyclical and the Syllabus and used them as arguments to foster nationalism. The espousal of the dogma of the infallibility of the Pope by the Vatican Council (1869-1870) was the cause for a more pronounced opposition. In Prussia, Bismarck instituted his *Kulturkampf*, a campaign against the Catholic Church; Austria annulled her Concordat of 1855; and Gladstone pointed out the need for resisting the expansion of papal authority in temporal matters. The capture of Rome by the Italians in 1870, destroyed the temporal power of the Pope. During the remainder of his Pontificate, Pius IX became a virtual "prisoner of the Vatican" and concentrated his attention on organizing the Clerical and Conservative elements throughout Europe. Pius IX's uncompromising conservatism sharpened the division between clericals and anti-clericals.

Progress and Readjustment. During the pontificate of Pius IX the Catholic Church had shown no signs of sympathy with the intellectual and social tendencies that had been gaining strength throughout the nineteenth century. But upon the death of Pius an era of adjustment and conciliation was inaugurated by the statesmanlike and modern-minded Leo XIII (1878-1903). Without abandoning any of the Church's historic dogmas, Leo nevertheless managed to bring about a rapprochement with both the political and the intellectual opposition. His policy was helped by the growing realization of the inadequacy of scientific materialism as a final philosophy and the skill with which Catholic dialecticians succeeded in accommodating Catholic theology to scientific discovery.

THEOLOGICAL RECONSTRUCTION. The renewed study of the works of Thomas Aquinas served as a basis for an agreement between Christianity and Science. Darwinism was explained by suggesting that the creation story be accepted as an allegory and that Darwin's theory did not provide for spiritual evolution.

CATHOLIC SCIENTISTS. The investigation of science was fostered by Leo XIII and helped to show that one could be a scientist and still be a good Catholic. The scientific work of the Catholics, Pasteur and Mendel, was notable. Louis Pasteur (1822-1895) revolutionized organic chemistry by his experiments with bacteria. Few men have contributed more to the well-being of the human race than he with his treatment for rabies, his preventive for the scourge of anthrax, his process of the pasteurization of milk to decrease infant mortality, and his explanations of fermentation. Gregor Mendel (1822-1884) experimented with plants to determine the influence of heredity upon the offspring. Mendelism has been greatly enlarged upon since 1900.

CATHOLICISM AND SOCIAL REFORM. Leo XIII changed his early views which were opposed to nationalism and began to feel that democracy could be made to serve the Church as monarchy had. The encyclical *Rerum novarum* (1891) discussed the problems of capital and labor. The encyclical opposed Socialism but urged the employer and employee to coöperate. While it upheld the right of private property, it denounced the concept of economic liberalism that labor is a commodity and urged reform legislation to bring about a more just distribution of wealth.

PIUS X (1903-1914) AND SCIENCE. The enlightened pontificate of Leo XIII led many to agitate for a change in the Catholic dogmas. The Modernists claimed that dogma was evolutionary, that the Church must revise its theology in accordance with modern ideas, and that the Church must not interfere with the state. The movement, which had made considerable headway, was denounced by Pius X in his encyclical *Pascendi* (1907) and it was effectively stamped out by 1914.

THE RISE OF SOCIALISTIC MOVEMENTS

After 1871, the increase in the number of urban workers and the accompanying problems led many bourgeois capitalists to forsake the old policy of laissez faire and to allow partial government regulation of industry. As previously mentioned, Leo XIII made a bid for the support of the masses through social legislation. The Socialists made up a third group, who were trying to win the workingmen to their principles. Socialism was an even greater menace to the bourgeois supremacy than Clericalism.

Early Types of Socialism. The beginnings of Socialism were a direct outgrowth of the Industrial Revolution. The changed system of production brought into sharp relief the distinction between two sorts of property; productive or capital, and commodities for individual use. Many men, contrasted the great increase in productivity made possible by the use of machinery, with the terrible poverty of the mass of the workers. They were convinced that the evil was in some way connected with the private ownership of capital under the old concept of property rights. Socialism demands the complete control of capital and means of production by society as a whole for the benefit of all. Many different ways were proposed of arriving at this goal.

UTOPIAN SOCIALISM—ROBERT OWEN (1771-1858).   Robert Owen was one of the first Socialists. A successful manufacturer, Owen set up a model factory village at New Lanark where he stressed good working conditions, fair wages, public schools, good homes, and coöperative stores. In New Harmony, Indiana, Owen attempted to set up another Utopia, but failed.

SAINT SIMONISM—SAINT SIMON (1760-1825). The founder of Socialism in France was Saint Simon. He favored an industrial state, which would be organized and directed by scentists and engineers. His scheme resembled that of "Technocracy" popularized in America about 1932.

SOCIALISM BASED ON HARMONY — CHARLES FOURIER (1772-1837). Fourier advocated a society based upon small, self-supporting units called *phalanges*. He thought that most human misery arose from the unnatural limitations imposed by the existing economic and social system, and that if every one was allowed to do as he liked he would select a congenial occupation, thus contributing to a harmonious and happy society. Many experiments were conducted, the most notable being the famous Brook Farm in America, but all were short-lived.

GOVERNMENT OWNERSHIP — LOUIS BLANC (1811-1882). The revolutions of 1848 in France gave Blanc an opportunity to institute the national workshops through which he hoped to eliminate unemployment and relieve the pressure of competition which kept wages at the poverty level. However, these workshops were never given any real trial and were discredited by the political factions.

Scientific Socialism—Karl Marx (1818-1883). The basis of modern socialism is taken from the Marxian type which was the work of the German, Karl Marx. Marx was born of influential bourgeois parents in the Rhenish Prussia. He was an extremely industrious student and his interest in philosophy and history was greater than in law, the field which the elder Marx had designated for his son. Hegel's philosophy of the freedom of man was influential in determining the liberal characteristics of Marx. The agitation of Marx for freedom of the press in Germany was not successful and he later went to Paris where he became identified with the working class socialists. While in Paris, Marx made the acquaintance of Blanc, Proudhon, Bakunin, Heine, and Engels. Friedrich Engels (1820-1895) was the most important of these new friends and was to be the lifelong co-worker of Marx. In 1845, Marx was forced to leave Paris because of the radical writings in the *Vorwärts* which he edited. Marx spent the next three years in Brussels.

"COMMUNIST MANIFESTO" (1848). A statement of the principles of the workingmen's clubs, which was prepared in 1848 by Marx and Engels, became the basis for the new socialism. The *Communist Manifesto* maintains that eventually capital will be concentrated in the hands of a few and that it will then be possible for the proletariat to rise up and establish the communist (social) state. The aims of the Socialists are, (1) to organize the proletarians, (2) to increase political power of the proletarians, and (3) to do away with bourgeois property ownership. The *Manifesto* ends with this challenge to the workingmen: "Proletarians of all countries, unite!"

MARX IN ENGLAND (1849-1883). While the revolutions of 1848 were going on, Marx returned to Paris to witness the inauguration of the Second French Republic. The spread of the revolution to Prussia made it possible for Marx to return to his native land, but the period of reaction which set in was strong enough to curb both liberal and socialist tendencies and Marx was forced to leave Prussia once more. Marx found refuge in England and remained there until his death. *Das Kapital* was Marx's philosophy of political economy, the first volume of which appeared in 1867. Another accomplishment of his English exile was the organization of an international workingmen's society for the extension of the new socialist doctrines.

SIGNIFICANCE OF THE WORK OF MARX. The contributions of Marx to socialism may be summed up as follows: (1) the organization of socialist theories; (2) the extension of Socialism into the field of political democracy; (3) the development of a philosophy of Socialism which stressed the historic importance of economic factors, the evolution of present society through class conflicts, and the eventual change of the existing society; and (4) the growth of class consciousness by the workingmen of the world.

THE INTERNATIONAL WORKINGMEN'S ASSOCIATION (1862-1876). The International was the attempt of Marx to organize his followers. For several years, congresses were held which were supported by groups in many European countries and the United States. However, the International failed because of, (1) the lack of capital, (2) the growth of nationalism, (3) the defeat of the Communist uprising in Paris (1871), and (4) internal strife between Socialists and Anarchists.

NATIONAL ORGANIZATION — FERDINAND LASSALLE (1825-1864). The organization of Socialism was accomplished, not through the efforts of Marx, but through those of another German, Ferdinand Lassalle, who established a Social Democratic party in Germany. This later was to fuse with the German portion of the International and to accept the Marxian principles. Marxian Socialism developed rapidly in Germany and by 1914 socialist political parties, patterned after the German type, were founded in every civilized country.

Clerical and Bourgeois Opposition to Socialism. Although opposed to each other on most political issues, the Clericals and the bourgeoisie carried on a strenuous campaign against the new force—Socialism. The Church opposed socialism for its anti-religious philosophy, its revolutionary plans to change the existing social structure, of which the Church was an important part, and its tendency to wean the masses away from the Church. Socialism sought to take away from the bourgeoisie the privileges which they had fought for centuries to obtain. Hence, the bourgeoisie had to direct their attention against not only the Clericals, but also the Socialists.

The Strict Marxists and the Reformists. The Strict Marxists held fast to Marx's central doctrines of the increasing concentration of capital and the inevitability of a social revolution resulting from the sharpening of the class war. They were opposed to imperialism and nationalism and insisted upon the identity of interests of the working class all over the world. They had no faith in palliative social legislation that could only delay, not promote, the radical reform they deemed necessary.

The Reformists, however, fostered nationalism to a certain extent and favored adequate military protection. They pointed out that the predictions of Marx regarding the increasing concentration of capital ownership and the increasing sharpness of the class war were not, in fact, being fulfilled, and they urged that Socialists give up their expectations of revolution and work for gradual reforms through parliamentary methods. They sought to enlist the support of the agricultural classes and the trade unions.

ANARCHISM

The Leaders of Anarchism. Anarchism, like Socialism, was the product of the Industrial Revolution, but unlike the latter it would gain its end by doing away with all compulsory government. William Godwin (1756-1836) is known as the father of Anarchism, but it was Pierre Joseph Proudhon (1809-1865) who made it popular. During the period when the Industrial Revolution was expanding over Europe, Proudhon gave vent to his anarchistic doctrines. His works, which included *What is Property* (1840), *System of Economic Contradictions*, and *Of Justice in the Revolution and in the Church*, became the basis for his opinions on Anarchism. Other notable anarchists were Prince Kropotkin, Count Tolstoy, and Bakunin.

Principles of Anarchism. Briefly, Proudhon believed that there should be no private property, but that each individual has the right to use it; that there should be no authoritarian government, but that each man should have absolute liberty; that Anarchism would be put into effect not by violence, but by education; and that the new anarchist state would be held together by a system of voluntary contracts which would react to all wrong doing on the basis of the Golden Rule. The essence of Anarchism is found in its extreme reliance upon the individual.

Violence and Anarchism—Mikhail Bakunin (1814-1876). Although the founders of philosophical anarchism were opposed to all force and violence, their bitter attacks on the injustice of all forms of government led many of their followers to advocate the destruction of government by any means available. Bakunin, a Russian, had a background which included association with the radicals in Berlin, the acquaintance of Proudhon, and an exile to Siberia, from which he escaped after eleven years. His insistence upon violence ended with his expulsion from the Marxian Socialists. Terrorism in the form of bombings, murderous attacks upon capitalists and royalists' representatives were carried on. The object was to arouse the people against, and to destroy completely, all governments.

Syndicalism. Syndicalism is a form of anarchism which organized the workers in whole industries so that through the organizations they would be able to control the entire industry. Syndicalism started in France and quickly spread throughout Europe, into Great Britain, to America, and even far away Australia. Once in control of an industry, the anarchist could use the strike and sabotage to embarrass the employer, to reduce his profits, and to arouse the workmen.

CHAPTER VI.

GREAT BRITAIN
1867-1914

The period 1867-1914 in England is marked by the achievement of political democracy, an immense industrial and commercial expansion, the growth of a new imperialistic spirit, important social legislation, and grave problems arising out of the relation between Great Britain and Ireland.

Political Democracy. One of the demands of the Chartists in the 1830's and 1840's had been universal manhood suffrage. At that time the demand was considered revolutionary. But by reform bills in 1867 and 1884, the demand was substantially satisfied. Nevertheless, the movement toward dominance of the government by the bourgeoisie, that had begun in 1832 with the enfranchisement of the wealthy middle class, continued even after the working class had received the right to vote, since for many years the new voters followed the lead of their industrial and commercial superiors. The advance of democracy did not, as gloomy prophets had confidently predicted, bring about any general movement on the part of the poor to confiscate the property of the rich, nor did it result in mob rule, nor in any noticeable lowering of the standards of intellectual and executive ability in public office. The English people throughout their history have shown a profound conservatism and dislike of revolutionary change. There has always been a feeling of loyalty on the part of the masses toward the aristocracy, complemented with a feeling of responsibility on the part of the leaders for the welfare of the masses, that has prevented, to a great extent, such large scale uprisings for the redress of injustice or the relief of intolerable economic distress as have characterized many countries of continental Europe. Thus it happened that as the vote was granted first to urban workingmen and later to agricultural laborers there was no immediate political reaction: property continued to be safe; cabinets continued to be formed from Eton and Harrow graduates; the hereditary House of Lords continued to exercise legislative powers and a veto over the acts of the House of Commons; and nobody moved to establish a republic. Yet, in the long run, the coming of complete democracy could not fail to alter fundamentally the whole structure of political and social life; it broke down centuries-old class distinctions; it required the adoption of new techniques by political leaders; it gradually forced to the front a serious grappling by government with the complex problems of social reform.

Industry and Commerce. In the period 1867-1914 the industry and commerce of Great Britain expanded enormously, and there was a nearly steady rise in the general standard of living of the whole population. The potentialities of the Industrial Revolution in bringing comparative comfort to the bulk of the people now began for the first time to be realized. In 1847 John Stuart Mill had declared "Hitherto it is questionable if all the mechanical inventions yet made have lightened the day's toil of any human being," but there could be no question about the matter in 1914. Real wages (average wages in relation to average prices) had risen about 50 per cent in the fifty-year period before the outbreak of the World War, while during the same time hours of labor had been steadily falling, and the worst excesses of child labor had been abolished. There was not only more wealth and more power for the few, but more comfort and leisure for the many. Yet the tendency toward concentration of wealth in the hands of the capitalists, that had marked the early stages of the Industrial

Revolution, continued through the half century before the World War in a somewhat different form. Replacing the individual factory owner of the early days there arose the great joint-stock corporations, the legal ownership of which was vested in thousands of shareholders, but the efficient management of which remained in the hands of a small group of bankers and industrialists.

The New Imperialism. Toward the close of the nineteenth century there came a powerful resurgence in England of imperialistic ideas and ambitions. Stimulated by Benjamin Disraeli during his Prime Ministry (1874-1880), the revival of imperialism seemed at first to be motivated chiefly by the ideas of national pride and patriotism that were enjoying a great vogue throughout Europe. Very soon, however, it became clear that underlying the patriotic motive, and perhaps unconsciously leading it, was a strong economic motive. The pressure of foreign competition (especially German), the approaching saturation of the home market for manufactured goods, the demand for cheap sources of raw materials, the need for undeveloped areas for the investment of ever growing surpluses of British capital, all contributed to the new enthusiasm for empire-building. This imperialism found literary expression in Rudyard Kipling's poems, political expression in Joseph Chamberlain's movement to make the Empire a great economic unit fenced about with tariffs, commercial expression in such organizations as the British South Africa Company of Cecil Rhodes, diplomatic expression in the treaties with the other imperialist powers arranging for trading concessions and "spheres of influence" in such backward regions as Persia and China, and military expression in wars against the African natives, against the Afghans, and against the Boers. In the early Victorian period such outstanding Liberal Party leaders as Cobden and Bright had gone so far as to declare that the whole idea of imperialism was an anachronism of the days before the Industrial Revolution and free trade, and they suggested that Great Britain cut herself loose from any political connection with the colonies. While the Liberal Party never accepted this view in full, its greatest leader, Gladstone, was opposed to imperialistic expansion and regarded the rise of the "jingo" spirit with the greatest abhorrence. But the pressure of popular patriotism, led and exploited by men with axes to grind, was too powerful to be resisted.

Social Legislation. The social legislation of the period 1832-1867 was meagre and timid. The majority of the members of Parliament, the new capitalists who had not, like the older British aristocracy grown up in the tradition of *noblesse oblige*, felt little responsibility for the immediate welfare of the people outside the economic class that supported them with votes, and this class was, on the whole, content with its own unexampled prosperity and incredibly smug toward the mass of the population who bore on their backs the burden of the prosperity. Isolated humanitarians such as Lord Ashley succeeded in getting a few measures of reform accepted, but the dogma of laissez faire with its cheerful assumption that all things worked together for good for those who kept their noses to the grindstone, and that the maximum of progress was concomitant with the minimum of government, kept even humane leaders of the Liberal Party in a coma of inaction on social issues, while the Conservative Party, drawing its chief support from the great landlords, could hardly be induced to sponsor any measures that proposed to tamper with their time-honored rent rights. With the coming of democracy, however, this apathetic attitude would no longer serve. Members of Parliament had to keep awake to the welfare of their working class constituents, and these constituents grew steadily more aware both of their needs and of their power. After 1875 laissez faire became a less and less respectable philosophy, and by the beginning of the twentieth century all parties, Liberals, Unionists, Conservatives, and the new Labor Party, were committed to the general view that it is the business of government to promote the social and economic welfare of the whole people by direct political action. Many who clung to the old-fashioned ideas were shocked out of their complacency by the revelations of the poor physical condition of the men recruited to fight the Boer War (1899-1902). "We are all socialists now," was the expression of the Liberal leader William Harcourt. The decade preceding the outbreak of the World War saw a veritable "revolution by due process of law" in social legislation. This

"British New Deal" enacted a mass of legislation of the type that in former years had been denounced as interference with property rights, and only the coming of the war prevented a showdown battle over a really radical program sponsored by David Lloyd George.

Irish Problem. Throughout the period 1867-1914, the perennial problem of Ireland defied the efforts of Liberals and Conservatives, coercionists and conciliators, Home Rulers and Unionists alike. Neither the growth of industry and commerce, nor the rise of democracy, nor the spread of education, nor the movement toward religious tolerance, all of which were relied on by one group or another to bring a solution, seemed to advance much the cure of that four-hundred-year-old cancer in the political body. It was a tangled mess of race, religion, and economics that the best political brains of England struggled with in vain. "The landlords have been as greedy and insolent a set of tyrants as ever ground the face of the poor in any country in the world." So wrote John Morley in 1882, and he can scarcely be said to have overstated the case as far as the central economic issue was concerned. But there was so much more to the Irish problem than the rapacity and hard-heartedness of the landlords that it is understandable why no practical solution could readily be found.

DEMOCRATIC REFORM (1867-1914)

Gladstone and Disraeli. For twenty years following the death of Palmerston in 1865, English politics revolved about the personalities and programs of the leaders Gladstone and Disraeli. Gladstone in his early years was a Conservative, but his support of the repeal of the Corn Laws alienated him from that party. Under the Liberal Ministry of Lord Palmerston, he was Chancellor of the Exchequer. His fame for reorganizing the budget raised him to a commanding position in his party. Under Gladstone, the Liberal Party for thirty years stood for free trade, laissez faire in economics, gradual parliamentary reform, economy in public expenditure, nonaggressive foreign policy, and local self-government.

The rise of Disraeli was handicapped by his eccentricities and Jewish ancestry, but his brilliance and force of personality triumphed over prejudice. He entered politics as an individualist rather than the wheel-horse of any particular party or set of principles, and his entire career was marked by opportunism and contempt for mechanical formulas. During the twenty-year period of conservative demoralization that followed the repeal of the Corn Laws, Disraeli's abilities as a caustic and persistent critic of the administrations of Lord John Russell and Palmerston made him a rather unwelcome hero to the Tories, and upon the retirement of Lord Derby in 1868, Disraeli assumed the titular leadership of the party.

Reform of 1867. The failure of Gladstone's attempt at reform in 1866, gave Disraeli an opportunity to frame a bill and have it passed. Gladstone's bill, which extended the franchise to the £14 householders of the counties and the £7 householders of the boroughs, was too democratic for a right wing faction of the Liberal party (the "Adullamites") and so they joined with the Conservatives to defeat the bill.

By sponsoring a Reform Bill in 1867, Disraeli played an amazing political trick, for he had been the most savage of the opponents of Gladstone's bill which he said would produce "a horde of selfish and obscure mediocrities, incapable of anything but mischief, and that mischief devised and regulated by the raging demagogue of the hour." Actually Disraeli's bill, after modification by the opposition, turned out to be much more radical than Gladstone's mild measure. The law provided that (1) 58 seats in the House of Commons were to be transferred to the industrial boroughs, (2) the franchise was extended to include £12 tenants and £5 leaseholders in the counties, and (3) the right to vote was given to a male citizen in the boroughs if he occupied a separate dwelling or was a £10 lodger. The practical effect was to grant nearly universal manhood suffrage in the cities.

Ballot Act (1872). The successful Act of 1867 was not enough to prevent the election of the Liberals in 1868. Through the efforts of Gladstone, the Ballot Act was passed (1872) which provided that the Australian secret ballot was to supplant the old method of voting by voice.

Other Reforms (1884-1885). The Representation of the People Act (1884) made the electoral qualifications in the counties the same as in the boroughs, and two million rural workers were added to the voting list. The bill for redistricting the seats (1885) divided the counties so that there would be one member of the House of Commons for each 50,000 people. With the exception of annual parliaments and payment for members, all the reforms of the Chartists had been obtained.

Parliament Act of 1911. The House of Lords was made up of hereditary peers, elected peers and Anglican prelates. The great objections were that the peers were unfit for duty because of prejudice, that the Anglican Church had representation which made it possible for that church to gain concessions and finally, that the Lords were opposed to Liberalism.

The Lords had continually opposed the reform measures, and their failure to accept the Finance Bill of the Liberal Ministry, which had passed the House of Commons (1909), caused Prime Minister Asquith to appeal to the people. Upon being returned to office, the Liberals framed a bill to curb the Lords. The proposal of a competing bill by the Conservatives resulted in another general election and another Liberal victory. The Liberal bill became a law in 1911, only after Asquith threatened to have the king create enough peers to get a majority in the House of Lords. The new act provided that (1) money bills passed by the Commons became a law one month after being submitted to the House of Lords; (2) other public bills would become a law if passed by three successive sessions of Parliament over a period of two years in spite of rejection by the Lords; and (3) the maximum duration of Parliament would be five years. The Parliament Act of 1911 thus ended with victory the 600-year struggle of the House of Commons to become the supreme executive and legislative power in the British nation.

Tradition and the British Government. The constitution of Great Britain is composed of treaties, important acts like Magna Carta, Petition of Right and Reform Acts, statutes, the Common Law, and a set of traditional practices which make the constitution extremely flexible. In theory, King George is a divine right monarch, but in practice, he is merely a figurehead. The House of Lords has been retained, but it has been stripped of much of its power and is now a kind of honorary body to which those who have rendered services to the nation are frequently appointed. It still acts as a balance-wheel of conservatism, however, since cabinets are unwilling to risk the prolonged battle that would result from legislation offensive to the Lords. The real center of the government is the House of Commons which is elected by almost universal suffrage (since Equal Franchise Act of 1928). There are 690 members and each receives a salary of £400 annually.

Parliamentary Government. The cabinet, which is composed of the heads of the governmental departments, is dependent upon a majority in the House of Commons for its power. Under the guidance of the prime minister, the cabinet not only enacts, but executes, legislation. When the cabinet fails to have the support of the majority of the members in the House of Commons, the prime minister and his cabinet may resign and allow the king to appoint a new prime minister, or he may ask the king to dissolve Parliament and call a new election. The responsibility and efficiency of the cabinet is greatly increased by keeping the Commons in touch with the people, by centralizing authority, and by having a nonresident requirement for M. P.'s. Bills are given three readings, namely (1) introductory, (2) debate on general provisions and reconsideration by the committee, and (3) vote for acceptance or rejection. If a bill passes the Commons it is sent to the Lords and if favored, is passed on to the crown for signature.

Centralized Government. The Parliament at Westminster legislates for the whole of Great Britain and executes laws for all, except Ireland and Scotland, who have some voice in the administration. For the most part, the local government is controlled by the (1) home office, (2) board of trade, (3) local government board, (4) board of education, and (5) board of agriculture. Besides these central forces, there are in the counties, a clerk, a treasurer, a constable, coroners, a county council, and education officials. In the boroughs, there are mayors, aldermen, and councilors for carrying on the government.

Political Parties in Great Britain. The evolution of the political parties in Great Britain during the nineteenth century mirrors the reform movements of the period.

WHIGS AND TORIES. During the agitation for the reforms of 1832, the Tories, who were in power, continued in the old dogmatic conservative manner to ignore the demands of the bourgeoisie. The Whigs, who had already started a reform movement, received many middle class representatives into their party.

LIBERALS AND CONSERVATIVES. The two parties were definitely lined up under the leadership of Gladstone (Liberals) and Disraeli (Conservatives). Disraeli tried to get the support of the people through his Reform Act of 1867, but Gladstone won the election of 1868. In the next six years, the Liberals introduced the ballot box, extended the franchise, and fostered education. In 1874 Disraeli came into office and concentrated on a vigorous foreign policy, but his neglect of the domestic affairs made it possible for Gladstone to become Prime Minister again in 1880. Later, Gladstone consented to support the Irish Home Rule movement (1886) in order to maintain his majority in the Commons, and in so doing he split the Liberal party.

LIBERAL UNIONISTS AND UNIONISTS. Joseph Chamberlain (1836-1914), a successful manufacturer who had entered politics, believed Gladstone's old-fashioned liberalism was out of date. He wished the Liberal Party to take an active lead in social reform proposals, which meant a break with the tradition of laissez faire and the idea that "the best government is the least government." He was also more imperialist minded than Gladstone. When Gladstone gave his support to the Home Rule for Ireland Bill, Chamberlain left the Liberal party and with a group of radical Liberals formed the Liberal Unionist Party, which later combined with the Conservatives to form the Unionist Party (1895). The new party had in its ranks, not only the nobility, clergy, and gentry of the Conservative group, but many professional and business leaders. Chamberlain fostered a tariff policy which was to have (1) held the empire closer together by preferential arrangements, (2) stimulated British industry, and (3) increased the revenue to allow the construction of a large navy. However, the Unionist party split on this program and the Liberals returned to power (1906).

LABOR PARTY. With the enfranchisement of the worker, the vote of labor became more and more important. Labor organizations began in 1899 to fight for representation in the Commons. The election of 1906 found fifty-four representatives of the new party in the Commons. In 1924 the party had become strong enough to control a majority in the House of Commons and thus install the first Labor government under Prime Minister Ramsay MacDonald.

THE NEW LIBERAL PARTY. As the opposition government during the Unionist supremacy (1895-1905), the Liberals were seeking a way to return to power. The election of the Liberals in 1906 by an overwhelming majority can be explained by: (1) their willingness to inaugurate a system of land reform which would greatly benefit the lower classes (Henry George's *Progress and Poverty* influenced many Liberals); (2) their opposition to Chamberlain's tariff and the advocacy of free trade; and (3) their condemnation of the Boer War (1899-1902) as unjustifiable. The poor physical condition of the recruits for the war revealed the need for regulating industry and the old doctrine of laissez faire was cast aside for an aggressive campaign to better the conditions of the lower classes.

LIBERAL LEGISLATION (1906-1914). The Liberals, under Sir Henry Campbell-Bannerman and Mr. Herbert Asquith, carried out a constructive program. Free trade was maintained, the budget reorganized and taxes were levied so as to place the greatest burden on the rich. The advanced character of the Liberal program aroused fear and bitter opposition among Conservatives, and the political battle ultimately led to important constitutional changes embodied in the Parliament Act (1911). Attempts were made to satisfy the Non-Conformists by establishing denominational schools, by regulating the liquor traffic, and by the disestablishment of the Anglican Church in Wales, but the Lords were able to block the first two and the last was passed with the aid of the Parliament Act. The Parliament Act (1911) was part of the democratic program of the Liberals. Considerable social legislation was passed which improved the condition of the masses. Finally, the Liberals passed a Home Rule Bill for Ireland.

IRELAND (1867-1914)

Religious Problems. The persecution of Catholics in Ireland began with Henry VIII, who attempted to impose Anglicanism upon the people. The passage of time and continual coercion did not deter the Catholics. A small portion of the population was Protestant (Ulster District) and this group with the aid of Great Britain attempted to suppress the Catholics. The first step towards religious freedom was the Emancipation of 1829, which removed political inequalities, but the Catholics still paid tithes to support the Anglican Church. Complete liberty came with the disestablishment of the Protestant Episcopal Church as the state church of Ireland (1869).

Agrarian Question. The major causes for contention in the land problem were revealed in the demand of the peasants for the "three F's"—fair rent, fixity of tenure, and free sale. Absentee landlords were interested only in the rent paid them and not in the conditions under which the peasant was living. The demand for the "three F's" was exceptionally strong after 1850, and in 1870 Gladstone's Land Act was passed to prevent the landlord from taking advantage of the tenant. It was not satisfactory, and a second act was passed in 1881 providing for a land court to fix rents, protect the peasants' tenure, and allow them to sell their improvements. This court succeeded only in reducing the rents. The Land Purchase Act (1891) allowed the tenant to borrow from the government in order that he might purchase his holdings on a basis that would be less than his present rent. The Acts of 1896 and 1898, which provided for a free Irish peasantry and autonomous local government, helped to improve the agrarian situation.

Home Rule Agitation. The spirit of nationalism in Ireland had continually opposed British domination from the twelfth century. Under Daniel O'Connell, peaceful attempts were made to sever the union of Ireland and England.

O'Connell's attempt was followed by the Fenian Revolts in Ireland and America (1867). The passing of the Disestablishment Act and the Land Act did not satisfy the Nationalists under Charles Stewart Parnell and a Home Rule Party was organized which gained eighty-six seats in Parliament. Parnell adopted the policy of embarrassing the government by obstructive filibuster tactics. Neither coercion nor minor concessions proved effective in dealing with the Parnellites. In the meantime Ireland was in a continual state of uproar verging on open rebellion. Finally, in 1886, Gladstone came to the conclusion that the only solution to the Irish problem was Home Rule. He proposed a Home Rule Bill in 1886, but it was defeated by a group of Liberals who joined the Conservatives. A second bill was introduced in 1893 and although it passed the Commons, the Lords defeated it. It was not until 1912 that the Liberals, under Asquith, proposed another bill. The new bill met with serious opposition and the Protestants of Ulster were afraid that the Catholics would gain complete control, even though the bill denied the proposed bicameral parliament the right to have a state religion. Although civil war seemed probable in Ireland, Asquith proceeded with his bill and, in spite of the outbreak of World War I, it became a law in 1914 as the Government of Ireland Act which instituted Ireland, except Ulster, as a Free State. However, the new government was not to go into effect until after the war.

SOCIAL PROGRAM OF THE LIBERAL MINISTRY (1906-1914)

Protective Legislation. The conditions in the factories and mines before 1900 were deplorable. The opposition of the factory owners to provisions demanding sanitary working conditions, a living wage, shorter hours of employment for women, and the withdrawal of children from industry was strong enough to prevent much improvement. The same evils were found in the mining industry. However, in 1878, the few factory regulations which had been passed were brought together in a Consolidation Act. A Code of Mines

Regulations was passed in 1872 which excluded women and children under twelve from underground labor and provided for some safety regulations.

MINIMUM WAGE REGULATIONS. The new Liberal government in the Trade Boards Act of 1909, gave the state the right to regulate the wages in the "sweated trades." Three years later (1912), the strike of the miners led Mr. Asquith to pass a Minimum Wage Law which provided that each district could determine the amount of wages through a local board.

CARE OF THE UNEMPLOYED. The unemployed may be divided into the physically handicapped or permanently unemployed and those temporarily unemployed through depressions or other causes. Workingmen's Compensation Laws were passed in 1897, 1900, and 1906 which provided that a weekly sum should be paid in case of accident and a lump sum in case of death. The Children Act (1908) provided for the proper care and treatment of the young. The same year, an old age pension bill was passed which gave a small pension to those over seventy who were in need. The large group of unemployed, mentioned above as the temporary group, were aided by an act of 1909 which created government employment bureaus. The National Insurance Act (1911) was another attempt to solve the unemployment problem. Lloyd George's bill provided that the workers in the building and engineering trades would pay a fee while they worked as an insurance against unemployment. This Act also provided for insurance against sickness.

Education of the Lower Classes. Before the coming of democracy, education was the luxury of the well-to-do few. After the Reform Bill of 1867 had granted the franchise to the urban working-class, it became increasingly evident that mass education was indispensable in a country with mass votes. An Education Act (1870) provided for the establishment of non-sectarian schools as well as financial support for religious schools. An attempt was made in 1906 to create a system of universal public, non-sectarian schools, but the Lords blocked the bill. However, industrial schools were established, medical attention was given the pupils, and meals were given the poor. In 1913, there were 6,500,000 children in school and $150,000,000 was being expended annually.

Importance of Trade Unions. The new comforts and privileges of the workingmen were gained to a great extent through the trade unions. For a long time legal restraints had prevented the growth of the unions. The famous Taff Vale decision of 1901 was a particularly heavy blow to organized labor, as it established the principle that a union might be held legally responsible for damages sustained by an employer as a consequence of "illegal" strike activities. But the passage of the Trades Disputes Act (1906), which safeguarded the union funds from suits and allowed picketing, the act which provided for the payment of members of parliament (1911), and the right to use trade unions for political purposes (1913), gave the lower classes the basis for an effective opposition.

The New Theory of Taxation. The Liberals placed the burden for carrying their programs into effect upon those who had large incomes, inherited property or money, and used luxuries. The new tax policy was aimed at the landlords who owned and controlled vast lands. Lloyd George's land reforms were held up by the opening of World War I, but the necessary start had been made.

CHAPTER VII.

THE THIRD FRENCH REPUBLIC, 1870-1914

The Third French Republic began under the worst possible conditions—a crushing defeat had just been sustained in a great foreign war; a revolutionary movement in Paris (the Commune, 1871) was put down only at the cost of much bloodshed and party bitterness; social discontent, political factionalism, and foreign military occupation all added to the burdens of the government. But with astonishing energy, France pulled herself out of the ruin of *l'année terrible,* and although a threatening monarchist-republican turbulence continued during the following eight years, with the selection in 1879 of Jules Grévy as President of the Republic, the critical period of political reconstruction was survived and the Republic was established on a firm basis. The next thirty-five years was a period of national growth, economic and social improvement, and external peace. Among the important underlying conditions of French politics of the period should be noted (1) the dominance of the bourgeoisie, (2) the Church-State problem, (3) chauvinism, and (4) cabinet instability.

Dominance of the Bourgeoisie. As in England, political democracy in France resulted in the control of affairs by the bourgeoisie, not by the lower classes. This was due to the superiority of bourgeois leadership and organization. Nevertheless, in the latter part of the period, the laboring classes became increasingly articulate, and through the formation of powerful labor movements were able to influence affairs in their own interest to a considerable degree. But even the social legislation of the period 1890-1914 represented rather the prudent enlightenment of the bourgeoisie than the success of working-class agitation.

Clericalism and Anti-Clericalism. The strongest political undercurrent of the period was the strife between the Republic and the Catholic Church. In the critical period 1871-1879 the Church had actively favored the Royalists, believing that the Republic represented the ideas of the old French Revolution which had ruthlessly confiscated the property of the Church and had made secularism its guiding policy. After the triumph of republicanism in 1879 the struggle continued. In 1892 Pope Leo XIII attempted to compose the quarrel, advising Catholics in France to accept the establishment of the Republic and cease their Royalist agitation, but his encyclical had little effect. Beginning in 1900 the Republic entered on a campaign against the religious schools and against the clerical orders, and in 1905 passed a Separation Law repudiating the Concordat of 1801 and disestablishing the Catholic Church in France. The battle between Church and State permeated all political life.

Chauvinism and *La Revanche*. The military defeat of 1870-1871 rankled in the breast of France—"a nation of patriots"—and few Frenchmen accepted the result as final. The forty-three-year period between the Franco-Prussian War and the World War was one of unprecedented military preparation throughout Europe. In France there was widespread dreaming of *la revanche*—a new war in which France would overwhelm and humiliate Germany as France had been humiliated in 1871. The army became an important factor in politics. The upkeep of an enormous military machine bore heavily on the nation's economic resources. The spirit of chauvinism—aggressive military patriotism—pervaded large sections of the population, and was heavily exploited by ambitious politicians.

Cabinet Instability and Factionalism. An outstanding feature of French parliamentary government has been the instability that has characterized her rapid succession of cabinets, and the numerous factions, or *blocs*, making up the Chamber of Deputies. No single party has ever been able to obtain an actual majority in the Chamber, and every cabinet must be supported by a coalition of *blocs*, The numerous cabinet changes, however, have not conduced to rapidly changing governmental policies, as in most cases the fall of a cabinet results merely in a change of personnel. In France, unlike Great Britain, a cabinet change does not result in a new election of representatives.

GOVERNMENT OF
THE THIRD FRENCH REPUBLIC

The Third French Republic was proclaimed by a coalition of Republicans, Liberal Monarchists, and Socialists who had all opposed Napoleon III. The permanent characteristics of the National Assembly were determined by the eventual control of that body by the Republicans.

National Assembly (1871-1875). The first National Assembly was composed of five hundred Monarchists who favored peace and two hundred Republicans who wanted to continue the Franco-German War. Thiers was made head of the executive power. The first act of the Assembly was to move to Versailles and to ratify the treaty of Frankfurt (1871) and restore peace.

THE PARIS COMMUNE (1870-1871). The Paris Commune, which had been organized to look after the interests of the workingmen during the siege of Paris, was composed of bourgeois Radicals, Marxian Socialists and Anarchists. The Commune opposed the National Assembly because of its monarchist membership and because of the economic conditions in the city of Paris, which had been aggravated by acts of the Assembly. Finally, the Commune revolted against the

Assembly, but the whole-hearted support given the government by the rest of France ended in a bloody victory for the Assembly. The imprisonment, deportation, or death of many of the Socialists and Radicals left France comparatively conservative after the Commune revolt.

ACHIEVEMENTS OF THE ASSEMBLY. Although the National Assembly was supposed to have come to an end after ratifying the Peace, it passed a law making Thiers President and proceeded to administer the affairs of government. The finances were reorganized and the last payment to Germany on the five billion franc indemnity was paid in 1873. To prevent a repetition of 1870-1871, the military machine was completely renovated, service in the army was put on a basis of universal conscription by the Army law of 1872, and a system of fortifications along the German frontier was constructed. The Assembly also reorganized the whole system of local government.

POLITICAL FACTIONS IN NATIONAL ASSEMBLY. The Monarchists had a large majority, yet they were divided into Imperialists (followers of Napoleon III), Legitimists (supporters of the Count of Chambord, heir of traditional monarchy), and Liberal Orleanists (upholders of the claims of the Count of Paris, heir of the Duke of Orleans, Louis Philippe). The Legitimists' and Orleanists' failure to arrive at a compromise prevented the formation of a constitution based on monarchial principles. The attempt of the Count of Paris to effect an agreement with the Count of Chambord resulted in the latter's insistence upon "divine-right" monarchy and the White Flag of the Bourbons (1873). The union of the Monarchists, which had seemed possible under the new President, Marshal MacMahon (1872-1879), was made impossible by this so-called "Chambord Incident," and the Orleanists joined with the Republicans. MacMahon was recognized as President with a term of seven years (1873), and in 1875 provision was made for the election of future presidents. Thus the National Assembly, originally hostile to the establishment of a republic, was gradually forced to republicanism by the inability of the two leading groups of Royalists to agree. Some other laws were passed at this time which were to be the basis of the French Constitution (Constitutional Laws 1875). The first real election, under the Third Republic, returned a Republican Chamber and a Monarchist Senate.

Government of the Third French Republic. The French government established by the Constitutional Laws of 1875 was a highly centralized parliamentary type similar to that of Great Britain. The legislature consists of a Chamber of Deputies (602 members) elected by universal manhood suffrage for four years and a Senate (300 members) chosen by indirect election for nine years. As a result of the indirect method of election and the long term of office, the Senate is usually an extremely conservative body, reflecting, like the British House of Lords, the viewpoint of the wealthy and socially elite class. The president, who is elected by the National Assembly for a term of seven years, is a mere figurehead in practice, although theoretically he is supposed to have specific powers. Unlike the American executive republic, the French system is parliamentary. As in England, the Ministry makes and executes the laws and its power is dependent upon a majority in the Chamber of Deputies.

Rise of the Republicans. President MacMahon was the leader of the Monarchists and he used his powers to increase the prestige of that group. Léon Gambetta (1838-1882) who was noted for his hostility to Napoleon III's imperialism, was the leader of the Republicans. He was not in sympathy with the ideas of the radicals; he favored the bourgeoisie and opposed the Clericals. By compromising with the Liberal Monarchists, Gambetta was able to help mould the Constitution. To increase the number of Republicans, Gambetta attacked the Clericals and pointed out that the Monarchists were aiding the Church and that the Church was aiding the Monarchists. Finally, MacMahon called for a new election because he believed that the people would repudiate Gambetta's attack on Clericalism. However, the election gave the Republicans a majority in the Chamber and in 1879 they gained control of the Senate. President MacMahon resigned (1879) and Jules Grévy, a moderate Republican, was elected by the Assembly. This marked the end of serious efforts to overthrow the Republic and restore a Monarchy. Gambetta became Premier in

1881, symbolizing the full victory of the Republicans, and from that date to 1914 the Republicans constantly gained in power at the expense of the Monarchists.

Political Factions. The French have many political groups; not two (sometimes three) well organized political parties as in Great Britain and the United States. A cabinet in France is always a coalition. The presence of many of the former cabinet officers in the succeeding one helps to retain stability in governmental policies. The fifty cabinet changes in France from 1871-1914 were not as conducive to instability as the nine in Great Britain during the same period.

Monarchists. The Monarchists occupied the extreme Right and although greatly reduced in numbers (26 in 1914), they continued to champion militarism and Clericalism.

Unified Socialists. The extreme Left was occupied by 102 Deputies (1914) of the Unified Socialist group. This faction was the best organized and was formed in 1905 under the leadership of Jules Guesde and Jean Jaurès.

Action Liberale. The Liberal Action group of the Right had a popular backing of over 1,350,000, but they were able to get only 34 seats because of the French system of voting. This faction supported Clericalism, the Republic, and social legislation.

Republican Bloc. The middle of the Chamber was made up of Republican groups who could determine the policy of the Republic by coöperating. The major factions in the Bloc were the Progressists, Republicans, Radicals and Radical Socialists. The Bloc was held together by its anti-clericalism until 1910, but after that, the new issues of tax reform, military conscription, electoral reform, and the insistence of the Radicals for further opposition to Clericalism, weakened the Bloc and established a new line-up with the Unified Radicals of the Right and the Federation of the Left (1914).

PROBLEMS AND ACHIEVEMENTS (1880-1914)

Economic Improvements. Internal improvements were fostered—roads were built, canals dug, railroads subsidized, and new harbors constructed. Agriculture was patronized and encouraged through helpful legislation. A high protective tariff policy aided the growth of industry. An aggressive colonial policy brought to the Republic a colonial empire, second only to Great Britain's, and increased French trade from about 350,000,000 francs to two billion francs. The Clericals did not oppose imperialism since it provided new lands for missionary fields and the new lands offered a new motive for nationalism and imperialism. To support this colonial aggrandizement, the government developed a formidable army and a strong navy. The French proved themselves the most successful of the world's nations in establishing a community of interest between the foreign empire and the mother country, and although the costs of administration were high, France was well repaid by the loyalty with which her subject nationalities responded to her call to arms in 1914.

Social Legislation. Social legislation was enacted by the Republicans to improve the lot of the proletariat, to satisfy Socialist demands, and to gain the support of the masses. Between 1892 and 1913, legislation similar to that passed in Great Britain was enacted. The protection of women and children in industry, a ten-hour day, and a day of rest were provided for in the Act of 1892. Hygienic conditions and medical care were provided for in 1893, trade unions were recognized (1884), workmen's compensation was required (1898), and old age pensions were voted (1911).

Individual Rights and Privileges. Liberty, the old watchword of the French Revolution, became a reality under the Third Republic. Freedom of speech and press were granted in 1881, and in 1901 the Associations Act gave all groups, except the monastic organizations of the Catholic Church, the right of association. The criminal law was modified, children were protected by proper legislation, and the right of divorce was once more recognized (1884).

Opposition to the Clericals. The growth of Anti-Clericalism was closely associated with the Monarchist-Republican struggle of 1871-1879. The Clergy had almost unanimously supported the Royalists. Gambetta, the Republican leader, led the attack with his battle cry "Clericalism, that is the enemy!" With the firm establishment of the Republic, a strong group arose determined to destroy the political influence of the Church, to get rid of religious control of education, and to withdraw state financial support. Church-State relations were theoretically regulated by the Concordat of 1801 between Napoleon and Pope Pius VII, but both sides of the controversy violated the Concordat.

The control of the Church over education was broken by the Ferry Laws. Children must attend a primary school—public or private. Public schools were to be supported by the state, no religious instruction was to be given, and only laymen might teach in them. The loss of educational control aroused the Clericals *en masse*.

The Boulanger Episode (1887-1889). General Boulanger (1837-1891) took advantage of his popularity to get a large Monarchist backing from the army, the Orleanists, and the Imperialists to attempt to overthrow the Republic. His election as deputy from six departments and finally from a Paris district gave him an opportunity to act, but he hesitated. In the meantime the Senate preferred charges of conspiracy against him. Boulanger fled to Belgium. Without a leader, the followers of Boulanger returned only 38 deputies in the general election (1889), whereas the Republican groups controlled 366 deputies. The Boulanger episode is important because (1) the prestige of the Republic was increased, (2) the military regulations were modified in order to decrease the number of Monarchist officers, and (3) the Monarchists lost considerable popular support for aiding Boulanger.

The Dreyfus Affair. The Anti-Semitic sentiment, which Edouard Drumont aroused through his newspaper, was supported by the Monarchists who hoped to discredit the Republicans. The assertion that the Jews were trying to control the French military machine to keep Germany informed, received added weight upon the exposure of the Panama Canal scandal (1894) and the conviction of Alfred Dreyfus, a Jewish captain, for selling military secrets to Germany (1894). The affair became important when Colonel Picquart, new head of the espionage system of the army, reached the conclusion that Dreyfus was innocent and that Major Esterhazy, a Monarchist, was guilty (1897). The army chiefs returned a verdict of

acquittal for Esterhazy, not because they believed him innocent, but to retain the "honor" of the army. The whole affair
was crystallized by Émile Zola, the author, who accused the
Anti-Semitics and the army officers of convicting an innocent
man. The confession of one of the forgers and the flight and
suicide of Esterhazy (1898) resulted in a new court-martial at
Rennes giving Dreyfus executive clemency although still considering him guilty. However, in 1906, the Rennes verdict was
annulled and Dreyfus was made a major in the army. Picquart, who had been disgraced, was vindicated. The Dreyfus
affair crushed Monarchism, formed a Republican Bloc, gave
the Republicans control of the army, and increased Anti-Clerical legislation.

Anti-Clerical Legislation (1901-1907). The Anti-Clerical
legislation was aimed directly at the opposition. The Associations Act of 1901 made it illegal for a religious organization to
exist without governmental sanction, and no member of an
unauthorized group was allowed to teach in any school. This
Act was strictly enforced and it served to force undesirable
religious groups out of the country, to weaken the private
schools and to develop the public schools. A rupture between
the Vatican and France ended with the separation of Church
and state (1905). The Concordat of 1801 was denounced and
all creeds were considered equal in France. This separation
was bitterly opposed by the Clericals, but they finally accepted
a compromise proposed by Briand (1907), by which they recognized the separation and the cessation of financial help from
the state, but they remained free to manage their internal
affairs and use their churches for worship.

CHAPTER VIII.

THE GERMAN EMPIRE 1871-1914

The foundation of the German Empire was the most important European event of the nineteenth century. It created an entirely new center of gravity in international affairs and represents as complete a break with the Europe of 1815-1871 as that era represents a break with the *ancien régime* of pre-French Revolutionary days. The most pressing European problem of the period 1871-1914 was that of adjusting the old European system to the new Germany. The failure of the statesmen of Europe to solve this problem brought about the World War. Important elements in German history (1871-1914) were (1) great industrial development, (2) militarism, (3) reactionary form of government, and (4) social legislation.

Industrial Expansion. The Industrial Revolution came to Germany late and made slow progress during the period 1830-1865. With the achievement of political unity, however, a great stimulant was given, and Germany became an industrial country almost overnight. The years 1870-1875 are called by the Germans the *Grundjahre*, or foundation years, in the establishment of the German industrial economy. Factories sprang up as if by magic. Railway trackage was nearly doubled. Shipbuilding received a tremendous impetus. Coal and iron production advanced by leaps and bounds. During the next thirty-five years German industry passed competitor after competitor; in 1914 Germany stood on practically even terms with Great Britain and the United States as a great industrial power. In many ways Germany's late entrance into the international industrial race was an advantage rather than a handicap—she was able to start with the most modern machinery and methods, unhampered either by traditionalism or by the drag of large capital investment in obsolescent equipment. Once launched on a career of industrialization, the Germans proved to be perhaps the most inventive and efficient people in the world; the British, especially, watched the rising giant, partly in admiration and partly in fear, as they contrasted their own methods of "muddling through" with the scientific organization, the patience for detail, and the genius for thoroughness of the Germans.

Militarism. Germany became a united nation, as Bismarck said, "not by speeches and majority resolutions, but by blood and iron," and during the period 1871-1914 the military tradition was never allowed to flag. The German army kept continually growing; a large naval program was begun in 1898; by 1914 she had the most powerful fighting machine in the world. In no other nation was the military profession so highly honored; in no other nation was there greater subordination of the civil government to the requirements of the soldiers; in no other nation was preparation for war carried through with such grim completeness, such attention to detail, such national energy and enthusiasm. Yet German militarism was not different in its origin and nature from French or Russian militarism or British navalism. All the nations of Europe were engaged, to the limits of their national capacities, in arming to the teeth—each fearing the armaments of its neighbors, each government feeling, in the words of Sir Edward Grey, that "it would be criminal and a betrayal of its own country not to take every precaution, while every government regards every precaution of every other government as evidence of hostile intent."[1] It was Germany's genius for organization and Germany's industrial growth rather than any

1 From *Twenty-Five Years* by Edward Grey. Published by F. A. Stokes Co.

uniquely aggressive attitude that made the German military establishment the most formidable in the world.

Reactionary Form of Government. Unlike Great Britain and France, Germany took hardly any steps toward democracy during the period 1867-1914. Bismarck, Germany's greatest statesman, was an implacable enemy of democratic ideas, and Germany had no long tradition of legal resistance to the encroachment of the state upon the rights of the individual as in Great Britain, or of democratic revolution as in France. For the French Revolution watchwords of "Liberty, Equality, and Fraternity," the Germans may be said to have substituted the ideals of System, Efficiency, and Discipline. Their great historical hero was the enlightened divine right monarch, Frederick the Great. For the long parliamentary tradition of such an institution as the British House of Commons, the Germans had no feeling. And so aristocracy and feudalism continued to flourish not, as in Russia, in the midst of a backward material civilization, but along with the most advanced science, scholarship, industry, and public education in the world. In the early twentieth century Germany seemed to many observers in democratic countries to be a huge anachronism—its science and industry leading the world, its politics sleeping in the eighteenth century. In the period 1908-1914, there developed a strong movement in Germany favoring democratization of the government, but down to the outbreak of World War I little had been accomplished.

Social Legislation. In spite of its undemocratic institutions—perhaps, indeed, partly because of them—Germany led Europe in social legislation. "In Prussia," declared Bismarck, "the kings, not the people, make revolutions." Earlier than any other nation Germany adopted large scale social insurance legislation, old age pensions, universal education, and other measures that made the state an active partner with capital and labor in the economic process. The shibboleth of laissez faire never attained much popularity in Germany, partly because the industrial experience of England had seemingly demonstrated its impossibility, and partly because the bourgeoisie failed in Germany to acquire the overwhelming predominance that they attained in England and France. Bismarck frankly embarked upon a program of social legislation as a means of gaining the loyalty and support of the working-men and preventing the growth of socialism and other movements deemed subversive by removing the causes of discontent. He had to meet the opposition of the bourgeoisie, who denounced his schemes as socialistic, but he cared nothing for names and catchwords. "Give the workingman the right to employment as long as he has health, assure him of care when he is sick and maintenance when he is old, and the socialists will sound their birdcall in vain. Thronging to them will cease as soon as the workingmen realize that the government is earnestly concerned with their welfare." Such was Bismarck's program. No other statesman in Europe could boast of so advanced a point of view. Had Gladstone said such a thing in England, his Liberal Party followers could scarcely have believed their ears.

THE GOVERNMENT SYSTEM

The government of the German Empire was provided for in a constitution which was accepted by the members of the North German Confederation and the southern states of Germany.

The Executive. The king of Prussia was given the title of German Emperor with the power to control the military and political policies of the state. The Emperor was the head of the army and navy; he appointed the chancellor, declared defensive wars, and made treaties with other nations.

The Legislature. A bicameral legislature was composed of a Reichstag (membership based on population) and a Bundesrat (membership based on states). Membership in the Bundesrat was not the same for each state but varied according to its size and importance, and all the delegates from a single state voted as a unit; hence Prussia with 17 out of 61 votes had a predominating position. The election of 236 of the 397 representatives to the Reichstag from Prussia, gave that state a decided advantage in this House also. Certain delegated powers were given to the federal government and all others were reserved to the states. The aristocratic Bundesrat was the real law-making body; the popular Reichstag was checked by the Bundesrat. The Reichstag had no power over the executive branch of the government as in Great Britain and France; in many respects it was scarcely more than a debating society in which public affairs were discussed but not acted upon. The effective power of the government was in the hands of the Imperial Chancellor.

The Imperial Chancellor. The favored position of Prussia was further strengthened by providing for the Emperor's appointment of an Imperial Chancellor, who remained in office during the pleasure of the Emperor. The Chancellor was the agent of the Emperor. He could address the Reichstag, preside over the Bundesrat, and cast the seventeen votes of Prussia. Also, he proposed legislation and executed it.

Stability of the Government. The acquiescence of the Germans to the undemocratic federal constitution is explained by (1) their traditional acceptance of absolutism from the time of the Great Elector, (2) the efficiency of the new government in consolidating the Empire, and (3) the development of democracy in the state and local governments.

CHANCELLORSHIP OF BISMARCK

Bismarck became the first Imperial Chancellor of Emperor William I in 1871 and for the nineteen years that followed proceeded to dominate not only the domestic affairs of Germany but also the field of European politics.

National Legislation. To meet the changed conditions, the whole legal system was revised and extended to include the whole Empire. Codes of civil and criminal procedure were drawn up (1871-1900). The financial conditions were improved by (1) regulating coinage, (2) giving the Bundesrat control of banks (1875), and (3) establishing an Imperial Bank (1876). A railway bureau helped to unify the railroads. Bismarck continued to place faith in the army, and a standing army of 400,-000 men was retained; service was still compulsory.

Political Parties. There were five important political parties in Germany during Bismarck's Chancellorship.

NATIONAL LIBERALS. The National Liberals were composed of a large group of the bourgeoisie and the patriots who favored nationalism. This party supported Bismarck.

CONSERVATIVES. The Conservatives were mostly agriculturalists of Prussia who were benefiting by the policies of Bismarck.

PROGRESSIVES. The Progressives opposed Bismarck and his autocracy and tried to arouse the people to democracy, but the success of the Chancellor's policies drowned their protests.

CATHOLIC (CENTER) PARTY. The Catholic or Center Party opposed the nationalistic policies and supported the idea of Particularism (States' Rights). Bismarck opposed the Catholics for several reasons: (1) he did not want to interfere in Italy as they wished him to, (2) the doctrine of the infallibility of the Pope aroused fear that the Church intended to reassert an authority in political affairs, and (3) the conflict between science and the Church was increasing. The *Kulturkampf* was a name given to the struggle between the Church and state in Germany between 1873-1883. The attempt of Bismarck to interfere with the Church through his "May Laws" was met by sturdy opposition from the Catholics. The struggle was finally neutralized by the appearance of a socialist group which Bismarck hated more than the Catholics. After 1876 the Center Party was important because of its independent position in the Reichstag.

SOCIAL DEMOCRATS. The organization of the followers of Marx and Lassalle into a Social Democratic Party (1875) which stood for political democracy, anti-militarism, and social legislation, aroused Bismarck. In 1877 the Socialists polled 500,000 votes and got twelve seats in the Reichstag. An attempt upon the life of the Emperor gave Bismarck an opportunity to enact a series of "Exceptional Laws" for suppressing Socialism (1878-1890) in spite of the opposition of the Progressives and Centrists. The anti-Socialist legislation did not succeed in its purpose. Socialist agitation continued through underground channels. In fact, during 1881-1890 the number of seats in the Reichstag controlled by the Socialists increased from 12 to 35. The year 1912 saw 110 Socialists in the Reichstag.

Bismarck's Economic Policy. Bismarck contested the rise of Socialism with a new economic policy which centered around imperialism, social legislation, and a protective tariff. The German Chancellor discarded the doctrine of laissez faire and the National Liberal party which supported it.

IMPERIALISM. The early opposition of Bismarck to colonial enterprises was gradually overcome as merchants and missionaries gained concessions in Africa and Oceania. These commercial posts were recognized as protectorates (1884-1885) and later as crown colonies.

SOCIAL LEGISLATION. Bismarck sponsored social legislation in order to remove the causes upon which Socialism was developing and to maintain military efficiency, which was dependent upon the health and happiness of the German people. Between 1881 and 1890, laws were enacted insuring workmen against sickness (1883) and accidents (1884); regulating the labor of women and children in industry (1887); providing for a day of rest (1887); and requiring compulsory insurance of workingmen against old age and incapacity (1889). Many other laws were passed which improved factory conditions, allowed trade-unions to grow, and provided for labor exchanges.

PROTECTIVE TARIFF. Bismarck's protective tariff (1879), which was supported by the Center and Conservative parties, served to protect infant industries, to provide the federal government with revenue, and to decrease its dependence upon the states for money.

Foreign Policy of Bismarck (1871-1890). The foreign policy of Bismarck centered around his efforts to isolate France and to prevent her from waging a "war of revenge."

GREAT BRITAIN. Bismarck's opposition to imperialism (1871-1882) helped to decrease Britain's fear of the German Empire. The Chancellor also felt that Great Britain would not join with France, because of her policy of isolation from continental affairs, unless British imperialism was challenged.

RUSSIA. Although the Russian expansion program made her lean toward a French alliance, autocratic Russia was politically nearer militaristic Germany than republican France. Bismarck's aid in the Polish Insurrection (1863) and in the reëstablishment of the Russian fleet in the Black Sea (1871) helped the Chancellor's cause, and Tsar Alexander II joined Emperor Francis Joseph and William I in an alliance known as the Three Emperors' League (1872-1876).

AUSTRIA-HUNGARY. The lenient treaty of 1866 made the people of Austria-Hungary grateful to Germany. France could not expect an alliance with the Dual Monarchy.

ITALY. In the seventies, the Italians were more friendly to Germany than France because (1) they still remembered Napoleon III's breach of faith in 1859 and (2) they were grateful to Germany for ceding Venetia to Italy (Treaty of Prague, 1866).

TRIPLE ALLIANCE (1882-1915). Although Germany had the backing of Italy, Russia, and Austria-Hungary as individual nations, it was almost impossible to bring them into a group alliance because of the animosities among them. Bismarck's attempt to satisfy both Russia and Austria after the Russo-Turkish War ended in bringing Austria closer, but Russian friendship was threatened. The Iron Chancellor finally concluded a secret agreement with Austria-Hungary (1879) which bound each to support the other in a defensive war. In spite of the fact that Austria was the traditional foe of Italy, that country finally joined Austria and Germany in a Triple Alliance (1882). Italy joined this secret alliance because she feared isolation and resented the French attempt to establish a protectorate over Tunis (1881).

GERMANY AND RUSSIA (1881-1890). The assassination of Alexander II (1881) and the accession of the autocrat, Alexander III, made it possible for Bismarck to revive the League of the Three Emperors for two terms of three years each (1881-1887). However, the aggrandizement of both Russia and Austria in the Balkans made a third renewal impossible. In order to keep Russia tied to Germany, Bismarck signed a secret treaty with Russia pledging neutrality. It mattered not to the wily Bismarck that in the secret agreement of the Triple Alliance he promised to support Austria if she were attacked by Russia or any other power. France was isolated; nothing else mattered.

Dismissal of Bismarck (1890). William I was succeeded by Frederick III (1888) who died three months after his accession. The new king, William II (1888-1918), was an autocrat with *divine right* leanings. He had not been in office long before he came into conflict with his grandfather's Chancellor, who had been the real ruler of the empire. Finally, Bismarck was asked to resign (1890) and he returned to Lauenburg. Until his death (1898) he continued to criticise the policies of the new Emperor.

GERMANY UNDER WILLIAM II

Political Parties (1890-1914). The major parties in the Reichstag were (1) Centrists, (2) Conservatives, (3) National Liberals, (4) Progressives, and (5) Socialists. In spite of the opposition of the Emperor and the former Chancellor, the Socialists, in 1912, polled 4,250,000 votes (110 seats) as compared to 2,000,000 votes (90 seats) by the Centrists, 1,120,000 votes (45 seats) by the National Liberals, and 1,500,000 by both the Progressives and Conservatives.

Of the minor political groups there were (1) the Guelfs, who protested against the annexation of Hanover to Prussia (1866), (2) the Danes of Schleswig, who wished the return of this land to the Danish king, (3) the residents of Alsace-Lorraine, who urged the return of their land to its former owner, France, and (4) the Poles of Posen, who demanded national independence and persisted in their claims in spite of persecution by Prussia.

Economic Growth (1890-1914). The growth of Germany during this period was phenomenal. The increase in population (from 41 million in 1871 to 65 million in 1910) was over 50 per cent. Industry and commerce thrived under satisfactory working conditions. In 1914, Germany was the second largest manufacturing country in the world and her exports had increased threefold from 1890.

Chancellor Count von Caprivi (1890-1894). Caprivi, with the help of the National Liberals, fostered colonial expansion and enacted reciprocity agreements with Austria-Hungary, Russia, Rumania, and Italy, which lowered the import duties on grain in order to gain concessions for the manufactured goods which were exported. These agreements aroused the agrarian interests against Caprivi.

Chancellor Prince Hohenlohe (1894-1900). The discontent of the agrarian interests prevented internal development, but it allowed William II and his Chancellor to foster imperialism. The beginnings made under Bismarck were furthered. Colonies were obtained in the Pacific (Caroline, Pelew, Marianne, and two of the Samoan islands), and a concession on the Shan-tung peninsula in China was acquired. On four continents, avenues were opened to allow the investment of German capital. The development of land armaments was supplemented with a naval force that rivaled Great Britain's. The rise of the German navy was due to (1) increased imperialism, (2) the development of nationalism, (3) the efforts of the Emperor, and (4) the activities of Admiral von Tirpitz as secretary of state for the navy. A naval base resulted from the acquisition of Heligoland (1890) and the completion of the Kaiser Wilhelm Canal (1896) connecting the North and Baltic Seas. The naval building program, when it was started in 1898, increased the cost of the navy from thirty million dollars to one hundred twenty million dollars in 1913.

Chancellor Prince Bernhard von Bülow (1900-1909). Bülow, as a landowner, was more sympathetic toward the Conservatives than his two predecessors, and in 1902 a new tariff law renewed the old protective rates. In addition to his efforts in behalf of the agrarian interests, he also kept the National Liberals in line by an aggressive foreign policy which threatened to dissolve the Triple Alliance, and did make possible a Triple Entente composed of France, Russia, and England (1907). The opposition of the Socialists and Centrists to the foreign and domestic program was stifled by the Chancellor and William II.

Chancellor Bethmann-Hollweg (1909-1917). The coming of a new Chancellor did not mean a change in policy, but rather a continuance of the old, because the real Chancellor was the Emperor. During the first half of Bethmann-Hollweg's chancellorship, the German Empire became more and more unified, until in 1913 the Army Bill had the support of all the political parties in the Reichstag. As a solidified whole, Germany entered World War I.

CHAPTER IX.

SPAIN, PORTUGAL, ITALY BELGIUM. 1870-1914

Spain (1800-1875). During the first three quarters of the nineteenth century Spain was the most turbulent state in Europe. Yet it is difficult to trace any politics of principle or any clear cut conflicts of great ideas or great interests. Such conflicts existed, of course, but they seemed unable to organize themselves. For the most part, the revolutions and civil wars of the period seem essentially meaningless, like the feudal wars of the Middle Ages. Indeed, nineteenth century Spain, as indicated by its slowness in accepting the Industrial Revolution, in many important respects adhered to a medieval and feudal political, social, and economic structure. Napoleon's intervention, which led to a revolution, was followed by the reign of Ferdinand VII (1814-1833), who was noted for his extreme absolutism. The inheritance of the throne by his daughter, Isabella II, resulted in a war of succession between the Carlists and the Christinists. Isabella II was finally recognized, and after an inglorious reign (1833-1868) was forced to flee to France. A new constitution was drawn up (1869), and when Prince Leopold of Hohenzollern-Sigmaringen declined the throne, Prince Amadeo of Savoy became king (Jan. 1871). King Amadeo did not satisfy the people, and upon his abdication (1873), a republic was proclaimed. The republican experiment was unsuccessful, and Alphonso, the son of Isabella II, was made king. This restoration of the Bourbons, in the person of Alphonso XII, started an era of reform.

The Reign of Alphonso XII (1875-1885). Alphonso XII was only eighteen and yet, with the help of Martinez Campos (1831-1900) and Cánovas del Castillo (1828-1897), he established law and order. A new liberal constitution was drawn up. It remained in force until 1931 and provided for a Cortes of two houses: a Senate (360 members) and a Congress of Deputies (406 members). The executive power was vested in a ministry, responsible to the Cortes. Alphonso XII protected the Catholic Church and allowed it to establish organizations and to administer education. Cánovas del Castillo organized a Conservative party to carry out his program. The finances of the nation were organized, the army improved, agriculture and industry promoted, and foreign lands gained by the marriage of Alphonso XII to Maria Christina of Austria. The death of Alphonso (1885) left the throne in the care of Maria Christina (1885-1902) until the posthumous Alphonso XIII became of age. With the help of the Liberal leader, Sagasta (Prime Minister, 1886-1890) and Cánovas del Castillo, Maria Christina was able to hold the monarchy together. Sagasta prepared a civil code and introduced trial by jury, liberal press and association laws, and universal manhood suffrage (1890). The disastrous war with the United States (1898) resulted in the end of Spanish control in Cuba, Puerto Rico, the Philippines, and Guam. The last vestiges of the vast colonial empire consisting of the Carolines and a few other islands were sold to Germany in 1899.

Alphonso XIII (1902-1931). The Republican influence which was to cause Alphonso XIII to flee in 1931 was not apparent as late as 1915. The King proceeded to improve the general economic conditions by developing natural resources, reducing taxes, reorganizing the finances, and curbing militarism. Commerce increased tremendously. Agriculture, which was the most important occupation, received an added impetus under favorable conditions. The activities of the Socialists and Anarchists resulted in liberal legislation after the death of Cánovas del Castillo (1897) and Sagasta (1903). Universal manhood suffrage was made compulsory (1907). Illiteracy was decreased through an elementary public school system. Anti-clerical legislation was defeated by the Conservatives and Moderate Liberals after the Protestant faith was recognized, and a curb placed upon the organization of Catholic religious groups (1909-1910). The unhappy experience of Spain in northern Morocco, which had been acquired in 1912, aroused the Spaniards against any attempt to revive imperialism, and the anti-military riots prevented the development of a strong army. Although under Alphonso XII and Alphonso XIII Spain made conspicuous superficial progress toward modern liberalism as it was then understood in Europe, little was accomplished toward fundamental solutions of social and economic problems and the nation remained in a state of suppressed and unorganized discontent.

PORTUGAL

Portuguese Monarchy (1834-1910). The history of nineteenth century Portugal is very similar to that of Spain. The reign of Queen Maria II (1834-1853) was like that of Isabella II of Spain, in which court intrigues, general lawlessness, and military coups prevailed. In 1852 a constitutional provision was made for direct election of deputies and popular participation in local government. Under Luiz I (1861-1889) several political groups appeared. The Regenerators (Conservatives) and the Progressives (Liberals) were the strongest, but the anti-clerical Republicans, Miguelites, Carlists, and Socialists were important. The reign of Carlos I (1889-1908) was characterized by several financial crises and by the corrupt practices of the Regenerators and Progressives. The attempt of Carlos I to govern through his Prime Minister João Franco resulted in the assassination of Carlos I and the Crown Prince (1908). The ascension of Manoel II (1908-1910), young son of Carlos I, the exile of Franco, and the strife between the Regenerators and Progressives led to the Revolution of 1910. The monarchy was overthrown and a republic proclaimed.

Portuguese Republic (1910-1915). The constitution of the Republic provided for a Cortes, a president (four-year term, elected by Cortes), and a ministry responsible to the Cortes. Dr. Manoel Arriaga was the first president. The Republicans confiscated church property, separated the church and state, stopped public payment of the clergy, and expelled church organizations (1911). This anti-clerical legislation aroused the clericals against the Republic. The failure of the Republican leaders to improve the condition of the working classes resulted in a period of strikes, riots, and political agitation. The army alone was able to hold the Republic against internal dissension.

THE RISE OF BELGIUM

Government of Belgium. The Constitution (1831) provided for a "constitutional, representative, and hereditary monarchy." The king was given power to initiate legislation, but all other acts had to be approved by a minister responsible to a parliament of two houses—a Senate elected for eight years and a Chamber of Representatives elected for four years.

Economic Growth. Rapid economic development in Belgium followed the introduction of improved methods of cultivation by the farmers, and the expansion of trade and industry. Internal improvements were made, and commerce was encouraged until in 1911 Belgium exports and imports were valued at over one and a half billion dollars.

The Catholic Party. The king was required to be a member of the Catholic Church, yet the constitution guaranteed religious liberty. However, the question of education created a difference of opinion. The Catholic party wished to make moral and religious instruction under the clergy compulsory, while the Liberals favored secular schools. During the Liberal supremacy, religious instruction was abolished. The Liberals were not important after 1885, but they were succeeded by an anti-clerical Socialist party. The Catholic party remained in control of the government from 1884 to 1914. They restored religious instruction and reduced illiteracy by supporting an aggressive educational program.

The franchise was extended, and proportional representation introduced. The condition of the working classes was improved through social legislation which protected trade unions (1898), provided for old age pensions (1900), and encouraged better living conditions. The acquisition of the Belgian Congo (1908) resulted in an increased emphasis on militarism. Compulsory military service was provided for in the Act of 1909 and the important cities of Liége and Antwerp were fortified.

ITALY (1871-1914)

The new Italy was a centralized state and not a federation of states. The enormous task of economic and social consolidation was evident in the contrast between the wealthy north, with its comparatively advanced industrial development, and the south, with its poverty, ignorant peasantry, and meager industries. Legislation was enacted after 1871 which served to decrease illiteracy, to improve means of communication and transportation, and to bring the sections closer together. The tax rate, which resulted from the internal improvements, rose steadily until it was higher, per capita, than that of any other European country. The northerners complained that the south was getting all the benefits, and the southerners claimed that the north monopolized public offices.

Government of Italy. The government of Italy is patterned after that of Great Britain. The old Sardinian *Statuto* (1848) provided for the frame-work of government. A parliament (composed of an elective Chamber of Deputies and an appointive and aristocratic Senate) and a ministry responsible to it had complete authority. The king was a figure-head. Universal manhood suffrage was provided for in 1912 as a result of the demands of the Catholics and Socialists.

Position of the Church. Cavour's suggestion of "a free church in a free state" was not followed. To clarify the papal problem, the Law of Papal Guarantees (1871) was passed. This law granted the Pope (1) sovereign rights similar to those of a king, (2) complete control of the Vatican city, (3) use of Italian communicative services, and (4) an annual payment of 3,225,000 lire for his lost territories. Pius IX refused to accept this arrangement; he made himself a "prisoner" in the Vatican and forbade Catholics to participate in the Italian government. This non-participation of Catholics weakened the government and aggravated the breach between Church and State. In 1905 a partial reconciliation occurred when Pius X practically rescinded the previous injunction against coöperation with the state by Catholics, but the "Roman Question," that is, the question of the temporal power of the Pope and of his relation with the Italian government, remained a thorn in the side of Italian statesmanship.

Political Parties. The trend of events in Italy from 1870 to 1876 was determined by the leaders of the Right. This group was responsible for the constitution, the Law of Papal Guarantees, organization of local districts, development of the army and navy, and the improvement of railways. In 1876, the statesmen of the Left came into power. Agostino Depretis (1813-1887) tried to make Italy a great power, but in his attempt he upset the finances and allowed corrupt practices. After the death of Depretis (1887), Francesco Crispi (1819-1901) continued the policies of militarism, imperialism, and nationalism through dictatorial methods. The defeat of the Italians at Adowa, Abyssinia (1896), and the assassination of the King, Humbert (1878-1900), who had supported both Depretis and Crispi, resulted in the latter's downfall.

Reign of Victor Emmanuel III (1900–1946). The new king introduced a new era. Industrial conditions improved and commerce increased. Legislation was passed (1) benefiting women and children in industry, (2) providing for insurance against accidents, sickness, and old age, (3) allowing for a day of rest each week, (4) recognizing trade unions, and (5) encouraging cooperative marketing. The failure of these reforms to benefit the agricultural classes (one-third the population) led many Italians to emigrate to countries that offered more favorable conditions. The political factions had a different line-up in the twentieth century. The Clericals became powerful after 1905. They strenuously opposed anti-clerical legislation but fostered social reform. A small group of Republicans still persisted, but the fact that they controlled only seventeen seats in the Chamber in 1913 reveals the stability of the monarchy. The Socialists made great advances after 1900, and they had seventy-eight representatives in 1913. The unrest of the proletariat gave the Syndicalists a chance to enlist many in its program of violence. However, the unifying force was an intense national patriotism, which was powerful enough to command the loyalty of the Italians.

CHAPTER X.

THE RUSSIAN EMPIRE
1855-1914

In population and potential resources Russia is the greatest of European states. Yet up to the beginning of the eighteenth century she contributed almost nothing to the political, intellectual, and social life of Europe. She was a vast but little known and little regarded eastern empire. In the eighteenth century, under such aggressive and ambitious sovereigns as Peter the Great and Catherine the Great, Russia emerged as an important European Power, and during the Napoleonic Wars she took the largest share (except, perhaps, Great Britain's) in breaking Napoleon's plans for European hegemony. This brought her actively into the "Concert of Europe" after the Congress of Vienna. During the Metternich Era she was a bulwark of reaction, and it was Russian troops that turned the scale against the revolutionists of 1848 in central Europe. But in the nineteenth century Russia lost much of her prominence. The Industrial Revolution made very slow progress in Russia, and the French Revolution, even slower. In 1850, when England and France were developed industrial countries dominated by the bourgeosie and profoundly stirred by the forces of economic and political liberalism, Russia was a "backward" country with a medieval social and economic structure. Because of her great physical size it was impossible for any other nation to cause much military damage, but since her resources were undeveloped and her social organization antiquated, she could not threaten the domination of Europe. Her interests in the Black Sea region brought her into conflict with the Turks and, through the Turks, with England and France, while her racial connections with the Slavic peoples of the Balkans made her a rival of Austria-Hungary; but until the beginning of the twentieth century these international difficulties were of a local character. Toward the end of the nineteenth century, however, the Industrial Revolution began to effect a "westernization" of Russia, and her enormous population and territory became again a specter in the minds of many European, especially German, statesmen. If Russia were ever to be developed to the degree her potential resources made possible, it was obvious that no power in western Europe could withstand her. It was German fear of Russia, on the eve of the World War, that more than anything else precipitated that conflict.

REFORM AND REACTION UNDER ALEXANDER II

Reform of Alexander II. The predecessor of Alexander II, Nicholas I (1825-1855), had been an unwavering autocrat. He had crushed Liberalism, yet he had not completely eliminated the demand for reforms; so when Alexander became tsar, there was a group ready to test the new, inexperienced ruler. Alexander II wished to be an autocrat, but lacking the personal force of his father, he decided to sanction internal reform.

EMANCIPATION OF THE SERFS (1861). The majority of the peasants were attached to the soil of the large estates of the nobility and lived under a system of feudalism similar to that which existed in medieval Europe. Alexander II took the first step in improving the lot of the serfs through a decree which freed the serfs in 1861. Many of the peasants left the farms and went to the cities to work in the new factories.

LOCAL ADMINISTRATIVE REFORMS — ZEMSTVOS (1864). The administration of local governmental affairs was to be carried on by zemstvos (assemblies) which were provided for in each Russian district and province by a decree in 1864.

JUDICIAL REFORMS (1862). A decree in 1862 provided for a system of courts similar to those of the United States to displace the old system of secret and arbitrary courts. Provision was also made for trial by jury, public court proceedings, tenure of office for judges, and a codification of the laws.

Reactionary Policy of Alexander II (1865-1881). Alexander's ardor for reform was considerably cooled by the Polish Insurrection (1863). Also, after ten years as tsar, Alexander felt capable of handling the Russian Liberals, and a policy of reaction was begun. The power of the zemstvos was curtailed, a strict censorship of the press was instituted, and political offenders were exiled. This reactionary policy resulted in considerable opposition to the Tsar.

NIHILISTS. The Nihilists were a group of intellectual radicals who opposed the political, social, and religious institutions of Russia and favored the growth of science and reason.

ANARCHISTIC SOCIALISTS. The Anarchistic Socialists of Russia were the followers of Mikhail Bakunin. Since they had been denied the right of reform through legislation, they sought to arouse the artisans and peasants to violence in order to effect their aims.

TERRORISTS. The attempt of the Tsar to suppress the Nihilists and Socialists resulted in the formation of a group who sought to terrorize the government. The Terrorists succeeded in killing many government officials in spite of the Tsar's secret police. Alexander II finally relented and signed a decree providing for a special commision to suggest administrative reforms. On the very day he signed the decree (March 13, 1881) Alexander II was assassinated by a Terrorist.

RUSSIA (1881-1905)

Alexander III and Autocracy. Alexander III (1881-1894) had the help of two extremely capable men to maintain autocracy. Konstantine Pobedonostsev (1827-1907) was a champion for reaction. He opposed even the slightest reforms and attacked parliamentary government, secular education, and the press. Plehve (1846-1904), as head of the police, concentrated his efforts on crushing all opposition to the government. His harsh, repressive measures carried out by a ruthless but highly efficient secret police, made him perhaps the most hated person in all Russia, but he succesfully stamped out all articulate revolutionary discontent. The imperial government became more centralized, and all elements of freedom in local government and secular education were removed. In spite of the efficiency with which the liberal tendencies had been thwarted, incompetence and corruption permeated the whole imperialistic government. The tsarist government had been able to maintain autocracy in Russia because of (1) the loyalty of the Tsar's assistants to the central government, (2) the control of the Greek Orthodox Church by the Tsar, (3) the administration of education, which was extremely meager, being in the hands of the Church (Russia's illiteracy was greater than that of any other European country), (4) the successful coercion of liberal movements, (5) the peasants' conception of the Tsar as a "Little Father," (6) the conservative agrarian group, (7) the history and tradition of the autocracy under leaders like Peter the Great and Catherine the Great, and (8) the prevalent opinion that democracy could not successfully cope with the problems of the Russian people.

Russification. The Russian Empire was composed of many groups of Slavic peoples who spoke different languages and had different customs. The problem facing the leaders in Russia was the development of a nationalistic state out of the heterogeneous population. In Russia there were to be found (1) the Great Russians of the grandduchy of Muscovy (50,000,000), (2) Little Russians of southwestern Russia (20,000,000), (3) White Russians of Lithuania (5,00,000), (4) Lithuanians (2,500,000), (5) Poles in Poland, (6) Finns in Finland, and numerous other peoples in Bessarabia, Esthonia, Livonia, Caucasia, and even in Asia to the Pacific coast. The Pan-Slavists supported the autocracy because they believed that it would unite all the Slavs within the Empire and then make it possible to extend Russian influence to all the Slavs throughout Europe.

With the aid of Plehve and Pobêdonostsev, Alexander III attempted to consolidate the Russian people by suppressing small nationalistic groups and all forms of worship except those of the Orthodox Church. In Poland, the Russian language and customs were imposed upon the people, and in Lithuania, the Catholic Uniates (Orthodox Christians who joined the Roman Catholic Church) were persecuted. The Jews suffered under Pan-Slavism because of their tendency to segregate themselves from others and because of their loyalty to custom and tradition. Stringent legislation discriminated against them, and as a result of pogroms (Anti-Jewish riots) their property and lives were endangered. To escape this persecution many emigrated to the United States. Throughout the Empire the process of Russification was put into practice.

Nicholas II (1894-1917) relied upon Pobêdonostsev and Plehve to carry on the program of Russification, and the following were all connected with the plan: (1) the Massacre of Kishinev (1903) in which thousands of Jews were killed; (2) the Russo-Japanese War, which was an attempt to extend Pan-Slavism to the Orient, and (3) the substitution of Russian for Finnish officials in Finland.

Influence of the Industrial Revolution. The Industrial Revolution did not affect Russia until the latter part of the nineteenth century, and then a marked increase in commerce and industry followed. This increase was due to the presence in the cities of cheap labor and the investment in Russia of foreign capital (chiefly French) with which railroads were built (Trans-Siberian Railway, 1891-1905). Arraigned against Plehve, who obstinately opposed industrial growth, was Serge de Witte (1849-1915). As the finance minister of Alexander III, Witte fostered railway construction, a protective tariff, and social legislation which would benefit the worker. However, in 1903, Plehve succeeded in getting Nicholas II to dismiss Witte. As the Industrial Revolution gained momentum, the opposition to the autocracy increased. The landowners urged agricultural reform, and the reports of the zemstvo committees were antagonistic to existing conditions. Marxian socialism appealed to the industrial workers and the poor peasants.

Besides the opposition of the landowners and the socialists, there was a group of middle class liberals who wished to extend their economic independence at the expense of the autocracy. Finally, the lesser nationalities welcomed the chance to ally themselves with either Socialists or Liberals in order to weaken the central government and further their own nationalism.

THE REVOLUTION OF 1905

Revolutionary Movement (1905-1906). The assassination of Plehve, the demands of the zemstvos for representative government, and the increased local freedom failed to stir the Tsar. But the Russo-Japanese War (1904-1905) served to reveal the depth of corruption and incompetency in the Russian administration. Discontent increased, laborers struck, and the peasants pillaged and destroyed. Finally the Tsar weakened under the continual evidences of dissatisfaction, and he granted religious toleration, promised a national assembly, and repealed anti-Jewish legislation. The reactionary ministers were dismissed.

OCTOBER MANIFESTO (1905). A manifesto issued in October 1905 guaranteed individual rights and provided for the popular election of a Duma or parliamentary assembly. Another decree in December 1905 provided for universal manhood suffrage.

RUSSIAN DUMA (1906). The new Russian legislature was a bicameral body composed of a lower house called the Duma and an upper house, not chosen by popular election, known as the Council of the Empire.

REVOLUTIONARY FACTIONS. Once the reform had been promised, the Revolutionists split into many groups. The radicals under the leadership of Profesor Milyukóv became known as "Cadets," and they sought to have a federal type of government with the monarch limited by a democratic parliament. The Octobrists accepted the reforms of the Tsar as being sufficiently liberal. The rise of the reactionaries and their organizing of the "Union of the Russian People" (1906) instituted a reign of terror to prevent liberal reforms and aided the Tsar.

First Duma (1906). The terrorism of the reactionaries made it possible for the Tsar to dismiss de Witte and to appoint the conservatives, Goremykin (Premier) and Stolýpin (Minister of Interior). The Duma met in May 1906 and the insistence of the Cadets that the Duma control the country led to its dissolution by Goremýkin, Stolýpin, and the Tsar, without establishing parliamentary government. The attempt of the Cadets to adjourn the Duma to Viborg was a failure and resulted in the death and banishment of thousands of the Revolutionists.

Second Duma (1907). The members of the second Duma favored the confiscation of the great landowners' property and ministerial responsibility to parliament. Unable to make the leader in the Duma accept his program, the Tsar dissolved this body in June (1907).

Third Duma (1907-1912). In order to prevent a repetition of what had happened in the first and second Dumas, the Tsar by arbitrary decree modified the election laws so that the members would be Octobrists and Moderate Conservatives. With the more liberal groups making up a weak minority, Stolýpin proceeded to punish the Revolutionists effectively and to use the Duma as a consultative body. This Duma ratified the decree which allowed the peasants to become landowners and provided for the redemption of dues. Some social legislation was supported. A large Russian naval-building program was also fostered. Stolýpin was assassinated in 1911 and was succeeded by Kokovtsev.

Fourth Duma (1912-1914). The fourth Duma was controlled by the reactionaries, and they endorsed provisions for governmental control of the liquor traffic and the lengthening of military service. In 1914, Goremýkin succeeded Kokovtsev as Prime Minister.

The Finnish Constitution (1906). The disorders in Finland at the time of the Japanese War and the revolutionary movement of 1905-1906 ended with a great national strike in 1905. Nicholas II was fearful of the result, and to prevent a worse disorder, granted the Finns a constitution to replace the one which had been abrogated in 1899. The new constitution provided for a unicameral legislature, proportional representation, and universal suffrage. The continual friction between the Tsar and Finland was approaching a climax when World War I opened.

CHAPTER XI.

THE OTTOMAN EMPIRE
1815-1914

Political Weaknesses. After 1683, when the Turks were defeated at Vienna, the Ottoman Empire began to decline. As a result of the Treaty of Karlowitz (1699), Austria obtained most of Hungary and later, by the Treaty of Kuchuk Kainarji (1774), Russia received Azov. Russia also gained concessions in the Crimea and won recognition as the protector of the Orthodox Churches in Constantinople. The success of Austria and Russia in taking Turkish territory was made possible by the failure of the Sultan to rule efficiently, to stamp out corruption, and to command respect.

Religious Controversy. The Mohammedans refused to grant religious toleration to the Christian "cattle." Many Christians were terrorized, their property stolen, and their lives blotted out by ruthless Turks. If the Christians in the Balkans had united with Russia against the Turks, they could have thrown off the Turkish yoke, but the insistence upon nationalism by the different states prevented any joint action.

Nationalities in the Turkish Empire. Within the Turkish Empire, the outstanding nationalities who were demanding political independence, were the Serbs, Bulgars, Rumans, and

Greeks. The Albanians had nationalistic ambitions, but they were weakened by being scattered throughout the Empire. Nationalism was fostered through encouraging the language and literature of the would-be states. By subordinating the church of the Serbs, Rumans, and Bulgars to the state, the nationalists were able to use this strong arm for patriotic motives. With the glorious exploits of their ancestors constantly being dinned into their ears, the nationalist groups demanded their freedom from Turkey and their recognition as independent nations.

THE BALKAN REVOLTS

Montenegro and Serbia. Montenegro, in 1799, was able to gain recognition from Turkey as an independent state. The activities of Karageorge and Obrenovich in Serbia resulted in the autonomy of the Serbs (1830).

Greece. With the help of European powers Greece was able to defeat the Turks in the Greek Revolt (1821-1829) and to set up a kingdom with the Bavarian prince, Otto, as king. The new king introduced German despotism into the new state and caused the Greeks to dislike him almost as much as they disliked the Turks.

Rumania. The Treaty of Adrianople (1829) recognized the autonomy of Moldavia and Wallachia under Russia. By controlling the Rumanian provinces Russia gained a commanding position in the Black Sea region, a foothold she had sought since the time of Peter the Great. The interest of Russia in the dismemberment of Turkey was watched by those European powers who did not wish to see "the sick man of Europe" suffer in such a way as to increase the power of Russia. Hence, in the Crimean War, Great Britain and France helped the Turks defeat the Russians (1854-1856). The Treaty of Paris (1856) made Russia stop interfering in Moldavia and Wallachia. In spite of European opposition, the principalities finally won recognition as a united state—Rumania (1862).

Russo-Turkish War (1877-1878). Great Britain championed the cause of the Balkans after the Crimean War and won the friendship of the Serbs and Greeks. On the other hand, Russia had not given up her cherished desire to control the Balkans and finally was ready to wage a war to gain this end. The cruel suppression of uprisings in Bosnia, Herzegovina, and Bulgaria offered a pretext for the Tsar to declare war upon the bankrupt, inefficient Turkish Empire. The Turks offered stern opposition, but the Russian victories at Plevna (1877) and Adrianople (1878) were decisive, and peace was arranged.

TREATY OF SAN STEFANO (1878). The Treaty provided for the independence of Serbia, Montenegro, and Rumania; a new Bulgaria was granted autonomy; the Dardanelles and the Bosporus were opened to peaceful commerce at all times; Turkish forts along the Danube were to be destroyed; and Russia was to get a large part of Armenia, a large indemnity, and a part of Dobrudja, which she hoped to exchange with Rumania for Bessarabia.

TREATY OF BERLIN (1878). The Treaty of San Stefano aroused the British and Austrians against Russian supremacy in the Near East and caused them to insist that this Treaty be ratified by the powers who had signed the Treaty of Paris. Although Russia objected, a threat of war by Great Britain resulted in the Congress of Berlin (1878) for the purpose of revising the Treaty of San Stefano. The Treaty of Berlin (1878) was a compromise on the demands of Great Britain, Austria-Hungary, and Russia.

Russia obtained the desired territory of Bessarabia (Rumania, most of Dobrudja). The Armenian districts of Ardahan, Kars, and Batoum were also given to Russia.

Austria-Hungary was given the privilege of occupying Bosnia and Herzegovina and of maintaining garrisons in Novi-Bazar.

Great Britain was allowed to occupy Cyprus to insure the Sultan's pledge to institute reforms beneficial to the Christians.

The Bulgaria which Russia had created was divided into Bulgaria (autonomous), East Rumelia (autonomous, but with military and political control by the Sultan), and Macedonia (ruled by Turkey).

The independence of Serbia, Montenegro, and Rumania was recognized, but they had to bear a part of the Sultan's debts.

Greece was promised additional territory, and in 1881, Thessaly was given to her.

MODIFICATIONS OF THE TREATY OF BERLIN (1885-1913). The attempt of Great Britain to save the Turkish Empire was not successful. By the revolution of Philippopolis (1885), Eastern Rumelia was added to Bulgaria, which was declared a kingdom (1908). Austria-Hungary annexed Bosnia and Herzegovina (1908) even though the treaty merely gave her the right to occupy them. In the next few years Turkey was almost completely stripped of her European territories.

OTTOMAN POSSESSIONS OUTSIDE EUROPE

Union of Crete With Greece. The Cretans opposed the Turks because of religious oppression and because of their desire to join with Greece as a national state. A series of revolts on the island from 1821-1897 did not gain the support of the European powers, and Turkey was always able to prevent the island's annexation to Greece. However, in 1897, the Cretans were granted autonomy. The attempt of Venizelos to unite Crete with Greece (1905) was not successful. It was not until 1913 that the Treaty of London recognized this union.

Egypt's Struggle for Independence (1800-1914). The Pasha of Egypt had a difficult time controlling the Mamelukes (military group) and ousting the French under Napoleon. An Albanian adventurer, Mehemet Ali (1769-1849), gained important concessions in Egypt and even had the Sultan appoint him Pasha (1805). Mehemet Ali became all-powerful in Egypt. However, the splendid army which he sent against the Greeks (1821) was able to retain only Crete for the Sultan, and Mehemet was not able to control Morea and Syria. The adventurous Albanian and the Sultan disagreed. Mehemet sent an army to obtain Syria, and the Sultan declared war on him, but the Egyptians easily won and, with the aid of certain European powers, Mehemet was made governor of Syria, Damascus, Aleppo, and Adana (1833). As a result of the Syrian revolt (1839), Mehemet was stripped of these possessions but recognized as hereditary ruler of Egypt (1841) paying tribute to the Sultan. In 1914, the Khedive of Egypt (since

1866) assumed the title of Sultan and was recognized by Great Britain and France as absolutely independent of Turkey.

Conquest of Algeria and Tunis by France (1830-1881). Algeria was considered as a part of the Ottoman Empire and was under the control of a dey. In 1830 the French expelled the dey because of a diplomatic quarrel. The complete subjugation was temporarily prevented by Abd-el-Kader, who waged a holy war against the Christians. His surrender to the French in 1847 made Algeria a French colony. Tunis was controlled by an independent prince who was but slightly obligated to the Sultan. The French occupied Tunis in 1881 and ignored the Sultan's claims to it.

Italian Control of Tripoli and Cyrenaica-Libya. The Ottoman Empire continued to have a limited control over the independent provinces of Tripoli and Cyrenaica, but as a result of the Turco-Italian War (1911-1912) Italy annexed these provinces, which became known as Libya. Thus Turkey's sway in Africa came to an end.

THE INDEPENDENT BALKAN STATES

Greece. The Greeks rose up against Otto I and deposed him in 1862. The new king, George I, (1863-1913) was a son of the Danish king. He consented to a constitution (1864) which provided for a single chamber legislature elected by universal manhood suffrage. The prosperity of the Greeks encouraged their nationalistic desires for the annexation of the Greeks in Crete, Salonica, and the Aegean Islands. Eleutherios Venizelos championed the Greek cause and skillfully prepared for the necessary war with Turkey. With the help of Serbia and Bulgaria in the Balkan War (1912-1913), Greece received the desired territories, and the Greeks became a united nation. Constantine I (1913-1922) succeeded his father George I, who was assassinated in 1913.

Rumania. The independence of Rumania (1878) did not satisfy the Rumans because (1) they had not wanted to give Bessarabia to the Tsar, (2) the provision for religious toleration gave the hated Jews the right to own land, and (3) the Rumans had been forced to buy the Rumanian railways built by German speculators. Rumania became a kingdom in 1881 with the Prussian prince, Charles, as king. The problems facing the new kingdom centered around (1) the desire to annex the territories of Bessarabia, Transylvania, Bukowina, and southeastern Hungary, which were inhabited by Rumans, (2) the foreign policy toward Russia and Austria-Hungary, and (3) the development of a prosperous and powerful nation. Feudalism had been abolished (1864) and small farms were given to the peasants from the confiscated estates of the monasteries. Natural resources were developed and social legislation passed. With the economic conditions improved, Rumania developed an army that was the largest one to be found in the Balkans.

Serbia. Four years after Serbia's independence had been recognized, she became a kingdom with Milan Obrenovich as the ruler. King Milan was not very popular because of his aristocratic background and because of the agitation of the Radicals, who were the followers of the Karageorge family. The abdication of Milan in favor of his son, Alexander (1889), when the granting of a liberal constitution failed to win the people to his side, did not relieve the political unrest. Alexander's decision to substitute Russian for Austrian friendship aroused the enemies of the administration and led to the assassination of the king, his queen, and his advisers (1903). The conspirators placed Peter, grandson of Karageorge, upon the throne and restored the constitution of 1889. Under Peter, the Serbians concentrated on a nationalistic policy which would bring all the Serbs of the Balkans into one large state. Since many of the Serbs lived in the provinces of Bosnia and Herzegovina, this "Greater Serbia" program could not be realized without a conflict with Austria-Hungary. The movement, therefore, turned to revolutionary propaganda and secret organizations directed against the territorial integrity of Austria-Hungary and became the most dangerous of the "irredentist" problems of Europe.

Montenegro. Montenegro, whose independence had been recognized in 1878, prospered under Prince Nicholas, who advanced education, industry, and political democracy. A constitution was adopted (1905) providing for a parliament elected by universal manhood suffrage. Montenegro became a kingdom in 1910.

Bulgaria. The annexation of Eastern Rumelia (1885) by Bulgaria made it possible for that state to become more prosperous and to improve the condition of its independent small farmers. Education was fostered. Like the other Balkans, Bulgaria's nationalistic designs on territories kept her in trouble with foreign powers. At first the new prince, Ferdinand of Saxe-Coburg, refused to be the tool of the Tsar, and through his minister, Stefan Stambolov, nationalism was furthered. After the assassination of Stambolov (1895), Ferdinand cultivated the friendship of the Tsar and, with Russian support, Bulgaria became an independent kingdom (1908).

The Later Ottoman Empire. The spirit of reform, which resulted from the Treaty of Berlin, was ignored by the insincere Sultan, Abdul Hamid II, who ruled with autocratic power. Conditions within the Empire grew steadily worse, as a study of the independent kingdoms established between 1878-1910 reveals; the "Sick Man of Europe" was nearing extinction. A group of patriotic Turks favoring reform organized the "Young Turks," and with the support of the army a coup d'état in 1908 was successful and the Constitution of 1876 was restored. Turkey became a constitutional monarchy. It was at this time that Austria-Hungary annexed Bosnia and Herzegovina outright, and Bulgaria became entirely independent. The opposition of the Sultan and Kiamil Pasha, the grand vizier, to the Young Turks' Committee of Union and Progress resulted in a march on Constantinople, the deposition of the Sultan (1909), and the selection of Mohammed V, young brother of the Sultan, as ruler. The Young Turks then proceeded to nationalize all the people within the empire, but the Balkan states strenuously objected, and in 1912, the Greeks, Bulgarians, Serbs, and Montenegrins formed a secret alliance against the Turks.

THE BALKAN WARS (1912-1913)

First Balkan War (1912-1913). In spite of the insistence of the European powers that the *status quo* of the Balkans must not be changed by a war, the states of Serbia, Greece, and Montenegro joined Bulgaria in a war against Turkey, when the Turks refused to grant Macedonia autonomy (1912). The Turks were no match for the Balkan allies, and an armistice was concluded, but the peace conference at London was unsuccessful and actual fighting was resumed. The fall of Adrianople to the Serbs and Bulgars and the surrender of Scutari to the Montenegrins ended the conflict.

Treaty of London (May 1913). The Treaty of London cut into the last of Turkey's European possessions. Albania was made an autonomous state and Crete was allowed to join Greece. But the victorious allies could not agree to a disposition of the European spoils. Bulgaria's demand of the lion's share was blocked by Serbia. The failure of the powers to agree led to another conflict.

Second Balkan War (July 1913). The Serbs, Montenegrins, and Greeks were joined by Rumania and Turkey in the war against Bulgaria. The Bulgarians found themselves hemmed in on all sides, and as the enemies advanced, the hopelessness of further opposition forced Ferdinand to sue for peace.

Treaty of Bucharest (August 1913). As a result of this treaty, Bulgaria ceded territory south of the Danube to Rumania; and Greece, Montenegro, and Serbia got most of Macedonia. A later arrangement between Turkey and Bulgaria resulted in Turkey's keeping Adrianople (Treaty of Constantinople 1913). In 1914 Albania was recognized as an independent principality with the German prince, William of Wied, at the head.

Results of the Balkan Wars. The Balkan states took from Turkey four-fifths of her European possessions and added it to their own territories. Hereafter, Turkey was to be important as an Asiatic, but not a European, power. After the wars, the Balkan states once more began to quarrel along nationalistic lines and made it easy for outside forces to interfere.

AUSTRIA-HUNGARY. The interest of the dual monarchy in the Balkans was primarily to extend the dominions to Salonica at the expense of the Serbs and Greeks.

Russia. The Pan-Slav movement of Russia intensified that country's desire to embrace the slavic peoples of Serbia, Montenegro, and Bulgaria. The policies of Austria-Hungary and Russia were bound to develop a breach between these powers.

Great Britain. The British support of Turkey was designed to protect her investments and commercial interests in the Near East and India. Great Britain knew that it would be easier to gain concessions from Turkey than from a power like Russia.

France, Italy, and Germany. France and Germany wished to protect their investments in Turkey and naturally opposed Russian aggrandizement. Germany had been successful in getting permission to build the Berlin to Bagdad railway through Turkish territory. The successful war of Italy in Africa had made that country content to avoid "The Sick Man of Europe."

Balkan Wars a Temporary Compromise. The powers were fairly well lined up in 1912 on the Balkan situation. The tendency of Great Britain and France was to support the Russian stand against Austria-Hungary. The successful dismemberment of the Ottoman Empire in Europe caused Rumans, Serbs, and Italians to dare to hope for the dismemberment of the Dual Monarchy. Austro-Hungarian meddling in the Balkans was an important cause of the assassination of the Archduke Francis Ferdinand in June 1914. The Near Eastern question was one of the important roots of World War I.

CHAPTER XII.

OTHER COUNTRIES OF EUROPE, 1870-1914

Heterogeneous Population. Within the Dual Monarchy of 51,300,000 people (1910) there were to be found (1) 12,000,000 Germans, (2) 10,000,000 Magyars, (3) 4,000,000 Latins, and (4) 24,250,000 Slavs, (Czechs, Slovaks, Poles, Ruthenians, Serbs-Croats, and Slovenes).

Government. The Ausgleich (1867) provided for an empire of Austria and a kingdom of Hungary. Political autonomy was granted in local government. The Hapsburg, Francis Joseph, was made Emperor of Austria and King of Hungary. He appointed a joint ministry for foreign affairs, army and finance, and sponsored a program dealing with trade treaties, tariff, public debt, and railways. A joint parliament, Delegations, composed of two bodies—60 Austrians and 60 Hungarians—assembled in separate rooms to make laws affecting the Dual Monarchy. Both members of the Dual Monarchy adopted the parliamentary system of government for carrying on its affairs. The presence of different races and nationalities caused considerable internal strife.

INTERNAL DISCORD. Arrangements for the ten year treaties on trade, taxes, and railways caused hard feelings because

131

the interests of the two powers were different. A tariff policy that helped industrial Austria was detrimental to agrarian Hungary.

FOREIGN POLICY. The Austrians and Hungarians were both insistent upon an aggressive foreign policy which would include (1) a strong army and navy, (2) the support of the triple Alliance, and (3) interference in the Balkans. The annexation of Bosnia and Herzegovina (1908) gave the Austrians and Hungarians an opportunity to exploit these provinces and even to extend their influence into Albania, western Macedonia, and Salonica. This foreign policy was to come into conflict with Serbia and lead to World War I. Francis Joseph (1848-1916) was the most important force holding together the Dual Monarchy.

Austria (1867-1914). The growth of political democracy received its greatest impetus through acts which made elementary school education compulsory (1896) and provided for universal manhood suffrage (1907). Among the political parties were (1) the Liberals, who were anti-clerical, (2) the Christian Socialists (Catholics), who defended the church, and (3) the Social Democrats, who were Marxian Socialists. Under Karl Lueger the Christian Socialists passed social legislation similar to that passed in other countries (1884-1910). The efficiency of the government was greatly impaired by the presence of many national groups in the Reichsrat. A concession to one group served only to arouse the others.

Hungary (1867-1914). In Hungary the Magyars were able to control the other nationalities. Political and social reform was limited to the type that would benefit the bourgeois Magyars. Agitation for reform threatened Hungary from within, as the World War threatened it from without. The protests of the people were revealed in the rise of nationalistic movements and in the emigration of over 1,000,000 people between 1896-1910.

THE SWISS CONFEDERATION

Government. The early government of Switzerland was merely a loose union of the cantons for defensive purposes, but in 1848, a constitution was adopted, after a short civil war, in which the Liberals (Federalists) won over those Catholics who wished local freedom. The Constitution provided for a government similar to that of the United States. German, French, and Italian were recognized as national languages.

New Powers of the Federal Government. The central government began to take over such powers as postal service, coinage, uniform custom duties, and standardization of weights and measures. The Constitution was revised to allow for a system of free elementary schools and the use of the referendum. Later (1891), the initiative was introduced, a national bank established, and a protective tariff passed. A National Militia was organized in 1874 as a protection against aggression.

Political and Social Reform. Social legislation was passed approving compulsory insurance against sickness and accidents. Universal manhood suffrage was prevalent in all cantons, and most of them used the referendum and initiative. Direct representation still exists in some of the smaller cantons.

Economic Welfare. The prosperity of the Swiss was due to (1) the increased growth of manufactures, which was stimulated by the protective tariff, (2) the large number of foreign tourists who spent considerable time and money in this scenic country, and (3) the thrift of the Swiss shepherds and farmers.

THE KINGDOM OF THE NETHERLANDS

Holland (1815-1890). During the reign of William I (1815-1840), Belgium was able to secure its recognition as an independent state and reduce the Netherlands to a state half as large as Portugal. However, it held several possessions beyond Europe—Java, Sumatra, Borneo, New Guinea, and the Spice Islands. A new constitution was granted by William II (1840-1849) in 1848. Royal ministers were made responsible to the States-General—a bicameral legislature. Local autonomy was guaranteed the states of the provinces. The problem of religious education during the reign of William III (1849-1890) was important. On the one hand, the Liberals wanted free, public, secular schools, while on the other the Protestants, Conservatives, and Catholics urged the establishment of parochial schools. The result was that (1) public schools without religious instruction were opened, (2) financial aid was given private parochial schools, and (3) attendance, either at public or private school, was compulsory (1900). The growth of political democracy was especially slow in the Netherlands.

Queen Wilhelmina (1890-1948). The popularity of the Queen was offset by the anti-German sentiment which developed after her marriage to Prince Henry of Mecklenburg-Schwerin. The Dutch concentrated on improving the national defense, and laws were passed strengthening the army and providing for naval construction. Through armed preparedness, the Dutch hoped to guard their neutrality.

SCANDINAVIA

Denmark. The Kingdom of Denmark was the smallest of the Scandinavian states in 1871, but it possessed a small colonial empire— Iceland, Greenland, and the islands of St. Croix, St. Thomas, and St. John. The revised Constitution of 1866 provided for parliamentary government through the Rigsdag—a bicameral legislature. The ministry was responsible to the Landsthing and not to the Folkething, which was elected by male citizens over thirty. The Folkething, supported by the peasants, demanded that the ministry be made responsible to that house, and finally, after a bitter struggle, this was done (1901). Christian IX (1863-1906) was succeeded by Frederick VIII (1906-1912), who favored democratic reform under the Liberals. During the reign of Christian X (1912-1947), the Constitution was amended to allow suffrage to all males twenty-five years old and to many women, and to abolish the appointive seats in the Landsthing. Iceland was given home rule (1903).

Sweden and Norway. The union of Sweden and Norway was not a popular one. Sweden was developing into an industrial nation with a landed nobility, while Norway was predominately agricultural, with an independent small farmer class. The government of Norway was more democratic than that of Sweden. The persistence with which the king seemed to favor the Swedes led to agitation for an independent

Norway. In 1905 the Norwegian parliament, angered by the
refusal of Oscar II (1872-1907) to appoint Norwegian consuls
to foreign cities, declared the independence of Norway, and
established a monarchy under Haakon VII (1905-1957) as a result of a popular plebiscite. This separation is remarkable as
almost the sole instance in modern history of a state's permitting
a discontented subject nationality to become independent without
resort to armed force.

In Sweden, laws were enacted which provided for universal manhood suffrage in elections to the Lower Chamber,
reduced property qualification for members of the Upper
Chamber, and introduced proportional representation in both
Chambers (1909). The growth of Socialism, which paralleled
the development of manufactures, caused the passage of social
legislation.

By 1913, there was universal suffrage in Norway, and
direct elections were substituted for indirect. The first women
to vote in general elections and to sit in the parliament of a
sovereign state were Norwegians. The king's veto was done
away with in 1913. Social legislation was fostered, but the
radical demands of the Socialists were not met. As in Sweden,
large numbers of Norwegians emigrated to other lands because of poor economic conditions.

CHAPTER XIII.

THE EXPANSION OF EUROPE

Old Colonial Movement. The old colonial movement that reached its height in the seventeenth and eighteenth centuries had been to a large extent a migration of population from impoverished, crowded, intolerant Europe to new and, it was hoped, more prosperous lands. The early explorers went forth in search of gold and adventure; the settlers that followed sought freedom and improved economic conditions. Governments supported exploring expeditions and fought wars with rival colonial powers for a variety of reasons—patriotism, monarchial prestige, and to establish trading monopolies that would bring a favorable balance of trade in the precious metals in accordance with the prevailing mercantilist theories of national wealth. There were conflicts for supremacy between Holland and England, and between Great Britain and France. However, the great long-term result of the early colonialism was that a new world had been discovered and Europeanized.

The New Imperialism. A renewed interest in exploration and colonization, which was to open up the whole world, was an important outcome of the French Revolution and the

Industrial Revolution. The leading powers in the world all took part in the new attempt to partition the world. The principles of democracy and nationalism for which they had fought were denied to the peoples who were annexed by the world powers. The chief characteristics of this movement were economic, patriotic, and religious. The economic root of the new imperialism was the rise of industrial and financial capitalism seeking new markets and new fields of profitable investment. For the purposes of the capitalists, actual political annexation and settlement were frequently unnecessary; economic penetration through the establishment of "spheres of influence" was sufficient.

THE PENETRATION OF CHINA

For centuries, the Chinese had held aloof from Europeans and had been content to live simple lives and enjoy their own culture. The isolation of China, which had been maintained except for a few instances such as Marco Polo's sojourn, the visit of Portuguese merchants at Macao, and the presence of the British in Canton, was threatened after 1840 by improved means of communication, by the eastward extension of the European powers, and by the filtering of European ideas into China.

The Opium War (1840-1842). The attempt of the English merchants to import opium into China from India resulted in a war between Great Britain and China. The British were successful in their attacks upon the Chinese ports, and the Treaty of Nanking (1842), which provided for the opening of Amoy, Ningpo, Foochow, and Shanghai to foreign trade, was accepted by the Emperor.

Second Chinese War (1856-1860). The murder of a French missionary and the seizure of a British ship caused these powers to oppose China in 1856. A treaty was arranged which gave Great Britain a foothold near Hongkong, opened six more ports to trade, allowed foreign ministers to reside at Peking, and promised the protection of Christian missionaries in China. An indemnity of 8,000,000 taels was also exacted.

Further Foreign Aggression in China. The Chinese Empire consisted of the eighteen provinces of China proper, the three provinces of Manchuria, Korea, and Mongolia, the provinces of Sin-kiang, Tibet, and several states in Indo-China. On all sides China was menaced by foreign enemies.

Russia obtained important territories on both sides of the Amur River, east of the Ussuri River, and north of Korea (1858-1860). A port of the province of Sin-kiang was later annexed.

The Chino-Japanese War (1894-1895), which was caused by Japanese interference in Korea, was won by Japan. The Treaty of Shimonoseki (1895) provided that an indemnity of $157,940,000 was to be paid to Japan. Formosa and the Liao-tung peninsula were given to Japan, and Korea became independent of China.

The treaty of Shimonoseki was opposed by Russia because of her own designs on this territory, and she influenced France and Germany to join her in advising Japan to give up these concessions. Japan, afraid to do otherwise, gave up all except the island of Formosa and accepted an additional indemnity.

The Germans proceeded to take Kiao-chau (1897) as a German base, and France took Kwang-chow Wan (1898). Russia gained important privileges in Peking, the right to build the trans-Siberian railway across Manchuria, and a lease on the much desired Port Arthur on the Liao-tung peninsula. Great Britain finally stepped in and occupied Wei-hai-wei (1898) in order to watch Russia and to prevent her from actually annexing Korea and Manchuria.

The Russo-Japanese War (1904-1905) was caused by Russia's humiliation of Japan at the end of the Chino-Japanese war and by the attempt of Russia to annex Manchuria. Russia was badly defeated, and by the Treaty of Portsmouth (1905) she gave up her lease of the Liao-tung peninsula to Japan; both countries agreed to withdraw from Manchuria and Japan was recognized as supreme in Korea. Ousted from Manchuria, Russia sought to annex a part of Mongolia, and during the revolution of 1912, she got important concessions in Outer Mongolia.

The French interfered in Indo-China. Between 1862 and 1885 France obtained complete control over Cochin-China and a protectorate over Cambodia and Annam.

The British control of India made it possible for Great Britain to extend her influence to the north and east. Burma, a tributary state of China, was annexed outright, and the independent states of Nepal and Bhutan came under British influence. Despite the attempt of China to retain her control over Tibet, Great Britain extended her power over Outer Tibet (1914) and greatly reduced Chinese influence in Inner Tibet.

Industrial and Commercial Changes. The antagonism of the Chinese to the Industrial Revolution diminished and by 1914 the Machine Age was gaining a foothold. The opening up of China to foreign trade and the granting of commercial privileges stimulated communication and commerce with China. From their spheres of influence, the "foreign devils" began to exploit the vast Chinese Empire.

China under the Manchus. The government of China was administered by a divine-right emperor assisted by a group of mandarins who carried on the actual administration. The government failed to reorganize the army and as a result the Japanese army, which had been Europeanized, easily won the Chino-Japanese War (1894-1895). It was not until 1898 that Emperor Kwangsu instituted some reforms which would partially Europeanize China. For his pains, the Emperor was dethroned by the reactionaries (1898), and his aunt, the Dowager Empress Tzu-hsi, became the real ruler and the champion of reaction. The reactionaries formed a society of "Boxers" dedicated to the stamping out of the "foreign devils." The Boxer Rebellion (1900) was crushed with great brutality by an army composed of Japanese, Russians, British, Americans, Germans, and French. China was forced to pay an indemnity of $320,000,000 and to grant more concessions to the Europeans. Once more a reform movement was instituted. A Young China Party under Sun Yat-sen inaugurated a republican movement, and in a successful revolution they overthrew the Manchu dynasty and established a republic (1912).

Republic of China (1912). The first President, Yüan Shih-kai, proved to be willing to accept reforms in education, industry, and the army but was opposed to parliamentary government. A rebellion against the monarchial practices of the President failed (1913). After this outbreak, Yüan Shih-kai dissolved the National Assembly and proceeded to introduce reactionary practices. His death in 1916 and the ascension of Vice-President Li Yüan-hung were advantageous to the republican cause.

THE EUROPEANIZATION OF JAPAN

Europeans were welcome in Japan for religious and commercial purposes from 1542-1587. The power of the Christians became so great, however, that the Emperor Hideyoshi ordered missionaries to leave (1587). A period of Christian massacres followed, trade was curtailed, and Japan held aloof from the rest of the world until 1853, when the American, Commodore Perry, sailed into the bay near Yokohama with his display of Western inventions. A treaty in 1854 promised shelter to ship-wrecked American seamen, allowed vessels to obtain supplies in Japan, and opened the ports of Shimoda, Hakodate, and later Yokohama (1858) to American merchantmen. These concessions were given also to Great Britain, Holland, Russia, and France.

Japanese Revolution (1867-1868). The Japanese Revolution was caused by the agitation of the feudal princes (daimios) against the hereditary shogun, who was the real power in Japan; by the realization, as a result of the bombardment of Kagoshima (1863) and Shimonoseki (1864) by the foreigners, that Japan must learn Western methods in order to compete with them; and by the revival of divine-right worship of the mikado—Shintoism. The Shogun, Yoshinobu, resigned in 1867 when he discovered that the reformers were gaining ground, and the new Mikado, Mutsuhito (1867-1912), became the real ruler of Japan. In 1868, most of the land of the Shogun was confiscated and feudalism was abolished by the voluntary surrender by the daimios of all their feudal rights. These reforms made a more highly centralized government possible, resulted in a national army which used European methods, and made the peasants landowners and taxpayers. The young Mikado encouraged the Europeanization of his Empire. In 1889, a constitution was granted which provided for parliamentary government.

The Industrial Revolution in Japan. The Machine Age took Japan by storm after 1875. Western methods and machines were introduced and encouraged. Commerce with foreign countries increased twenty-seven fold from 1877 to 1913. A capitalist class appeared which encouraged Japan to adopt an imperialistic policy for purposes of trade and as a haven for its surplus population.

Aggrandizement of Japan. The first imperialistic war (Chino-Japanese, 1894-1895) was a victory for the Europeanized army of Japan, and although Russia, France, and Germany prevented her from taking as much of China as she wished, Japan got Formosa and an indemnity of $180,000,000. The Russo-Japanese War (1904-1905) resulted in victories on land and sea for Japan, notably Mukden (1905) and The Battle of the Sea of Japan (1905). The Treaty of Portsmouth freed Korea and Manchuria from Russian influence and gave Japan half of the island of Sakhalin and an indemnity of $20,000,000. This war and an alliance with Great Britain (1902) gave Japan recognition as a world power. In 1910, Japan annexed Korea and proceeded to develop it.

RUSSIAN IMPERIALISM

The expansion of Russia to the Pacific began in 1579. During the next three centuries Russia obtained the Pacific port of Okhotsk (1638), territory on both sides of the Amur River, in which she established the imposing port of Vladivostok, and the island of Sakhalin (1875). Russia's attempt to expand to the south was blocked by Japan (1904-1905), and she was forced to give up Port Arthur and to keep out of Korea. The failure in Manchuria and Korea was partly compensated for by a successful campaign in Mongolia, which resulted in a Russian protectorate developed from the western part of this territory (1913). Between 1554 and 1885, Russia gained control of the numerous tribes which owed allegiance to the Turkish sultan and the Persian shah on the east and west shores of the Caspian Sea. The weak government of Persia was unable to cope with the interference of Russia and Great Britain within the kingdom, and in 1907 these powers signed an agreement which recognized the northern part of Persia as Russia's sphere of influence and the southeastern as Great Britain's. The advance of Russia to the Indian Ocean was blocked by Great Britain, who was afraid for her possessions in India, which were separated from Russia by the buffer state of Afghanistan. However, Russia did succeed in annexing Western Turkestan and in obtaining commercial privileges in Afghanistan, while Great Britain was given control of that state's foreign affairs. The Russian Empire in Asia was an immense territory embracing over six million square miles. The new territories were linked together by a vast railway system which extended from Petrograd to Vladivostok and the Chinese capital, Peking.

OTHER IMPERIALISTIC NATIONS IN THE FAR EAST

French Possessions. France still controlled several trading posts in India, and in eastern Indo-China had a colony which was larger than the mother country. The French capitalists invested their money in these territories and carried on a profitable commerce.

Dutch Colonies. The Dutch controlled the islands of Java, Sumatra, Celebes, and parts of Borneo and New Guinea. A profitable trade with these islands was carried on by the Dutch.

German Territories. The decision of Germany to foster imperialism came late and, as a result, her possessions were limited in quality and quantity. Germany's possessions included the bay of Kiao-chau in China and the following islands in the Pacific: Bismarck Archipelago (1884), Ladrone Islands, (except Guam) (1914), and two of the Samoan Islands (1899).

American Imperialism in the Far East. The Hawaiian Islands were obtained in 1898, and as a result of the Spanish American War, the Philippine Islands were annexed. The original plan of the United States to grant the Filipinos their independence was carried out in 1946 according to the Tydings-McDuffie law which the Philippine Legislature had accepted (1934).

EUROPE IN THE AMERICAS

The New and Old Imperialism. The old colonial system had planted in the New World French, English, Spanish, and Portuguese states which were similar to the mother countries in many respects. The new imperialism sought avenues to profitable investments in the New World.

Rise of the United States. After its war for independence (1775-1783), the United States spent the next century in expanding her "natural" boundaries. The expansion of the United States, territorially, was accompanied by economic growth. Rich natural resources and cheap immigrant labor helped to make the United States a great industrial nation with a group of wealthy capitalists, who clamored for new territories. Alaska was purchased in 1867, and in 1898, Hawaii, Puerto Rico, the Philippines, and Guam were obtained, and a protectorate was established over Cuba. The next year, two of the Samoan Islands were acquired. The Monroe Doctrine (1823), which aimed to prevent further European colonization in the Western Hemisphere, made it easy for the United States to act as a protector of the Latin-American countries, to invest capital, and to protect American interests there. The construction of the Panama Canal (1907-1914), which was accomplished after a revolution succeeded in creating the republic of Panama, was still further evidence of American imperialism.

Latin America. During the sixteenth century Spanish nobles and gentlemen adventurers created an American Empire for their nation. Cortez in Mexico (1520), Pizarro in Peru (1531), Mendoza in the Argentine (1535), De Soto along the Mississippi (1539-1542), Coronado beyond the Rio Grande (1540), and Menendez in Florida (1565) pushed out the frontier of Spanish territory. By 1575 approximately 175,000 Spaniards, organized politically in the viceroyalties of New Spain and Peru, were exploiting the resources of Central and South America, christianizing thousands of the natives and sending a steady stream of gold and silver to Europe.

CENTRAL AMERICA. The small number of Europeans living in the republics prevented the successful application of democratic government. Revolutions were frequent and the natives were easily influenced by politicians and military leaders. Costa Rica, which had a large Spanish population, was the only state which was able to maintain peace and prosperity in Central America.

SOUTH AMERICA. With the exception of the A-B-C Powers, the governments of the South American states were weak and inefficient. Revolutions and civil wars were common. The countries of Argentina, Brazil, and Chile prospered under stable governments. Arbitration was encouraged as a means for settling difficulties among them. Trade and industry were fostered. Immigrants from Portugal, Italy, and Germany were welcomed.

LAND PROBLEM IN LATIN AMERICA. The presence of large plantations was due to (1) the type of agricultural pursuits, (2) the vast colonial grants which had been made, and (3) the cheap Indian and Negro labor found in these countries. The "peons" (Indian farm laborers) were practically serfs. The unsatisfactory condition of the peon made him extremely susceptible to revolutionary propaganda.

FOREIGN INVESTMENTS IN LATIN AMERICA. The failure to establish efficient governments in Latin America prevented these countries from fostering internal improvements without foreign capital. Bankers in London, New York, and Paris poured vast sums into these countries. When a state failed to meet its obligations, the instruments of the banker's country were used to make the necessary collections. Beside these loans, foreigners invested capital to exploit natural resources and to construct internal improvements for private gain. The weak governments, which allowed this capitalistic imperialism, were prevented by the capitalists from becoming powerful.

THE EUROPEAN PARTITION OF AFRICA

Conquests in Africa to 1870. The vast extent of Africa was first revealed by the Portuguese explorers of the fifteenth century. Trade was carried on with the natives, but Portugal was not successful in controlling the continent. The Portuguese possessions in 1870 consisted of Portuguese East and West Africa, Portuguese Guinea, and the following islands: the Azores, Cape Verde, Madeira, Prince's, and St. Thomas.

South Africa was settled by the Dutch and British. The Dutch farmers, or "Boers," resented the British rule (since 1806), and they migrated to the north and established the Boer republics of Orange Free State and Transvaal ("Great Trek," 1836-1840). The two southern states of Natal and Cape Colony remained under British control.

Exploration of the Dark Continent. Great Britain and France had established several slave-trading posts and succeeded in acquiring the colonies of Gabun and Algeria before 1870, but the abolition of the slave trade by Great Britain (1807) and other countries (1807-1850) changed the interest in Africa to material commodities. Explorers set out to learn about the possibilities of the black man's continent. Missionaries were sent to convert the negroes. The work of Livingstone and Stanley revealed the commercial potentialities of Africa. Leopold II of Belgium encouraged the European countries to form committees as part of an "International Association for the Exploration and Colonization of Africa." The Belgian committee, with the help of Stanley, set up a Congo Free State with Leopold II as personal sovereign (1885). Business enterprise was fostered, not religious enlightenment. Leopold II and his capitalist associates reaped a fortune in the Congo, but the cruelty of their methods of exploitation shocked the conscience of the entire civilized world. Finally, reforms were instituted as a result of British and Belgian criticism of the treatment of the natives, and Leopold II turned the Congo Free State over to the Belgian parliament (1908).

The Imperialistic Policies of the Powers. The same reasons that prompted imperialism in Asia and America were paramount in Africa. Men like Cecil Rhodes and Lüderitz began to occupy territory and to claim it for the mother country. Up and down the continent they went carving out colonies. In order to prevent serious disputes over African territory, the leading powers arrived at certain understandings.

THE INTERNATIONAL CONFERENCE OF BERLIN (1884-1885). The important agreement of this conference provided that a power, upon annexation of territory in Africa, must notify the other powers in order to avoid any dispute. It also provided for the abolition of slavery and for freedom of trade in the Congo Free State.

ANGLO-GERMAN AGREEMENT (1890). Great Britain and Germany reached an agreement by which the former was to be recognized as protector of Uganda, and was thus enabled to connect British East Africa with her spheres of influence in the Nile Valley. Germany was given permission to extend Kamerun to Lake Chad, to control central Sudan, and to add a desired piece of land to German Southwest Africa so that it would be connected with the Zambesi River. Another clause provided for the establishment of a British protectorate over Zanzibar and Pemba in return for the cession to Germany of Heligoland, in the North Sea.

THE ANGLO-FRENCH AGREEMENT (1890). This agreement gave France control of Madagascar and the Sahara, and Great Britain was to be recognized as supreme in northern Nigeria.

ANGLO-FRENCH AGREEMENT (1899). The attempt of France to occupy eastern Sudan and the resulting Fashoda incident (1898) almost created a war, but France recognized Great Britain's claims to the Anglo-Egyptian Sudan and received the kingdom of Wadai, which linked up the French Congo with the possessions in the northwest.

ANGLO-FRENCH AGREEMENT (1904). This agreement allowed the British to establish a protectorate over Egypt and France to do the same in Morocco. Germany objected to a French protectorate in Morocco (1905), and a conference met at Algeciras (1906) to settle the dispute. At the conference the Germans were out-maneuvered, and France succeeded in getting her claims recognized. Great anti-French bitterness was thus created in Germany. The failure of the French to put down an uprising resulted in the dispatch of a German vessel to Agadir (Agadir Incident) to protect German interests (1911). The dispute was finally settled by the cession to

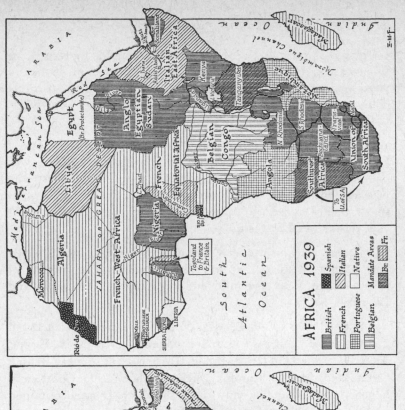

AFRICA 1939

Legend:
- British
- French
- Portuguese
- Belgian
- Spanish
- Italian
- Native
- Mandate Areas
  - Br.
  - Fr.

Togoland to France & Britain

To U. of S.A.

Mediterranean Sea — ARABIA — Red Sea — *Indian Ocean* — Morocco — Algeria — Libya — Egypt [Br. Protectorate] — SAHARA or GREAT DESERT — French West Africa — Nigeria — French Equatorial Africa — Anglo Egyptian Sudan — Italian East Africa — Belgian Congo — Angola — Northern Rhodesia — Southern Rhodesia — Southwest Africa — Bechuanaland — Union of South Africa — Mozambique — Madagascar — Mozambique Channel — South Atlantic Ocean — Rio de Oro — Liberia — Sierra Leone — Portuguese Guinea — L. Chad — L. Tana — Addis Ababa — Somaliland

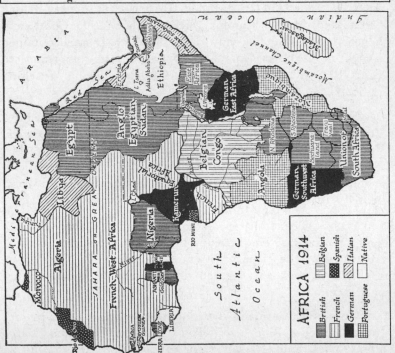

AFRICA 1914

Legend:
- British
- French
- German
- Portuguese
- Belgian
- Spanish
- Italian
- Native

Mediterranean Sea — ARABIA — Red Sea — *Indian Ocean* — Morocco — Algeria — Libya — Egypt — SAHARA or GREAT DESERT — French West Africa — Nigeria — Kamerun — French Equatorial Africa — Anglo Egyptian Sudan — Ethiopia — German East Africa — Belgian Congo — Angola — N. Rhodesia — S. Rhodesia — German Southwest Africa — Bechuanaland — Union of South Africa — Mozambique — Madagascar — Mozambique Channel — South Atlantic Ocean — Rio de Oro — Liberia — Sierra Leone — Portuguese Guinea — RIO MUNI — L. Chad — L. Tana — Adis Ababa — Somaliland

Germany of part of French Equatorial Africa in return for full sway in Morocco. Next Spain objected. France finally gave Spain a small strip along the northern coast of Morocco. This pushing and counter-pushing of the powers kept international relations in a state of tension.

ANGLO-PORTUGUESE AGREEMENT (1891). The ambition of Portugal to establish a belt of territory across Africa was prevented by the British and especially by Cecil Rhodes, who was anxious to extend British control in Africa. The Portuguese finally agreed to allow Great Britain to control what was termed as Rhodesia.

Extent of the European Colonies in Africa. By 1914, the European powers had appropriated the whole continent of Africa (except for the independent states of Abyssinia and Liberia).

GREAT BRITAIN. The possessions of Great Britain included the Union of South Africa, Bechuanaland, Rhodesia, Egypt, Anglo-Egyptian Sudan, Uganda, British East Africa, British Somaliland, British Gambia, Sierra Leone, Gold Coast, and Nigeria. The financial coup through which Disraeli obtained control of the Suez Canal was of tremendous importance to Great Britain because of the value of the Canal in reaching India.

FRANCE. During the nineteenth and twentieth centuries, France gained control of Algeria, Tunis, French West Africa, French Congo, Morocco, French Somaliland, and Madagascar. Throughout these extensive dominions the French ruled with a stern hand, encouraged commerce and industry, and prevented tribal wars.

ITALY. The Italians controlled Eritrea, Italian Somaliland, and Libya. The attempt to appropriate Abyssinia was frustrated by the emperor, Menelek, and in 1906, Great Britain, France, and Italy agreed to recognize Abyssinia's independence.

GERMANY. Germany had important territories under her control in 1914. They were Togo, Kamerun, German Southwest Africa, and German East Africa. The fact that these lands were not suitable for colonization made it necessary for the Germans to transform the natives into industrious workers so that Germany could get the products of their lands. Small beginnings were made in "civilizing" the savages.

OTHER EUROPEAN POSSESSIONS. Portugal, Belgium, and Spain had territories in Africa: Belgium had Belgian Congo, and Portugal controlled Guinea, Portuguese East Africa, and Portuguese West Africa. Spain was master of the colonies of Rio de Oro, Adrar, and small pieces of territory on the coasts of Guinea and Morocco.

Significant Dates

Government of India Act . .	1858
British North American Act .	1867
Jubilee Conference	1887
Boer War	1899
Australian Commonwealth Act	1900

CHAPTER XIV.

GREAT BRITAIN AND IMPERIALISM

Canada. The Canadian Rebellion (1837) revealed to the British government the necessity for adjusting the reasons for discontent in Canada. Although Great Britain recalled Lord Durham, who had been sent over to adjust Canada's grievances, his report became the basis for conciliation. Lord Durham's report (1839) recommended that Upper and Lower Canada be united (principle of confederation) and that the colonies be allowed to have responsible self-government. The first recommendation was carried out in 1840 and the second in 1847. In 1867, (British North American Act) New Brunswick and Novia Scotia joined with Quebec and Ontario to form the Dominion of Canada with a government similar to Great Britain's. The governor-general appointed the senate (life term), and the House of Commons was elected by the people. The cabinet was responsible to the Commons. During the next twenty-five years, internal reforms were made, a tariff levied to protect industries, and westward expansion was accomplished. By 1878 the whole of British North America, except for Newfoundland, became a part of the Dominion.

The provinces of Alberta and Saskatchewan were organized in the western territories in 1905. Newfoundland became an independent, self-governing colony.

Australasia. The colonies of Australasia held aloof from a confederation, until, in 1900, the Australian Commonwealth Act provided for the union of New South Wales, Queensland, Victoria, South Australia, West Australia, and Tasmania. New Zealand formed a separate dominion. The Australian government was similar to that of the United States. At the head there was a governor-general. The cabinet was responsible to the House of Representatives. Universal suffrage prevailed in Australasia. The Australians have tried to combat poverty to a greater extent than any other country by enacting social legislation.

New Zealand. The islands of New Zealand became a separate dominion (1907). Here, experiments in democracy and business were fostered. Woman suffrage was granted, and popular election of the senate was provided for. Government control of railways, insurance, and mines fostered state socialism. Protective social legislation was passed, and novel schemes of taxation were introduced placing the maximum burden on those best able to pay.

South Africa. Responsible governments were granted to Cape Colony (1872) and to Natal (1893). The Boers were able to retain control of the Orange Free State and the Transvaal for a time, but the British desire for expansion, conflicting with the Boers' attempt to retain control, resulted in the Boer War (1899-1902). The British won through sheer numbers, and the treaty provided for responsible governments for the Transvaal and the Orange Free State. Finally, the Union of South Africa, consisting of the four states, was established (1909). The Boers had a majority in the first parliament, and General Botha, a Boer, was the first premier. Some of the problems in the Union of South Africa centered around (1) the animosity between Boers and British, (2) the labor question, and (3) the discontented Indians of Asia, who had been imported as laborers.

Attitude of Great Britain Toward Self-Governing Colonies. The British exercised very little political control over these dominions before World War I. There was considerable agitation to bring the colonies into closer relations with the mother country, however.

IMPERIAL PREFERENCE. The plan to bring the colonies together through a preferential protective tariff failed because Great Britain refused to throw over free trade. But Canada, South Africa, Australia, and New Zealand all enacted tariffs which discriminated in favor of the United Kingdom.

IMPERIAL CONFERENCE. The desire for imperial federation was furthered through conferences at which the self-governing colonies were recognized as co-partners with Great Britain. The first conference of Queen Victoria's Jubilee (1887) was followed by others in 1894 (Ottawa), 1897, 1902, 1907, and 1911 (all in London), at which the Prime Ministers discussed the problems of the parts of the British Empire.

IMPERIAL DEFENSE. The attempt to bring the colonies closer by having them help bear the burden of the British navy was not successful, due to the failure of Canada to contribute money and ships. Each colony desired its own navy but could not afford to develop one. They did develop armies which proved very helpful in the Boer and World Wars.

THE CROWN COLONIES

British West Indies. The British controlled many of the West Indies. The islands had a legislative council appointed by the crown. The real authority came from the mother country.

Africa and Asia. The territories of Gold Coast, Nigeria, Gambia, Sierra Leone, Basutoland, and Swaziland were crown colonies, as were Ceylon, Hong Kong, and the Straits Settlements.

Naval Stations. The following naval and coaling stations in the temperate zones were inhabited by whites, but were not granted self-government: Gibraltar, Malta, Cyprus, Falkland Islands, and Bermuda.

Rhodesia and North Borneo. Rhodesia and North Borneo are examples of colonies governed by chartered companies. The government is the same as in crown colonies.

Egypt. Under Lord Cromer and Lord Kitchener, political and economic reforms were fostered. By controlling Egypt, Britain was able to extend her influence over the Sudan. The reasons for Great Britain's assuming a protectorate over Egypt were its financial chaos and the irresponsibility of the Khedive.

Other Protectorates. Besides over Egypt, Great Britain exercised a protectorate over the Malay States, India, British East Africa, Nyasaland, Somaliland, Bechuanaland, Nigeria, Gambia, and Sierra Leone.

INDIA

Means of Control. The conquest of India by the British was made easy because of (1) geographical divisions—Southern India, lowlands of the Ganges and Indus rivers, and the Himalayan mountain districts, (2) heterogeneous population, (3) diverse religions, and (4) political dissensions.

East India Company. With capable leaders like Clive, Warren Hastings, Cornwallis, Wellesley, the Marquess of Hastings, and Lord Dalhousie, the East India Company developed an empire. The corrupt practices of the company in India resulted in the passage of the India Act (1784), which provided for the nomination of high officials for India by the British ministry and for a Board of Control with a cabinet minister at its head. However, the introduction of reforms, the interference with the native religion, and the desire of the native princes for power resulted in a mutiny among the native soldiers (sepoys) in 1857, when they refused to use the new greased cartridges. The mutiny was finally put down (1859), but in the meantime, the East India Company lost its power, and India became a Crown dominion (Better Government of India Act, 1858). The government of India is vested in a Secretary of State for India (cabinet officer). The British Ministry appoints a viceroy who is assisted by an Executive Council and a legislature. Although the Indian Councils Act

(1909) granted a few concessions to the people, it was not satisfactory, and the criticisms of the Hindus became stronger.

Economic Value of India. Agricultural conditions were improved by irrigation, and more efficient methods of transportation made it easier to obtain products. Besides affording a source of wheat and other farm goods, India was valuable because of its trade, which was carried in British ships. In addition, English manufactured goods were sold in large quantities in India. Although Great Britain was primarily interested in India because of certain specific economic advantages, there were some British who put forth the "civilizing" argument as a reason for British control.

CHAPTER XV.

THE ARMED PEACE

The period 1871-1914 was, for the men who lived in it, an age of unparalleled peace, progress, enlightenment, and promise. For the first time in European history, there was a widely diffused feeling that mankind had won the battle of civilization—that the evils of war, pestilence, poverty, and ignorance belonged to a dying past. A few pessimists, indeed, pointed out the underlying instability in the state of the world, and those on the inside of diplomatic affairs knew that the peace of Europe was "at the mercy of an accident," likely at any time to be broken by a general war; but the average man understood little of the dangerous conflicts that went on underneath the surface. He trusted to his statesmen to keep his country out of serious trouble (although he was very sensitive of his country's "honor" and "prestige"), and he could see all around him the evidences of a new era of civilization and progress. Historians of the first decade of the twentieth century dwelt much on the material prosperity of the world, on the triumph of democratic principles of government in America and in Western Europe, on the spread of popular education, and on the prevalence of a better understanding among nations. While this general optimism had substantial grounds, it is difficult for our post-war generation to see civilization and progress as the essential characteristics of the period; we are more inclined to see the sinister forces that were slowly working forward to a world catastrophe. And so we often think of the period not as the "Age of Progress" that its contemporaries frequently called it, but as the "Armed Peace"— the breeding ground of World War I. But before reviewing this ominous aspect, we may briefly list some of the outstanding features that gave ground at the time for a hopeful outlook.

The Growth of Internationalism. The development of improved means of transportation and communication, the stimulation by education of interest in foreign countries, and the great increase in the number of people of sufficient means to be able to travel extensively led to much intermingling and interchange of culture among the peoples of Europe and between Europe and America. Many international societies were established, and men came together from all parts of the world for labor conferences, religious congresses, and scientific and economic meetings. Professorships were exchanged among the great universities. The preëminence of German scholarship led hundreds of students from England, France, and the United States to attend German universities for advanced degrees and to carry German methods of higher education back to their own countries. The idea that Europe and America together formed a great cultural and social unity—"Western Civilization"—gained strength. In addition to these ties of a common intellectual and cultural heritage, there were strong ties of mutual economic interest. International commerce and specialization of industry had made the nations of the world economically interdependent to a degree formerly undreamed of. It was easy to cherish the illusion that these international forces and interests made a great war impossible.

The Popular Peace Movement. During the forty-year period preceding World War I there was a remarkable increase in the number of people and organizations devoted to the promotion of peace. After 1891 an international peace conference was held annually at Bern, Switzerland. Many philanthropists, notably Andrew Carnegie and Alfred Nobel, contributed large sums to the cause of pacifism. Literary men and intellectuals in all countries waged a campaign of education against war. The rising body of Socialists, with strong groups in most of the leading parliaments of Europe, was set against war and the growth of armaments. Business men and financiers with large stakes in the continuing development of international trade and in the safety of foreign investments were also vigorous supporters of peace among the great powers, although not always opposed to small-scale wars in faraway lands for imperial aggrandizement. Religious men of all sects denounced war. Never had there been so widespread a movement demanding peace.

International Arbitration. The substitution of peaceful for warlike means in the settlement of international disputes gained much ground. Notable examples of arbitration were the settlement of the Alabama Claims (Great Britain and the United States, 1871-1872), the Dogger Bank Incident (Great Britain and Russia, 1904-1905), the Casablanca Case (Germany and France 1908-1909), and the Argentina-Chile dispute (1902).

The Hague Conferences. In 1899, at the invitation of Tsar Nicholas II of Russia, representatives of twenty-six nations met at The Hague to consider plans for the curtailment of armaments. On this question no agreement was reached, but the Conference set up an international tribunal for the arbitration of disputes and began a systematic codification of the international laws of war. A second Conference met in 1907, attended by forty-four nations. Again no agreement was reached on the crucial questions of armaments, but further conventions were adopted, providing humane restrictions on war practices. The Hague Conferences did not touch any of the real causes of war among nations, but the mere fact that such gatherings occurred seemed to augur well for future and perhaps more fundamental understanding.

THE BACKGROUND OF WORLD WAR

While the surface of European life thus seemed to promise much for the perpetuation of peace, there were powerful forces tending toward war. Chief among these were the excesses of nationalism, imperialism, and militarism. The con-

EUROPE
1914

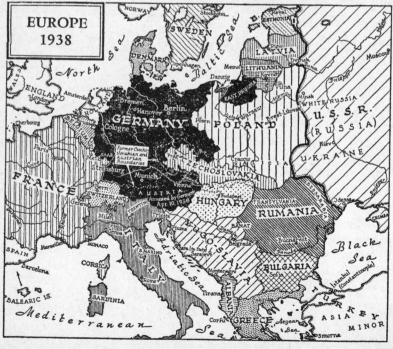

EUROPE
1938

flicting systems of alliances, the anarchy of international negotiations, the concept of unlimited national sovereignty, all made
it easy for a minor dispute to develop into a great catastrophe.
Nations were as sensitive to considerations of their "prestige"
and "honor" as were the proud noblemen of old dueling days.
All the statesmen lived in fear lest some rival power should
seize territory or form a coalition, or lest their own country
should be ignored in the settlement of some "European" question. Down to the year 1905, the mutual jealousies of the six
great powers prevented a clear lineup on one of two sides and
thus made general war less likely; after 1905 there developed
a crystallization of the alliance system—Great Britain, France,
and Russia stood against Germany and Austria-Hungary, with
Italy occupying an ambiguous position. After this separation
of Europe into two armed camps, incidents and crises became
increasingly dangerous. A series of crises occurred during the
years 1905-1914, and although in each case war was averted,
increasing bitterness followed each diplomatic defeat, and
increasing arrogance, each diplomatic victory. The losers resolved not again to be outwitted; the winners, to press their
advantages while the opportunity lasted.

THE ALLIANCE SYSTEM

The Triple Alliance. The defeat of France by Prussia in
1870-1871 and the formation of the German Empire gave
to Germany the unquestioned predominance in continental
Europe. But Bismarck feared, above all, a recovery by France
and a war of revenge. In Chapter VIII we traced his schemes
to isolate France and secure permanence for the 1871 settlement—he formed first the Three Emperors' League (1872-
1878; 1881-1887) and then the Triple Alliance of Germany,
Austria, and Italy. Conflicting interests between Austria and
Russia in the Balkans made a further renewal of the Three
Emperors' League impossible, but Bismarck concluded a secret
agreement with Russia, known as the Reinsurance Treaty
(1887), in which he sold out Austria's interests in the Balkans
in return for Russia's promise not to aid France in a Franco-
German war. But Caprivi, who followed Bismarck as German
Chancellor, allowed the Reinsurance Treaty to lapse (1890)
The conflict of interests between Italy and Austria over

Italia Irredenta and control of the Adriatic sea produced a serious weakness in the Triple Alliance. In 1902 Italy and France reached a secret agreement practically nullifying the Triple Alliance as far as Italy was concerned. Yet the Triple Alliance was renewed as late as 1913 because, although the German and Austrian governments knew that promises of Italian support were of doubtful value, they were by this time so terrified by the coalition of powers ranged against them— Great Britain, France, and Russia—that they were willing to grasp at any straw.

The Dual Alliance. France, isolated by Bismarck's policy for twenty years after the Franco-Prussian War, was anxious for an alliance with any power that would give her a chance to regain her lost position. The Russians were infuriated at Germany's refusal to renew the Reinsurance Treaty, and they had become increasingly dependent upon French capital for large loans for internal development. The Tsar also feared a coalition between the Triple Alliance and Great Britain. In 1891, therefore, France and Russia signed a secret agreement to consult together and decide on common measures in the event of a crisis threatening peace; in 1894 this agreement was made public and supplemented by a full-fledged military alliance. The Dual Alliance was confirmed and strengthened in the years following, and France, relieved of her fears of having to confront Germany alone, was able to pursue a more aggressive policy.

Position of Great Britain (1890-1904). With the formation of the Triple and Dual Alliances, continental Europe had separated into two hostile camps. Great Britain continued outside the alliance system and for some years pursued a policy of "splendid isolation." She had conflicts of interests with all the continental powers. Her rivalry with France in Africa came to the very verge of war in 1898 over the Fashoda Incident. Her relations with Russia were kept in a strained state by Russia's activities in Persia, Afghanistan, and the Far East. Germany was vigorously challenging her old-time commercial supremacy. At the time of the outbreak of the Boer War (1899-1902), Great Britain found herself cordially disliked in most of the foreign offices of Europe. A scheme was even set on foot to join France, Germany, and Russia in a coalition to force Great Britain to make peace with the Boers. Nothing came of this plan, but the British were painfully reminded of the dangers of their position. In 1900-1902 the British statesmen, Joseph Chamberlain and Lord Landsdowne, repeatedly approached Germany with offers of an understanding. They frankly threatened to seek allies elsewhere if no agreement could be reached with Germany. Bülow and Holstein, who directed Germany's foreign policy, did not believe Great Britain could ever reach a satisfactory settlement with the Dual Alliance, especially with Russia, and they refused the British offers. Rebuffed by Germany, the British turned first to Japan, with whom they signed a treaty in 1902, and then to France, with whom they reached an understanding (Entente Cordiale) in 1904.

The Entente Cordiale. In the period 1895-1902 no two powers of Europe seemed less likely to come to a friendly understanding than Great Britain and France. They had been traditional enemies for hundreds of years. France had just signed a military alliance with Russia, Britain's bitter imperialistic rival in Asia. Conflicting ambitions of France and Britain in Africa seemed irreconcilable. The French dreamed of an African empire reaching from the Atlantic to the Red Sea; the British were planning a Cape-to-Cairo railway and were intent upon extending their control of Egypt to the whole upper Nile valley. The press in both countries was given to the most inflammatory mutual denunciation; responsible statesmen often talked of war. Kitchener's seizure of the Egyptian Sudan in 1898 brought relations between the two countries to the boiling-point. But the failure of the British rapprochement with Germany in 1900-1902, the determination of Germany to embark on a naval building program, the changed attitude toward Britain on the part of the French government after the French elections of 1902, and the skillful diplomacy of the French ambassador to Great Britain, Paul Cambon, all contributed to a change of front. The most important factor in bringing the two countries together was probably the French determination to get control of Morocco, which they could not possibly do without first assuring themselves of the support of Britain. At length (1904) a deal was arranged, the essence of which was that Britain promised the French a free hand in Morocco in return for French recognition of Britain's virtual conquest of Egypt. Several minor commercial and colonial disputes were settled at the same time. Although this agreement was merely a statement of harmony and not an alliance, it was of great importance in ending Anglo-French rivalry and was consequently a terrific blow to the Triple Alliance.

The Triple Entente. Anglo-Russian relations were not at all improved by the Entente Cordiale between Britain and France. Indeed, during the Russo-Japanese War (1904-1905), Britain, as the ally of Japan, did everything possible, short of war, to hinder the Russians and bring about their defeat. With Russia, Britain had colonial disputes in Asia similar to those with France in Africa. But in 1905 new governments came to power in Britain and in Russia, opening the way for a settlement of the various sources of friction. In 1907 a treaty was signed arranging for the division of Persia into spheres of influence, for non-intervention in Tibet, and for Russian recognition of British supremacy in Afghanistan. Like the Entente Cordiale, this treaty with Russia was merely the burying of the hatchet; Great Britain was still uncommitted to the continental alliance system. But from 1905 on, the coöperation between Britain and France grew closer. Sir Edward Grey, the new British Foreign Minister, was inclined to suspicion and hostility toward Germany, while he had a sentimental attachment for France; Paul Cambon was tireless in his efforts to tie Britain to France by definite written pledges. Consultations between British and French military and naval experts were arranged. The result was that although no formal treaty binding Great Britain was concluded, the strongest possible moral obligation of Britain toward France was created. At the same time the French and Russian diplomats did all they could to create the impression throughout Europe that Britain, France, and Russia were as one, and this group of powers began to be called the "Triple Entente" and regarded as the counterbalance to the Triple Alliance. Thus the shifting and maneuvering of international diplomacy had at last brought about the necesary condition for a world war as distinguished from a war involving only some of the powers—Europe had separated into two hostile groups.

CHAUVINISM AND MILITARISM

Chauvinism. The disposition to saber-rattling, excesses of aggressive patriotism, threats of resort to force for the settlement of even trivial disputes were prevalent in all the great nations. Newspapers found it profitable for their circulations to indulge in the most unlicensed invective against foreign nations; politicians, hungry for applause and votes, exploited a never-failing reservoir of popularity by vain-glorious boasting about the achievements and historic destinies of their countries. Each nation had its war cult and its popular literature praising military glory. The pressure of the chauvinists was such that even pacifically minded statesmen were carried along by the current and forced to adopt aggressive policies against their better judgments; any yielding would at once be interpreted as a sign of weakness or cowardice, so that the alternatives in the diplomatic game were victory or political ruin.

Armaments. The enormous growth of armaments during the period 1871-1914 was one of the outstanding characteristics of the period. In all the continental countries, peace-time conscription, or universal military training, was in vogue. Huge standing armies were maintained, growing larger almost every year. In the meantime the progress of science and the Industrial Revolution were multiplying the effectiveness of weapons and continually adding to the cost and complexity of the modern military machine. The economic burdens imposed on all peoples by the tremendous non-productive military expenditures grew steadily more intolerable during the decade before the World War, yet no practical way of stopping the mad race was discovered. Each nation believed itself to be arming in self-defense and was unwilling to put any faith in promises made by other nations. An important cause of the growing estrangement between Great Britain and Germany in the years 1900-1914 was the German effort to create a large navy, which Britain regarded as a direct threat to her national safety. The Hague disarmament conferences of 1899 and 1907 came to nothing, as we have seen; in 1912 an attempt on the part of Great Britain and Germany to reach an agreement regarding naval armaments (the Haldane Mission) was also a failure. Although many statesmen saw that the international armament race was leading straight to bankruptcy or war, perhaps to both, they could not advocate that their countries relax their preparations in the midst of armed and threatening neighbors. They therefore did their best to pretend that great armaments were the best insurance for peace and that if all were armed, all would be safe. For in spite of all their aggressive talk, almost nobody in Europe really wanted a general war.

Militarism in Civil Government. Sinister as was the mere growth of military and naval establishments in itself, an even more dangerous manifestation was the increasing influence of the military leaders and of military considerations over the conduct of civil government. Questions of governmental policy came to be decided more and more by the necessities of the General Staffs and their plans for war. Particularly at a time of crisis, the pressure of military men upon the civilian government was likely to be irresistible; in their anxiety not to lose the advantage of the offensive if war should come, the soldiers were prone to jump to the conclusion that war was "inevitable" and, accordingly, would urge the fatal step of mobilization, thus actually making war inevitable. All the General Staffs had very technical and elaborate plans that could not be changed on the spur of the moment to conform to unexpected diplomatic developments, and which, therefore, tended to tie the hands of the diplomats. A notorious instance was the German "Schlieffen Plan," which made it literally impossible for Germany to go to war with Russia except by invading France through Belgium.

INTERNATIONAL ANARCHY

Concept of National Sovereignty. A necessary condition of civilized society is the reign of law and order—the strict limitation of the liberties of individuals by the concerted action of the state, by the power of social custom and opinion, and by the self-discipline imposed by religion and ethics. Among nations, no similar system for the preservation of order has yet developed. All nations claim to be "sovereign powers," subject to no law imposed from without. Essential in the concept of national sovereignty is the right to declare war or to make peace. No effective international machinery exists for adjusting disputes or for arranging a peaceful change in the *status quo*. In the final analysis important changes can come only through force or the threat of force. After World War I two important attempts were made to limit the concept of national sovereignty in the interest of peace—the League of Nations and the Kellogg-Briand Pact—but these attempts disappointed even their most ardent supporters. Before World War I even these feeble instruments of international order did not exist. While some restraint upon naked aggression was imposed by the necessity of placating public opinion and building up some sort of moral case, chauvinism and nationalism made public opinion uncritical: "Our country right or wrong" expressed the usual attitude of patriots in all countries.

Secret Diplomacy. The anarchic condition of international relations was aggravated by the practice of secret diplomacy, which lent itself to all kinds of corruption and double-dealing. An atmosphere of suspicion and fear was created. No nation knew when it might be sold out by its allies, what combinations and plots might be forming behind its back, or what statements by foreign diplomats could be accepted as truth. Men perfectly honorable in their private lives were willing to lie shamelessly in the service of their countries. Such instances of international duplicity as Bismarck's negotiation of the Reinsurance Treaty (1887), Italy's nullification of the Triple Alliance in her rapprochement with France (1902), and the secret plans for military coöperation between Britain and France (denied by Sir Edward Grey in the House of Commons) bring vividly to mind the prevalence of conspiracy and Machiavellianism in the dealings among great states and show why no nation felt it could trust any other.

NATIONALISM

The spirit of nationalism, or the emotional desire for unity and political independence among peoples having a common language and a common racial and cultural heritage, is a very old force in human civilization. The ancient Greeks, for example, made a sharp distinction between *Hellenes* who spoke Greek and *hoi barbaroi*—the rest of the world. Readers of the Bible may recall the intense national spirit of the Hebrews: their conviction that they were the *Chosen People;* their preservation through centuries of persecution of their cultural and religious traditions. But with the establishment of the Roman Empire and the rise of Christianity the spirit of nationalism died out. It was revived in the fourteenth and fifteenth centuries when the languages of Europe had become differentiated and the unifying influence of the Catholic Church began to decline. Through the sixteenth, seventeenth, and eighteenth centuries nationalism continued to grow, and it received an immense impetus from the French Revolution and the Napoleonic Wars. At the Congress of Vienna, nationalism was largely disregarded in favor of "legitimacy." During the nineteenth century the Vienna settlement was revised, in most cases by violent nationalistic upsurgence, as happened most notably in the cases of the unification of Italy and of Germany. But there remained in the period 1871-1914 many unsatisfied nationalistic ambitions, and the agitation of these ambitions, combined with the maneuvering of the great powers to take advantage of the situation constituted a constant menace to peace.

Alsace-Lorraine. These border regions between France and Germany had been seized by Germany at the close of the Franco-Prussian War. Inhabited by a mixed population, the provinces were claimed by nationalist patriots on both sides. A vigorous attempt was made during the forty-year period following 1871 to "Germanize" the provinces by restricting the use and teaching of the French language, encouraging immigration by Germans, and by many tactless and repressive measures. But repression served only to keep alive resistance and increase the bitterness of the French, who looked forward to *la revanche,* when the "lost provinces" might be regained.

Italia Irredenta. Trentino and the area around Trieste remained part of the Austrian Empire after the unification of Italy, although the majority of the population was Italian.

Austria-Hungary and Italy, although joined together in the Triple Alliance, could not be real friends as long as this source of irritation continued.

Austria-Hungary and the Balkans. The mixture of languages and nationalities in Austria-Hungary and the Balkans made this whole territory a caldron of agitation. In Chapter XI we traced the steps in the breakup of the Turkish hegemony in southeastern Europe. The Balkan Wars (1912-1913) deprived Turkey of her whole European empire except Adrianople and eastern Thrace. But many territorial questions remained unsettled; the four Balkan states of Greece, Serbia, Bulgaria, and Rumania continued to quarrel among themselves, while the great powers, with conflicting interests in the settlement, engaged in diplomatic intrigues.

A vague nationalistic movement known as Pan-Slavism was strongly at work among the peoples of the Balkans and the subject nationalities of Austria-Hungary. Pan-Slavism preached the cultural and political solidarity of all the branches of the Slavonic peoples. As the great Slav power, Russia appeared as the "protector" of the Slavs against Teutonic aggression. Many statesmen, privately contemptuous of the emotional talk of the Slavonic patriots, were willing to use the popular passion to further their own imperialistic schemes: Russia was anxious to get control of the Straits at the entrance to the Black Sea and was pleased to see a revolutionary movement weakening her Austrian rival; German expansionists cried up the menace of Pan-Slavism to gain patriotic support for their dreams of the *Drang nach Osten* or *Mitteleuropa* hegemony. Of the complexity of this nationalistic and imperialistic tangle Professor S. B. Fay has written: "Of all the major conflicts of interest which have been alleged as making it [World War I] 'inevitable,' the Balkan problems were those most nearly incapable of a peaceful solution."[1]

ECONOMIC IMPERIALISM

In Chapters XIII and XIV we traced the scramble of the European powers that resulted in the partition of Africa and in the European economic dominance of most of Asia. At bottom

---

[1] From *The Origins of the World War* by S. B. Fay. Published by The Macmillan Co.

this new imperialism was a struggle for markets, for raw materials, and for fields of investment, although it was largely supported by emotional patriots who had nothing personally to gain. The imperialistic rivalries exacerbated nationalist feelings and led to endless friction among the great powers. Particularly keen in the decade before World War I was the commercial competition between Germany and Great Britain. Nevertheless, economic imperialism, while a powerful force in the creation of the general war psychology of Europe, can hardly be accounted a direct cause of the World War, since economic competition cut across the lines drawn by the alliance system. It was strong between Great Britain and France and between Great Britain and Russia, just as it was between Great Britain and Germany.

INTERNATIONAL CRISES (1905-1914)

After the separation of Europe into two armed groups, diplomatic "incidents" became increasingly dangerous, more likely to develop into "crises," which might involve the whole continent in war. A series of these crises occurred during the period 1905-1914.

Moroccan Crisis (1905-1906). The formation of the *Entente Cordiale* was a shock and a defeat to German diplomacy. Determining not to be left out of the settlement of the Moroccan question, the German minister, Baron von Holstein, sent the Kaiser on a visit to Tangier in March 1905. The Kaiser made a speech recognizing the independent sovereignty of Morocco, and the German Foreign Office demanded an international conference to settle the future of the country. Theophile Delcassé, the French Foreign Minister, resented this challenge and advocated war with Germany. But Russia was exhausted by her war with Japan and because of internal disorder was in no condition to fight, while Great Britain, though offering strong diplomatic support, did not definitely commit herself. The French finally submitted to the German pressure, and Delcassé resigned. This was regarded as a humiliating defeat for French diplomacy. But the German triumph was short-lived, for at the Algeciras Conference which the Germans had insisted upon, they found themselves out-voted and out-maneuvered. Italy threw her diplomatic support on the side of the French on all important questions; in the end the Germans were able to salvage only the naked form of Moroccan independence. The French were given special financial powers and the right, with Spain, to police the country.

Balkan Crisis (1908). Bosnia and Herzegovina had been administered by Austria-Hungary since 1878, although the provinces were nominally part of the Ottoman Empire. In 1908, taking advantage of a revolution at Constantinople, the Austrian Foreign Minister, Alois von Aehrenthal, and the Russian Foreign Minister, Alexander Izvolski, arranged a deal by which Austria was to annex Bosnia and Herzegovina and Russia was to obtain the opening of the Straits to Russian battleships. Unfortunately for Izvolski, the opening of the Straits did not depend upon the good will of von Aehrenthal but upon the good will of Great Britain, and Britain was unwilling to abandon her traditional policy of keeping the Straits closed. Austria proceeded quietly and annexed Bosnia and Herzegovina; Russia received nothing as a compensation. The annexation aroused the greatest resentment in Serbia, where ardent Pan-Slavists had been nourishing plans for a "Greater Serbia" to include the South Slavs of Bosnia. For some months war seemed imminent between Austria-Hungary and Serbia. Into such a war, Russia would be practically forced by the pressure of her Pan-Slavists and her considerations of prestige. Russia, however, was unprepared for a great war. It was clear that Germany would support Austria. In the circumstances, Russia was forced to back down; the Serbs, unable to obtain Russian support, also backed down. Austro-German diplomacy won a victory. But bitter resentments were left by the crisis. The "Greater Serbia" agitation continued with redoubled vigor; Izvolski, outwitted and humiliated, was bent on revenge against Austria.

Agadir Crisis (1911). Since the Algeciras Conference the French had been steadily pushing their economic penetration of Morocco, and in 1911 they announced that certain towns would be occupied by French troops until "order" was restored. The Germans immediately suspected that the occupation would be a prelude to French annexation. In order to prevent this or to secure suitable "compensation" for themselves as a price of their consent, the Germans sent the warship *Panther* to the port of Agadir as a threatening gesture. A "crisis" at once developed. After considerable shaking of the mailed fist on both sides, the matter was adjusted by granting Germany two strips of land from the French Congo in return for German consent to the French protectorate over Morocco. Although France got by far the best of the bargain, chauvinists in the French Senate forced the fall of the ministry of Joseph Caillaux on the charge that he had truckled to the Germans.

Turco-Italian War (1911). Italy took advantage of the Agadir crisis to send to Turkey an ultimatum demanding Tripoli. While public opinion in Europe condemned Italy's "stiletto policy," the powers did not intervene. It was evident that Italy's allegiance to the Triple Alliance was extremely weak, since Germany was actively cultivating the friendship of Turkey, and the attack by Italy was very embarrassing.

Balkan Wars (1912-1913). Throughout the period of the Balkan Wars, the European diplomats were kept in a state of nervous excitement. Austria repeatedly threatened intervention; all the powers watched the situation jealously, fearful lest a rival should gain an advantage. A tremendous military-preparedness fever swept the continent.

THE OUTBREAK OF WORLD WAR I

Assassination of Archduke Francis Ferdinand. On June 28, 1914, the Archduke Francis Ferdinand, heir-presumptive to the throne of Austria-Hungary, and his wife were assassinated at Sarajevo, the capital of Bosnia, by a fanatic Serb patriot, Gavrilo Princip, a South Slav Austrian subject. The incident brought to a crisis the relations between Austria-Hungary and Serbia, which had been strained since the Austrian annexation of Bosnia-Herzegovina in 1909. The Austrian government, believing that the crime was the outcome of the revolutionary "Greater Serbia" movement, and that this movement threatened the very existence of the Dual Monarchy, determined to take strong measures.

The Austrian Ultimatum. Having obtained a promise of support from Germany (the "blank check" of July 5), and having converted the Hungarian Prime Minister, Count Tisza to his views, Count Berchtold, the Austrian Foreign Minister delivered an ultimatum (July 23) to Serbia containing ten humiliating demands. The ultimatum was deliberately framed with the intention of provoking a war with Serbia, as Berchtold felt that only by a punitive military expedition could the anti-Austrian agitation in Serbia be squelched. The Austrian government relied on the threat of Germany to prevent any effective interference by Russia. Insofar as the matter was considered at all, it was believed that, confronted by Germany, Russia would do no more than she had done in 1909 after Austria had annexed Bosnia-Herzegovina.

The Serbian Reply. On July 25 Serbia made a reply to the Austrian ultimatum, conciliatory in tone, but practically rejecting, as destructive of Serbian sovereignty, the two most important of the ten demands (those requiring that Serbia accept the collaboration of Austrian officials in Serbia for suppressing the subversive movement and for investigation of the Sarajevo crime). Austria pronounced the reply unsatisfactory and broke off diplomatic relations.

Actions of the Powers. During the seven days between the delivery of the ultimatum and the declaration of war by Germany on Russia (August 1), the diplomats of the five major powers worked feverishly to prevent a general war from breaking out. Unfortunately, while no power wanted war, none was willing to make concessions. Sir Edward Grey, British Foreign Minister, and Bethmann-Hollweg, German Chancellor, were particularly active in attempting to stop war. But Bethmann-Hollweg's frantic efforts to restrain Austria met the stubborn and reckless non-coöperation of Count Berchtold, while Grey was prevented from taking a strong and consistent stand by his secret commitments to France and by the necessity of obtaining the support of the British Cabinet and the British Parliament for any grave steps. The French statesmen confined themselves to a "stand firm," "united front" policy which they hoped would frighten the Germans into a peaceful diplomatic retreat. The Russian Foreign Minister, S. D. Sazonov, was determined to prevent, at any cost, an Austrian triumph, diplomatic or military, over Serbia, as such a triumph would humiliate Russia and damage her prestige with the Balkan Slavs. "Secure of the support of France," she determined to "face all the risks of war."

Mobilizations and War. On July 28 Berchtold, who found embarrassing the pressure of the Powers to restrain his proposed punishment of Serbia, declared war on Serbia. He intended by the declaration of war to "bring about a clear situation" and to "cut the ground from every attempt at intervention." But he misjudged the degree of Russian determination, and the effect of his *fait accompli* was to irritate Sazonov and Tsar Nicholas to the fatal step of sanctioning a partial mobilization of the Russian army (July 29). For technical military reasons (probably not fully understood by Sazonov and the Tsar at the time) a partial mobilization, if not followed at once by a general mobilization, would seriously dislocate the whole Russian military machine. When this was made clear to the Tsar on the afternoon of July 30, he felt absolutely compelled to permit a general mobilization, even though it was well understood that general mobilization was equivalent to European war. The Russian mobilization forced mobilization by Germany, and German mobilization would be followed in accordance with the "Schlieffen Plan" (well-known in all the foreign offices of Europe) by a German attack on France. The existing system of alliances and the irreversibility of a mobilization order once issued made the Russian mobilization tantamount to a declaration of general war. The formal declarations (Germany on Russia, August 1; Germany on France, August 3) were merely routine consequences.

Belgium and Great Britain. The German "Schlieffen Plan" provided for an immediate concentrated attack on France. It was believed by the German General Staff that unless France could be overwhelmed in a few weeks, the unlimited masses of Russian man-power would beat the skeleton German army in the east and win the war. It, therefore, seemed to the Germans a vital necessity to get at France by the shortest possible route. This route lay through Belgium. The invasion of Belgium united the dissentient elements in Great Britain and led to a British ultimatum and declaration of war on Germany (August 4). Yet it was the secret commitments of Sir Edward Grey to France, and the general orientation of British foreign policy against Germany that forced Britain into the war; the invasion of Belgium was important rather as an issue on which Parliament and public opinion could quickly unite than as a fundamental cause of Britain's entrance. In the midst of his agitation and chagrin, the German Chancellor tactlessly referred to the treaty of 1839 (guaranteeing Belgian neutrality) as "a scrap of paper." This blunder proved of great value to the British in mobilizing moral opinion against Germany after war was declared, but it had nothing to do with causing the declaration.

Responsibility for the War. Article 231 of the Treaty of Versailles fixed upon Germany and her allies the entire legal and moral responsibility for causing the war. The verdict was a natural result of years of propaganda and hatred. In the decade following the war, authorities with new materials and a calmer perspective, gradually revised this extreme emotional judgment. It became clear that all the nations had contributed to the conditions that made the war, and that, given these conditions, the conduct of the different statesmen in the crisis of July 1914 could not be condemned or praised on a "black-white" basis. All the important statesmen made what in the light of later developments we feel justified in calling "mistakes"; all of them lived in the atmosphere of Machiavellian statecraft, in which moral judgments are unrealistic. Different historians will appraise differently the various psychological and material forces that led up to the catastrophe, but they will not return to the simple view popular on both sides during the war that all the right was on one side and all the wrong on the other.

CHAPTER XVI.

WORLD WAR I

Magnitude. World War I was the most disastrous resort to arms up to that time. From whatever point of view we attempt to measure it—size of armies, extent of devastation, effects upon civilization—the fact that stands out is that no previous war is comparable. Twenty-seven nations, including all of the eight great powers, were engaged. The total number of men mobilized in armies on the Allied side was about 40,000,000; on the side of the Central Powers, about 21,000,000. The total direct cost of the War has been estimated to exceed $150,000,000,000. The cost in human life could not be accurately stated because of the large numbers who died of starvation and in other indirect ways, in addition to those killed on the battlefields. The toll certainly exceeded 15,000,000. Twenty years after the War's end it was seen more clearly that the ultimate results were even more terrible than the war itself.

New Methods. The forty years of peace among the great powers following the Franco-German war of 1870-1871, were years of great scientific and technological development. In the World War all the resources of the Second Industrial Revolution were called upon to produce new and destructive weapons, such as high explosive shells, poisonous gases, armored tanks, submarines, machine guns, and airplanes. Most of the fighting was done in trenches stretching across fronts hundreds of miles long. There were almost no "battles" in the old sense; the operations consisted chiefly of great artillery bombardments and "drives" to break through the enemy's trench barrier.

Nations in Arms. At the outset, few of the leaders, political or military, expected a prolonged war. As the months passed away without a decision, however, it became necessary to revolutionize the internal organization of the nations in order to meet the ever mounting demands for men and material. In all countries the governments reached out into the private lives of their citizens to secure a coördination and efficient direction of the national effort. In no country was this reorganization to create "a nation in arms" more thorough than in Germany, and to her superiority of internal organization must be largely attributed her astonishing power of resistance against overwhelmingly greater potential resources. The Allied Powers did not reach their full fighting strength until the later stages of the war, chiefly because of their early failure to realize the magnitude of the task and the necessity of sacrificing individual freedom for the sake of efficiency.

Supremacy of Industrialization. At the beginning of the war there was a tendency to estimate military strength in terms of man-power in armies, and there was a total lack of understanding of the immense drain of war upon a nation's industrial resources. This misconception caused Germany to over-estimate the strength of Russia and consequently weaken her attack on France at a critical moment, in order to throw additional forces to the eastern front. Russia, undeveloped industrially, proved able to accomplish little in spite of the bravery of the Russian troops (Russia's casualties were the largest of any combatant). The Allies, too, were slow to realize the importance of industry in keeping armies supplied, and sustained serious shortages of munitions on the Western Front in 1915. It was finally her industrial resources rather than the actual troops furnished that made the United States' entrance into the war such an important factor in defeating the Central Powers.

Propaganda. A relatively new feature of World War I was the widespread use of organized propaganda by all the governments, both for the purpose of maintaining popular support at home and of influencing foreign opinion. A particularly elaborate campaign was waged in the United States: the Allies skillfully built up the sympathy that many Americans felt for their cause at the start by books, newspaper articles, lectures, and the personal partisanship of influential Americans. Allied (chiefly British) propaganda in the United States was immensely successful in diffusing a belief in the justice of the Allied cause and in the "war guilt" of the Germans. The German propaganda was directed chiefly to creating a sentiment for neutrality and pacifism, since it was soon obvious to the Germans that there was no chance of gaining active American support. All the governments published "Rainbow Books" (so named from the circumstance that different colors were used to distinguish the different countries) setting forth supposedly official documents bearing on the origin of the war in such a way as to support the claim that the war was one of self-defense. Since the war, students of history have shown that all of these books contained deletions, omissions, and actual fabrications, sustaining the maxim that "in war, truth is the first casualty." All the governments likewise disseminated "atrocity stories" which had no foundation in fact but were effective in spreading germs of hate. As a result of the propaganda, whole populations were whipped up to a savage fighting fury unknown in previous wars, and it was the effect of the propaganda, above anything else, that created the atmosphere of hatred and vindictiveness at the Conference of Paris at the end of the war and prevented the framing of a peace of conciliation.

THE CAMPAIGNS OF 1914-1915

The Western Front. The original German plan for the War contemplated overwhelming France with the greatest possible speed. This was to be accomplished in accordance with the "Schlieffen Plan" by throwing a tremendous army through Belgium which was to wheel back and pocket the French army that would presumably be engaged in an attack in Alsace. Though a masterpiece of strategic conception in its original form, the Schlieffen Plan was so modified by Moltke, who followed Schlieffen as chief of the German General Staff, that it failed to produce the results expected. Moltke so weakened the right wing, or main German army advancing through Belgium, that it lacked the necessary mass to execute the enveloping movement. Though taken by surprise in the first weeks, the French Staff under Joffre recovered, and the French army displayed heroic powers of resistance. At the decisive First Battle of the Marne (September 5-12) the Germans were repulsed and their entire plan of campaign was wrecked. The Germans retreated to prepared entrenchments along the Aisne River, and the line of battle was quickly extended north and west to the English Channel. The war in the west lost the character of free maneuver and settled down to what was essentially a vast siege operation, punctuated by bloody "drives" to effect a break-through.

The Eastern Front. The Russians threw forward their armies on two general fronts, moving north and west from Poland against East Prussia and south against Austria-Hungary. In East Prussia they were met by the better equipped and better led German armies of Generals von Hindenburg and Ludendorff and crushingly defeated in the great battles of Tannenberg (August 25-30) and the Masurian Lakes (September 4-10). These two battles so shattered the Russian armies operating against Germany as to end any threat of invasion. Against the Austrians, however, the Russians won a series of victories, occupied most of eastern Galicia, and inflicted fearful losses of men and materials. The Germans, to relieve the pressure on the Austrians, counterattacked in Poland. By the end of the year the Russian campaign was at a standstill. In 1915 the Germans took the offensive on the eastern front, pushed deep into Poland, captured Warsaw and Vilna, and inflicted nearly 1,000,000 casualties on the Russians. Although Russia remained in the war and made a further great and costly effort in 1916, she was no longer a serious menace to the Central Powers.

The Balkans. The Austrians attempted to carry through their proposed punishment of Serbia, but they had inadequate forces, and the Serbs proved unexpectedly resistant. Three separate invasions were launched in 1914, but none was successful. Turkey entered the war on the side of the Central Powers, and Germany was anxious to clear the Balkans to permit free communication from Berlin to Constantinople. In 1915, after Bulgaria had joined the Central Powers, the conquest of Serbia, which the Austrians had failed to accomplish, was rapidly carried out by General von Mackensen. In the meantime, an extensive British naval campaign, supported by some land forces, had failed to break through the Turkish fortifications guarding the Dardanelles, so that the Central Powers continued to cut off the Russian Black Sea ports from outside shipments.

Italy. Early in 1915 Italy joined the Allies. She was induced to do so by the promise of the annexation of Trentino and Trieste—"*Italia irredenta.*" Her entrance proved of little military importance as she had neither large industrial resources nor a very good army. A new trench deadlock developed on the Austro-Italian frontier and kept considerable numbers of Austrian troops immobilized, but no decisive action took place.

THE WAR AT SEA

The British Navy. The importance of British sea-power in the ultimate triumph of the Allies can scarcely be overstated. Through her control of the seas, Britain was able to establish a blockade of Germany's coast, sweep all German shipping from the high seas, cut off free communication between Germany and the outside world, seize the German colonies in Africa, and maintain lines of communication through the Mediterranean between the western Allies and the Balkans. It was the strangle-hold of the British navy that drove Germany to the desperate submarine campaign that finally brought the United States into the war against her. It was the protection of the British navy that enabled the transportation of thousands of soldiers from Canada and the other Dominions and of millions of tons of supplies from the United States. England is the most dependent of all the great countries of Europe upon an outside food supply, and without the protection of her navy would have been blockaded and starved in a few months.

The German Submarines. Her fleet bottled up by the British, Germany resorted to a new weapon, the submarine. Early in 1915 she proclaimed the establishment of a "war zone" in the waters around the British Isles and announced her intention of sinking merchant vessels carrying food and munitions. The sinking of the *Lusitania* (May, 1915) with the loss of 1200 lives, including over one hundred American citizens, aroused the people of the United States and resulted in a long diplomatic correspondence. Sinkings and incidents continued during 1915, but in April, 1916, after an attack on the French steamer *Sussex*, in which some Americans were killed, the United States presented to Germany a virtual ultimatum that resulted in the cessation of unrestricted submarine warfare for nearly a year. During the submarine campaign the drift of American opinion turned strongly against the Central Powers.

THE CAMPAIGNS OF 1916

Verdun and the Somme. Relieved of pressure in the east, Germany attempted to force a decision in the west by "bleeding the French army to death" in a campaign to capture the powerful French fortress of Verdun. The attempt was beaten back by the French under Pétain, but only after ghastly sacrifices of life on both sides. The British conducted an offensive near the Somme River that pushed the Germans back for some miles at great cost of casualties but failed to bring any real results. Neither side was able to break the deadlock; it was a war of "attrition"—killing—in which the generals could think up no new ideas.

Russia and Rumania. The Russians made a partial recovery from their defeats of 1915 and tried hard to relieve German pressure at Verdun by resuming the offensive in the east. They won a heavy victory over the Austrians at Lutsk and occupied most of Bukovina, but were stopped by German reinforcements. In the meantime Rumania joined the Allies. The Russian victories that had induced her to abandon neutrality did not continue, and an army of Bulgars and Turks commanded by von Mackensen swept into Rumania and subjugated the country within a few months. The Rumanian conquest enabled the Germans to get much-needed supplies of wheat and oil.

THE CRITICAL YEAR (1917)

The Western Front. In the spring of 1917 the military stalemate so angered the Allied politicians that they consented

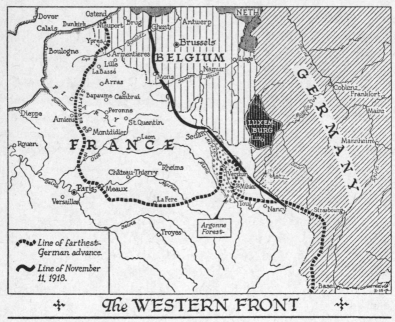

The WESTERN FRONT

to a reckless plan proposed by General Nivelle for a large-scale offensive to pierce the trench barrier. The offensive failed with great loss of life, and the futility and stupidity of the effort, recognized by the rank and file of the French army, caused great discontent and in some instances open mutiny. In England, France, and Germany, there was widespread defeatism as losses piled up without decision and as economic hardship undermined morale.

Entrance of the United States. In April 1917 the United States declared war on Germany. The precipitating cause was the German resumption of unrestricted submarine warfare on February 1. In addition to the submarine controversy was the fact that sentiment against Germany had long been growing in the United States as a result of propaganda and the sabotage activities of German agents. The economic interests of many American investors had become identified with the success of the Allied cause, and a vague feeling had developed that a German success would threaten the security of the United States and of civilization. President Wilson's famous statement "The world must be made safe for democracy" became the rallying cry of millions of well-meaning patriots who felt that America had drawn the sword, not for gain or hate, but in defense of a noble ideal. The entrance of the United States was the real turning-point of the war, although many months elapsed before American weight made itself felt. Germany made two more strong bids for victory, first by the submarine pressure on England, which reached a climax in the months of April, May, and June 1917, and second by a great land offensive on the western front in the spring of 1918.

The Withdrawal of Russia. The terrible military defeats sustained almost steadily from 1914 to 1917, the corruption and incompetence of the Tsar's bureaucracy, and the economic collapse of the entire nation combined to wreck the fighting will of the Russian people. A revolution broke out in Petrograd in March 1917, and the Tsar's government was driven from control. A provisional government, in which the leading figure was Kerensky, tried to carry on the war and establish a liberal regime. But the partial reforms proposed failed to satisfy the growing group of revolutionary leaders, while the decision to carry on the war speeded the disintegration of the army. In November the provisional government collapsed, Kerensky fled the country, and the Bolshevik group of advanced revolutionaries led by Lenin and Trotsky seized power. They were faced with enormous internal difficulties and immediately decided to make terms with Germany at any price. They tried to make peace according to the formula "No annexations and no indemnities," but finally accepted the crushing Treaty of Brest-Litovsk (March, 1918). The withdrawal of Russia enabled Germany to shift masses of troops to the western front for a final effort against the British and French.

THE TRIUMPH OF THE ALLIES

The Final German Effort. A great German drive opened on the Western Front in March, 1918. Deep pockets were pushed into the allied lines, nearly 800,000 casualties were inflicted on the British and French, and vast supplies of materials were seized. But the Allied lines did not break, while Ludendorff destroyed the German army by his frantic attacks. At the end of July it was clear that the drives had spent themselves, and the Allies, now reinforced by an American army of over 1,000,000, began a smashing counter-drive. The pressure of defeat had forced the Allies to a belated acceptance of unity of command, and General Ferdinand Foch was selected as the supreme commander.

Failure of the Submarines. During 1917 German submarines destroyed shipping faster than it could be constructed, and the Germans had good reason to believe that they would succeed in starving England before American help could arrive in force. But the British and American navies developed new methods of dealing with the submarine menace, and by the beginning of 1918 the convoy system and the so-called "Q-ships" had brought the danger under control. The submarines proved unable to impede the transport of American troops to France.

Allied Successes in the Near East. Of great importance in bringing about the final defeat of the Central Powers was the British campaign in the Near East where the Ottoman Empire was gradually overrun, and the whole German hegemony of the Balkans was threatened with disintegration. British forces under General Allenby captured Jerusalem in December, 1917, and in the following year, the Turks were forced out of the whole of Asia Minor. Allied forces from Salonika, Greece, attacked Bulgaria in September, 1918 and forced a surrender. The whole German southeast front began to crumble.

Breakdown in Germany. Four years of intense war effort had exhausted the German people. The shortage of food and its poor quality, the continuous drain of men, the failure of Ludendorff's costly drives, the growing realization that they confronted a world in arms finally broke the civilian morale. Austria-Hungary had been weakened throughout the war by the disloyalty of her subject nationalities and was on the brink of revolution. The main German army was being steadily driven back on the western front by the crushing blows of Foch. Thousands of soldiers who had served on the eastern front and had fraternized with the revolutionary Russians were infected with Bolshevism. The propaganda of the Allies, particularly President Wilson's peace program set forth in the "Fourteen Points," convinced many Germans that the war was lost and that reasonable terms could be secured if peace was made at once.

The Armistice. On September 29, 1918, the German military leaders informed the government that the war could not be won and demanded an immediate armistice. After considerable negotiations, during which the political and military situation grew rapidly worse for the Germans, the Allies presented their conditions on November 8. The terms were such as to render any resumption of the war on the part of Germany impossible. She was to surrender large quantities of military supplies and to evacuate the whole territory west of the Rhine. The Allied food blockade was to continue. The Germans accepted these terms on November 11.

CHAPTER XVII.

THE WORLD SETTLEMENT

Bulgaria (1918). Ferdinand of Bulgaria, who had been the leader in throwing his country into the war, abdicated on October 3, 1918, after the collapse of the army before the Allied advance from Salonika. Although the Bulgarians accepted Boris III as king upon the abdication of Ferdinand, the power of the monarchy was broken. An Agrarian and Socialist group under Stambulinsky controlled the government.

Turkey (1918-1923). The Young Turks, who had favored the German alliance, resigned during the Allied advances in 1918. Under Mustapha Kemal Pasha, a revolt was started in Anatolia against the Sultan, Mohammed VI (1918-1923), which spread throughout Turkey and ended with the dethronement of Mohammed VI and the establishment of the Turkish Republic (1923).

Austria-Hungary (1918). The restlessness of the subject nationalities of Austria-Hungary had been a grave source of weakness throughout the war. In the latter part of 1918 the central government lost all semblance of authority. The succession of military disasters, the terrible pressure of the food blockade, and the widespread defeatist propaganda had destroyed the morale of the people. On October 17 the government made a last effort to appease discontent by publishing a manifesto agreeing to autonomy within a federal state, but this concession came too late. Not autonomy, but independence was now the determined goal of the nationalities.

YUGOSLAVIA. The inclusion of all the South Slavs (Yugoslavs) in a "Greater Serbia" had been the specific nationalist ambition that caused the outbreak of the war. In July 1917 a group of Yugoslav leaders had met at Corfu and signed a declaration of their intention to form a new state, which was to be a "constitutional, democratic, parliamentary monarchy." Upon the collapse of the Austro-Hungarian government, the Slovenes, Croats, and Serbs broke away and joined with Serbia and Montenegro to form the "Kingdom of the Serbs, Croats, and Slovenes," with Peter of Serbia as ruler.

CZECHOSLOVAKIA. The territories of Bohemia, Moravia, and Slovakia formed a republic modeled largely on that of the United States, and selected Thomas Masaryk as President. The Czechs had been the most active and persistent of the rebellious nationalities. They had established cordial relations with the Allied powers as early as 1916, chiefly through the skillful diplomacy of Masaryk and Eduard Beneš. The state they established was therefore placed immediately in the privileged position of association with the victorious Allies.

HUNGARY. Unlike the Czechs, Slovaks, and South Slavs, the Hungarians were a dominant nationality, and up to the very end they supported the German Austrians and coöperated to carry on the war. When it became clear that the old Empire was breaking up, the Hungarian leaders attempted to salvage an integral Hungary from the wreck—that is, a Hungary that would include all the territory of the old Hungarian kingdom. This territory contained many Rumans, Slovaks, and Yugoslavs. The Hungarian Republic that was set up under the leadership of Michael Karolyi and his Independence Party was therefore confronted at once with the problem of settling with its own minorities. Karolyi, a liberal republican, attempted to introduce reforms which he hoped would placate these minorities and win lenient terms of peace from the Allies. But the Allies insisted upon treating the newly formed republic as an enemy power, and the subject nationalities refused to coöperate. The regime of Karolyi lasted only three months.

AUSTRIAN REPUBLIC. On November 11, 1918, the Emperor, Charles, abdicated. A coalition of Social Democrats, Christian Socialists, and German Nationalists established a provisional government, issued a constitution, and declared German Austria a republic. The change was accomplished with practically no violence, chiefly owing to the sensible conduct of Charles, who voluntarily released his former officials from their oaths of allegiance to him so as not to stand in the way of the "free development of the people whom he loved." It was the intention of the Austrian leaders to join the Austrian Republic with the new German Republic, but this plan was blocked by the Allies.

Germany. The almost universal support of the War by the German people cooled as the years passed bringing nothing but military deadlock, ration cards, and casualties. As early as 1916 the radical leader Karl Liebknecht was circulating his "Spartacus" letters denouncing the War and advocating a social revolution. By 1917 a powerful peace movement had developed. The Reichstag, which for three years had docilely voted whatever measures had been requested, began now to grow restive. There was much demand for liberal reform in the government. Matthias Erzberger, leader of the Center Party, came forward with a resolution calling for peace on the basis of the Russian formula: "no annexations and no indemnities." But the military leaders, Hindenburg and Ludendorff, had now assumed the real control of affairs, and they were determined to push the war forward to victory. They forced the resignation, in July, 1917, of the moderate Bethmann-Hollweg and secured the appointment, as Chancellor, of George Michaelis, a weak man who was not likely to oppose their policies. Michaelis' chancellorship lasted only four months. The Reichstag refused to support him and for the first time in German history was able to bring about the fall of an unsatisfactory ministry. Michaelis was succeeded by Count Hertling. Hertling attempted to carry on the government with the help of the Reichstag, but the necessities of the war placed more and more power in the hands of Hindenburg and Ludendorff. Not until September, 1918, when the military leaders admitted that the war was lost, was there a resurgence of demands for democratic reform. Then two revolutions followed in quick succession.

PARLIAMENTARY GOVERNMENT (OCTOBER 1918). On September 30, 1918, the Kaiser issued a proclamation granting full representative and parliamentary government, and on October 3, appointed the liberal Prince Max of Baden to carry the proposed reforms into effect. Unfortunately, the concessions had been forced from the Kaiser only by the desperate military situation, and this situation did not improve as a result of the change in government. While Prince Max was hurriedly pushing through liberalizing, constitutional changes, he was forced to sue for terms of peace. President Wilson notified him that no terms could be granted until the "military masters and monarchial aristocrats" of Germany were shorn of all power. At once there arose a popular demand for the abdication of the Kaiser. At the end of October a mutiny broke out among the sailors at Kiel, and revolutionary activity quickly spread throughout the country. Still William II refused to abdicate. Finally, the General Staff informed him that they could no longer protect him, and on November 10, he fled to Holland. On the previous day Prince Max had resigned at the demand of the Social Democrat leaders, Ebert and Scheidemann.

GERMAN REPUBLIC (1919). Chaotic conditions followed the resignation of Prince Max and the flight of the Kaiser. The armistice, bringing an end to the actual fighting of the war, was signed November 11, but the Allied blockade continued. Economic hardship was increased by the crippling of the nation's railway system that followed the surrender of 3,000 locomotives and 100,000 cars. The struggle between the Majority Socialists, led by Ebert and Scheidemann, and the Spartacists, or Communists, led by Karl Liebknecht and Rosa Luxemburg, nearly developed into civil war. But in January 1919 a mass demonstration in Berlin of Spartacists intended to overthrow the provisional government of Ebert, but dispersed without attempting to enforce their demands, and a few days later the leaders, Liebknecht and Rosa Luxemburg, were arrested and murdered. The Spartacist movement then collapsed. On January 9 elections for a national assembly were held. The assembly met at Weimar on February 6. A heavy majority of the delegates were Majority Socialists (Social Democrats), Centrists, and Democrats. On February 11 the assembly elected Ebert as president. A republican constitution was drawn up and adopted, July 31.

Independent Poland. Ever since its partition by Austria, Prussia, and Russia, Poland had hoped for independence. The revolts of the Poles against Russia in 1830 and 1863 were cruelly suppressed. In World War I the Poles of Russia found themselves fighting the Poles of Germany. Leaders favoring national independence were divided on whether to support Russia or the Central Powers. When Russia withdrew from the war, the Poles discovered that Germany had no intention of allowing a strong, independent Polish state, so they almost unanimously turned against the Central Powers.

With the collapse of the Central Powers, the Poles in Galicia, Posen, West Prussia, and Silesia demanded the right to join Poland. The new republic became a fact in November 1918 with Pilsudski as president and Paderewski as premier (1919).

PROBLEMS OF ESTABLISHING PEACE

Aims of the Allies. During the war the Allies had claimed that they were the champions of right and justice against their enemies, as typified by the Central Powers. But this claim was mainly propaganda. Right and justice in the minds of the Allied statesmen took the form of certain specific advantages. France wanted Alsace-Lorraine; Great Britain was anxious to curb Germany's sea-power; Italy wished *Italia irredenta;* the Balkan states desired complete independence; and Japan wanted to extend her power in the Pacific. The imperialistic designs of the several Allied Powers were set forth in a series of secret treaties which had been made during the war.

Wilson's Peace Program. The United States did not wish any territorial gains but entered the war "to make the world safe for democracy" and to end wars. In a message to Congress (January 1918), Wilson set forth his Fourteen Points as a program for a lasting peace—(1) abolition of secret diplomacy, (2) freedom of the seas, (3) removal of economic barriers, (4) reduction of armaments, (5) impartial adjustment of colonial claims, (6) evacuation of Russia, (7) restoration of Belgium, (8) cession of Alsace-Lorraine to France, (9) readjustment of Italian frontiers, (10) acceptance of the principle of self-determination, (11) evacuation of the Balkans by the Central Powers, (12) autonomy for non-Turkish nationalities and the opening of the Dardanelles to all ships, (13) creation of an independent Poland, and (14) the creation of an association of nations to guarantee independence to all nations. While some of these points coincided with the specific aims of the European Allies, the spirit of Wilson's program was quite contradictory to the spirit of the secret treaties. Nevertheless, the Fourteen Points were accepted by the Allies (with certain reservations) as the basis on which peace was to be made, and it was with this definite understanding that the Germans signed the armistice. The problem of the Peace Conference was to be the problem of reconciling the selfish and revengeful ambitions of the Allies with the idealism of the Fourteen Points.

THE PEACE CONFERENCE (1919)

The Peace Conference opened on January 18, 1919, just forty-eight years after the proclamation of the German Empire in the same palace at Versailles. The members of the Conference included such notables as Wilson, Lansing, and House of the United States; Lloyd George and Balfour of Great Britain; Clemenceau and Foch of France; General Smuts of South Africa; Orlando of Italy; and Venizelos of Greece. The real leaders were the "Big Four"—Clemenceau, Lloyd George, Orlando, and Wilson. Most of the work was done by experts. The terms were skillfully worked out so as to give an outward appearance of conformity with the Fourteen Points while actually providing for the maximum punishment of Germany and the maximum aggrandizement of the Allies. Wilson acquiesced to compromises in order to assure the organization of a league of nations. He recognized many of the injustices of the treaty but hoped that these might be removed by revision in future years through the medium of the League of Nations and the new world-order he hoped the League would bring. When the treaty was finally completed, the German representatives were admitted to the Congress to accept it. The Germans protested its severity, pointing out its inconsistency with the Fourteen Points, but their disarmament made them helpless, and they finally agreed to accept the treaty. On June 28, 1919, it was signed as the Treaty of Versailles. Other treaties were drawn up with the other countries.

TREATY OF VERSAILLES

Territorial Provisions. (1) Alsace-Lorraine ceded to France. (2) Posen and a corridor about sixty miles wide separating Pomerania from East Prussia and fronting the Baltic Sea ceded to Poland. (3) Small districts including the towns of Eupen, Malmedy, and Moresnet ceded to Belgium.

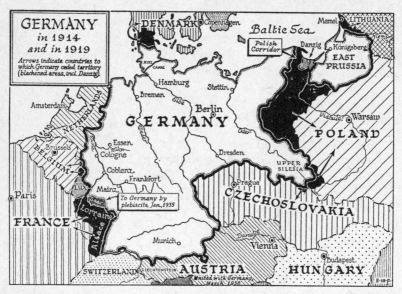

GERMANY in 1914 and in 1919

Arrows indicate countries to which Germany ceded territory (blackened areas, incl. Danzig)

To Germany by plebiscite, Jan. 1935

United with Germany March 1938

(4) City of Danzig and surrounding territory (about 700 square miles) organized as a free city under the League of Nations, its foreign relations to be controlled by Poland. (5) City of Memel and strip of territory northeast of River Memel (Nieman) ceded to the Allies (turned over to Lithuania in 1924). (6) Plebiscites to be held in Schleswig, Upper Silesia,

and certain districts in East Prussia. (As a result of the plebiscites, the northern part of Schleswig was ceded to Denmark; about 1,500 square miles of Upper Silesia, including the most valuable mines and industries, was ceded to Poland.) (7) All Germany's overseas possessions were surrendered. They were later turned over to Great Britain, France, Belgium, and Japan as mandates of the League of Nations.

Miscellaneous Economic and Territorial Provisions. (1) The coal mines of the Saar Basin were ceded to France with the privilege of repurchase by Germany after fifteen years. The Saar territory was to be administered by the League of Nations until 1935, when a plebiscite was to decide its ultimate disposition. (2) Germany lost all her commercial concessions and economic spheres of influence in China, Siam, Liberia, Egypt, Morocco, and other backward regions. (3) Luxemburg was severed from the German Customs Union and united economically with Belgium. (4) Complex arrangements were included to secure virtual Allied control of the German river system.

Military and Naval Provisions. The intention of the military provisions of the Treaty was to reduce Germany's armaments and means of armament to such a point as to render her helpless. (1) Germany's army was reduced to a maximum of 100,000 men. (2) Conscription was abolished, and voluntary enlistments were to be accepted for twelve-year periods for private soldiers and twenty-five-year periods for officers (to make impossible the building up of a trained reserve by rotation of service). (3) The German navy was to be reduced to a skeleton patrol with tonnage of ships severely restricted and submarines entirely prohibited. (4) The entire area west of the Rhine and a zone fifty kilometers deep east of the Rhine was to be demilitarized forever; all fortifications were to be destroyed and garrisons prohibited. (5) The manufacture of arms was to be supervised by an Allied commission, and all heavy armaments—tanks, bombing planes, and large caliber artillery—were prohibited. (6) Naval fortifications at Heligoland were to be destroyed. The Kiel Canal was to be demilitarized.

Reparations. Under the celebrated Article 231, Germany accepted responsibility "for causing all the loss and damage to which the Allied and Associated Governments and their nationals have been subjected as a consequence of the war imposed upon them. . . ." The legal claim for financial reparations, however, was based upon the qualifying note of the Allies that accompanied Wilson's Fourteen Points in the pre-armistice offer to make peace. The note declared that "compensation will be made by Germany for all damage done to the civilian population of the Allies. . . ." After much discussion it was decided that such expenses as pensions to ex-soldiers and allowances made to soldiers' families during the absence of the soldiers at the front could legitimately be included. As part payment on account of reparations, Germany was to turn over (1) her entire merchant marine, (2) large quantities of live stock, raw materials, coal, chemicals, etc., and (3) $5,000,000,000 in cash before May 21, 1921. The total amount of reparations was ultimately fixed by a Reparations Commission at $27,000,000,000. As this amount was vastly in excess of Germany's ability to pay, the actual effect of the reparations section of the Treaty was to impose upon Germany an economic serfdom from which she could never free herself without revision of the Treaty's terms.

Guarantees. The German area west of the Rhine was to be occupied (at Germany's expense) by Allied Troops for a period of fifteen years. The bridgeheads at Cologne, Coblenz, and Mainz were included. Evacuation of these zones was to take place in three stages at intervals of five years, provided the terms of the Treaty were faithfully kept.

Summary of Economic Effects of the Treaty. The losses inflicted on the German economy by the Treaty included: (1) One-eighth of her area and about one-tenth of her population, (2) Two-thirds of her iron ore, half of her coal, three-fourths of her zinc ore, half of her lead ore, and nearly all her potash, (3) Practically all her foreign investments, amounting to one-tenth of her total wealth, (4) One-sixth of her agricultural produce and one-tenth of her manufacturing plants

ADDITIONAL TREATIES

Treaty of St. Germain (September 1919). This treaty with Austria was similar to the Treaty of Versailles. It provided that (1) the Republic of Austria accept partial guilt for the war and hence liability for reparations, (2) no union be permitted between Austria and Germany, (3) the Austrian army be reduced to 30,000, (4) her navy be restricted to three police boats on the Danube, and (5) Austria recognize the independence of Hungary, Czechoslovakia, Poland, and Yugoslavia.

Austria became a small, impoverished country without access to the sea surrounded by the customs barriers of the newly arisen hostile states. No other nation suffered such great hardship in the years following the war.

Treaty of Neuilly (November 1919). This treaty with Bulgaria provided that Rumania should get Dobrudja; Yugoslavia most of Macedonia; and that Greece should get western Thrace and the Aegean coast. Bulgaria's army was to be reduced to 20,000 men, and her navy was to be practically abolished. She was also made liable for reparations.

Treaty of Trianon (June 1920). According to the treaty with Hungary, she gave up the Slovak provinces to Czechoslovakia; Transylvania to Rumania; Croatia to Yugoslavia; and Banat to Rumania and Yugoslavia. Hungary was thus reduced to an unimportant state of Central Europe. In none of the other treaties was the principle of self-determination (Point 10 of the Fourteen Points) so grossly violated as in the case of Hungary; nearly one-fourth of the Hungarian nationals were assigned to neighboring hostile states.

Treaty of Sèvres (August 1920). The problem of settling a peace with Turkey was extremely difficult because of the desires of the different Allied Powers. Finally, it was agreed that (1) Hejaz would be controlled by Great Britain; (2) Palestine, Mesopotamia, and the Jordan territory would be mandates of Great Britain; (3) Syria would be made a French mandate; (4) spheres of influence would be given to France in Cilicia and to Italy in Anatolia; (5) Greece would obtain Thrace, Adrianople, Gallipoli, the islands of Imbros and Tenedos, and the Dodecanese Islands which Italy had occupied; and (6) the Dardanelles would be internationalized. Although the Sultan signed the treaty, the National Assembly under Mustapha Kemal Pasha refused to ratify it.

The
BALKANS

Treaty of Lausanne (July 1923). Italy and France, jealous of the privileges conferred upon Great Britain and Greece in the Treaty of Sèvres, concluded separate treaties with Turkey, after the aggressive campaign of the Turkish army had blotted out Armenia and forced the Italians and

French out of Anatolia and Cilicia, respectively. Encouraged by Great Britain, the Greeks precipitated another Graeco-Turkish War (1921-1922). The army of the Turkish Nationalists was successful. It not only drove the Greeks out of Smyrna but also deposed Mohammed VI and made possible a new settlement of the Near East. The Treaty of Lausanne modified the Treaty of Sèvres by giving Turkey control of Anatolia, Armenia, Cilicia, Adalia, Smyrna, Constantinople, Gallipoli, Adrianople, and eastern Thrace. Turkey was not compelled to reduce her army and navy or to pay reparations. By her successful resistance to the dictated Treaty of Sèvres, she obtained independence from international control, and was actually in a better position to develop along national lines than she had been before the war.

Special Agreements. Besides the treaties already discussed, there were several agreements that are considered a part of the "Peace of Paris." Rumania was allowed to annex Bessarabia (1920), and Poland was given a limited mandate over Eastern Galicia. Italy's claims to Dalmatia, the port of Fiume, and the Adriatic islands caused considerable trouble. In spite of the opposition of the League, and without governmental sanction, D'Annunzio seized Fiume. By an agreement in 1920, Fiume was recognized as a free city, like Danzig, and Italy was given Zara, Istria (as far as Fiume), and a part of the Dalmatian coast. Treaties protecting the racial, linguistic, religious, and economic equality of the numerous national minorities included within the new national states were also consummated. It was recognized by President Wilson that nothing was "more likely to disturb the peace of the world than the treatment which might in certain circumstances be meted out to minorities." In spite of the minorities' treaties, the future was to confirm Wilson's judgment.

Alliances of 1919-1920. To insure the carrying out of the provisions of the "Peace of Paris," and to prevent a war of revenge by Germany, Great Britain and the United States promised to aid France in case of any aggression on Germany's part (1919). As the United States failed to ratify this treaty, France entered into agreements with Poland and Belgium

(1920). At the same time, the states of Czechoslovakia, Yugoslavia, and Rumania formed a "Little Entente" and proceeded to coöperate with France and her allies.

LEAGUE OF NATIONS

The last of the Fourteen Points called for the creation of a "general association of nations" to afford "mutual guarantees of political independence and territorial integrity to great and small states alike." The first twenty-six articles of each of the peace treaties set forth the "Covenant of the League of Nations." To Wilson and to many liberals and idealists, the establishment of the League of Nations redeemed whatever other mistakes and extravagances might be contained in the treaties and gave promise for a new departure in world affairs. It was hoped that the League would maintain peace, promote the solution of international disputes by the methods of law, make possible the reduction of armaments, and lead to general international coöperation. The horrors and costs of the War were fresh in the minds of the peoples of the world, and there seemed to be a better chance than ever before for nations to abandon their pretensions to absolute sovereignty in the interest of the common good.

Membership. The original membership of the League consisted of the Allied and Associated Powers ratifying the treaties, together with a group of invited neutrals. Future members were to be elected on application by a two-thirds vote of the existing members. In 1920 forty-two states were members, including all the Allied powers except Ecuador, Hejaz, and the United States; in 1931 sixty-two states were members, including all independent countries of importance except the Soviet Union and the United States. Between 1931 and 1938 five countries resigned from the League—Brazil, Costa Rica, Germany, Japan, and Paraguay—but Afghanistan, Ecuador, and the Soviet Union joined. In 1935-1936 one of the members of the League—Ethiopia—was forcibly consolidated with another member, Italy. In 1938 another member, Austria, was absorbed by a non-member, Germany. At the end of 1938 these changes had not been officially recognized by the League, but they appeared permanent.

LEAGUE OF NATIONS

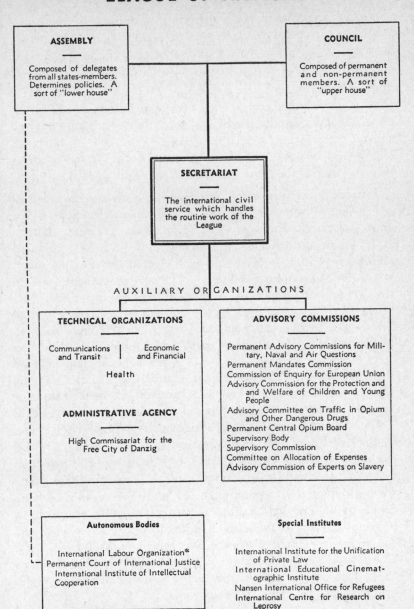

ASSEMBLY

Composed of delegates from all states-members. Determines policies. A sort of "lower house"

COUNCIL

Composed of permanent and non-permanent members. A sort of "upper house"

SECRETARIAT

The international civil service which handles the routine work of the League

AUXILIARY ORGANIZATIONS

TECHNICAL ORGANIZATIONS

Communications and Transit | Economic and Financial

Health

ADMINISTRATIVE AGENCY

High Commissariat for the Free City of Danzig

ADVISORY COMMISSIONS

Permanent Advisory Commissions for Military, Naval and Air Questions
Permanent Mandates Commission
Commission of Enquiry for European Union
Advisory Commission for the Protection and and Welfare of Children and Young People
Advisory Committee on Traffic in Opium and Other Dangerous Drugs
Permanent Central Opium Board
Supervisory Body
Supervisory Commission
Committee on Allocation of Expenses
Advisory Commission of Experts on Slavery

Autonomous Bodies

International Labour Organization*
Permanent Court of International Justice
International Institute of Intellectual Cooperation

Special Institutes

International Institute for the Unification of Private Law
International Educational Cinematographic Institute
Nansen International Office for Refugees
International Centre for Research on Leprosy

Assembly. The Assembly of the League consisted of the representatives of all the member states, each state being entitled to one vote. The Assembly was a deliberative, consultative, and advisory body, but without power to legislate or compel acceptance of its decisions. It made the budget for the League, elected the non-permanent members of the Council (see below), admitted new states to the League, and advised the reconsideration of treaties that had become inapplicable. The Assembly met annually at Geneva. However, no meetings were held after the Nazi conquest of Holland (1940).

Council. The Council originally was to be composed of one delegate from each of nine states: five "Principal Allied and Associated Powers" — namely, France, Great Britain, Italy, Japan, and the United States, who were to be permanent members,—and four lesser powers elected by the Assembly, who were to serve for fixed terms. The non-permanent seats on the Council were expected to rotate among the minor members of the League. As a result of the non-adherence of the United States, the permanent members of the Council were reduced to four, while the non-permanent were increased to six. In 1926 Germany was admitted and given a permanent seat on the Council. In 1934 the Soviet Union was admitted to the League and similarly given a permanent Council seat. But decline had already begun. Japan and Germany resigned in 1932-1933, Italy in 1937, and France in 1941. The Soviet Union in 1939 was expelled for aggression against Finland. During the political life of the League the Council was the principal executive power. Its functions were (1) to formulate plans for the reduction of armaments, (2) to advise on means to be taken by the whole League to protect member states from aggression, (3) to mediate disputes between members, and (4) to receive reports from Mandatory powers (see below). The Council met three times a year at Geneva and could be called into emergency session. All important decisions of the Council were required to be *unanimous*.

Permanent Secretariat. The Permanent Secretariat consisted of a Secretary-General appointed by the Council and approved by a majority vote of the Assembly, together with a staff of investigators, secretaries, interpreters, and clerks.

The functions of the Secretariat, prior to its dismissal in 1940, were (1) to collect and compile data on international problems, (2) to register treaties, and (3) to act as secretaries at deliberations of the Council and of the Assembly. A small staff remained at Geneva after the German conquests to carry on certain non-political activities for the League.

Supplemental Bureaus. A number of technical organizations and advisory committees were set up by the League for the handling of special problems.

Important Articles of the Covenant. The important articles of the Covenant intended to preserve peace were articles 10, 12, and 16.

Article 10. This article, described by Wilson as "the heart of the Covenant," was the main obstacle to ratification of the Covenant by the United States Senate. It was attacked as a blanket abdication of sovereignty and a commitment that might in the future require the United States to go to war when no question of American interest was involved. It read as follows:

"The Members of the League undertake to respect and preserve as against external aggression the territorial integrity and existing political independence of all Members of the League. In case of such aggression or in case of any threat or danger of such aggression the Council shall advise upon the means by which this obligation shall be fulfilled."

Article 12. This article provided that member nations submit "any dispute likely to lead to a rupture" to arbitration or judicial settlement or inquiry by the Council. League members further agreed in no case to resort to war until three months after the award by the arbitrators, the judicial settlement, or the report by the Council.

Article 16. This article provided for the coercion of any "covenant-breaking" state by the joint action of the members of the League.

"1. Should any Member of the League resort to war in disregard of its covenants under Articles 12, 13, or 15, it shall *ipso facto* be deemed to have committed an act of war against all other members of the League, which hereby undertake immediately to subject it to the severance of all trade or financial relations, the prohibition of all intercourse between their nationals and the nationals of the Covenant-breaking state. . . ."

"2. It shall be the duty of the Council in such case to recommend to the several governments concerned what effective military, naval, or air force the Members of the League shall severally contribute. . . ."

SUCCESSES AND FAILURES OF THE LEAGUE (1920-1939)

Preservation of Peace. A number of political disputes were satisfactorily settled by the League. The most important of these were (1) the Albanian boundary dispute (Greece, Italy, Yugoslavia) settled, 1921, (2) the Mosul Boundary dispute (Great Britain, Turkey) settled, 1926, (3) the Graeco-Bulgarian border violation dispute settled, 1926, (4) the Aaland Islands dispute (Sweden, Finland) settled, 1931 after ten years of negotiations, and (5) the Letician dispute (Columbia, Peru) settled, 1934. In some other cases, such as the Upper Silesia dispute between Germany and Poland in 1921, the Graeco-Italian dispute of 1923 in which Italy seized the island of Corfu to enforce a claim of indemnity from Greece, and the Chaco dispute between Paraguay and Bolivia settled in 1935, a settlement was effected through the instrumentality of the League, but the terms were what they probably would have been if the League had not acted. In serious disputes such as the Sino-Japanese disputes of 1931 and 1937, the Italo-Ethiopian dispute of 1935, the German seizure of Austria in 1938, and the partition of Czechoslovakia under a threat of force by Germany in 1938, the League's success was insignificant. The most serious effort was made in the Italo-Ethiopian case, when the League voted "sanctions" against Italy under article 16 of the Covenant. The "sanctions," however, did not include an effective blockade and did not cut off Italy from essential supplies of oil. In July 1936, having proved ineffective, the "sanctions" were withdrawn. In 1937 the League passed resolutions branding Japan as an aggressor and condemning her bombardment of open cities in China but did not adopt any coercive measures. In 1938 the League was not even appealed to in the cases of Austria and Czechoslovakia.

The Conference of Munich, September, 1938, appeared to have administered the coup de grace to the League as an instrument of "collective security" and substituted a new form of European Concert of Great Powers. However, the League did meet in a special session after the Russian invasion of Finland. It voted to expel Russia from the League and to send assistance to the Finns. The League also proved entirely unsuccessful in its purpose of reducing armaments.

Fostering of International Coöperation. While the League was disappointing in its handling of the problems of peace and disarmament for which purpose it was mainly founded, it more than justified its existence by promoting international coöperation in other fields.

ECONOMIC REHABILITATION OF AUSTRIA AND HUNGARY. Postwar conditions produced desperate economic distress in Austria. In 1922 the League Council arranged for a loan up to $135,000,000 and appointed a commissioner-general to supervise Austrian finances. Undoubtedly many thousands of Austrian people were saved from sheer starvation by these measures. Similar assistance was extended to Hungary in 1924.

GREEK AND BULGARIAN REFUGEE PROBLEMS. In 1924 the League arranged for a loan of $50,000,000 to Greece to assist in the care of more than 1,000,000 refugees ruined by the Graeco-Turkish war of 1922. In 1926 $11,000,000 was loaned to Bulgaria for the care of refugees.

MISCELLANEOUS SOCIAL PROJECTS. Under the auspices of the League a large amount of international social work has been accomplished of a sort that would have been difficult, if not impossible, without an organization representing a concert of the civilized world rather than of any single power. Coöperation in health and sanitation work, in the control of the traffic in narcotic drugs, in the suppression of slavery and the international traffic in women, and in the extension of scientific and intellectual relations has been fostered. These activities are frequently overlooked by critics of the League who fix their attention on the failure of the League to limit armaments and to outlaw war.

Mandates. The surrendered colonies of Germany and Turkey were turned over to the control of the Allied powers under a system of mandates, which made the governing powers responsible to the League for the welfare of the populations governed. While selfish exploitation of colonial possessions still continue, the mandate system represented a break from the old absolute sovereignty theory under which protest or even inquiry by foreign nations was considered an unwarranted interference.

Minorities. The League of Nations became responsible for the protection of the 30,000,000 people who, under the peace treaties, were included within the boundaries of foreign states. The mixture of races and languages especially in eastern and southeastern Europe is such that it is impossible to draw boundaries so as not to include large minorities within every one of the national states. The problem was complicated by economic and strategic considerations. The treaties previously mentioned (Special Agreements, p. 195) guaranteeing minimum rights to the minority nationalities were to be enforced by the League. But the problem of the minorities was never satisfactorily solved and remained one of the most dangerous threats to the League of Nations. The rise of dictatorial governments, the world economic depression of the 1930's, and the recrudescence of racial, religious, and political persecution greatly aggravated the difficulties. The prestige of the League of Nations sunk to a low ebb as a result of Hitler's successful resort to force in dealing with minority groups.

Saar Basin. Under the Treaty of Versailles the Saar Basin, an area, rich in coal, 740 square miles on the border between France and Germany was detached from Germany and administered by the League of Nations through a commission. The coal mines were to be turned over to France for exploitation for fifteen years, and a plebiscite was then to be held to determine the ultimate disposition of the territory. Between 1920 and 1926 the French government dominated the Saar administration and attempted by many improper means to detach the inhabitants from their German loyalty. On the complaint of Great Britain, the League instituted an investigation which resulted in more equitable treatment. In 1935 the plebiscite required by the Treaty resulted in an overwhelming victory for Germany, and on March 1, the League returned the Saar Basin to Germany.

Danzig. The city of Danzig and the surrounding area was made a "free city" under the League of Nations by the terms of the Treaty of Versailles. Its population was about 95% German. The League's administration was moderately successful during the first thirteen years and settled peaceably several economic and political controversies with Poland and Germany. With the rise of the Nazi government in Germany, however, new difficulties were created. Repeated appeals were made to the League to prevent the persecution of anti-Nazi elements in Danzig, especially after the elections of 1935 had returned a Nazi majority to the Volkstag, or legislature. These protests and appeals were, at the end of 1938, doomed to failure.

INDEPENDENT CREATIONS OF THE LEAGUE[1]

Permanent Court of International Justice. This organization, usually known in the United States as the World Court, was provided for in Article 14 of the League Covenant. The purpose of the Court was to decide questions of interpretation of treaties and obligations under international law. It could settle disputes between nations and also furnish the League Council or Assembly with "advisory opinions" on submitted questions. Forty-two nations, including France, Germany, Great Britain, and Italy, signed the protocol binding themselves to accept the jurisdiction of the Court in legal disputes. Other nations could voluntarily submit cases to the Court. The Court sat continuously at The Hague. It should not be confused, however, with The Hague Tribunal, established by The Hague Conference of 1899 for the arbitration of disputes. The World Court did not arbitrate, but delivered judicial decisions on legal questions.

International Labor Organization. Under Article 23 of the Covenant, the League undertook "to secure and maintain fair and humane conditions of labor for men, women, and children" in all countries. An International Labor Organization (I. L. O.) was set up within the framework of the League, but

---

[1] Continued to function after the beginning of World War II.

it was an entirely autonomous organization (like the World Court), and nations not members of the League could participate. The purpose of the I. L. O. was to study labor conditions throughout the world and make recommendations that were submitted to the governments of the various nations. More than fifty such recommendations were made, to the substantial benefit of laboring men, especially in the less advanced countries of South America and Asia.

THE UNITED STATES
AND THE WORLD SETTLEMENT

Repudiation of the League of Nations. The "Peace of Paris," especially the League of Nations, was unfavorably received in the United States. According to the United States Constitution, treaties with foreign powers must be ratified by a two-thirds vote of the Senate, and in the fall of 1918, Wilson had attempted to insure support for his program by appealing to the voters to elect Democratic candidates to Congress. The appeal was disregarded, and Republican majorities were returned to both houses. Wilson made little effort to conciliate the leaders of the new Senate, and did not take them into his confidence during the Paris negotiations. When he returned from Paris in 1919, he found himself faced by a strong opposition. The war fever had cooled, and a wave of disillusionment had swept over the American people. Wilson's personal popularity was fast declining. His supporters in the Senate controlled slightly more than one-third of the votes and were hence able to block any alternative treaty. But there was no chance of securing acceptance of the treaty as presented. The opposition consisted of two groups (1) "Irreconcilables," or "bitter-enders," opposed to all participation in the League of Nations, and (2) "Reservationists," led by Senator Lodge of Massachusetts, willing to vote for ratification if certain "reservations" (described by Wilson as "nullifying") were adopted. Wilson fought for ratification of the Treaty without change, although he was willing to accept "interpretative" reservations. For more than a year the Senate remained deadlocked. In the presidential campaign of 1920 the chief issue was support or repudiation of Wilson and the League of Nations he sponsored. Wilson himself wished the election to be "a great and solemn referendum" on the Treaty. The issue was, however, confused by the efforts of such prominent pro-League Republicans as William H. Taft and George W. Wickersham to maintain that the best way of getting the United States into the League was through the election of the Republican candidate, Warren G. Harding. But the overwhelming victory of Harding was taken as a mandate against American participation in the League. In 1921-1922 the United States signed separate treaties with Germany, Austria, and Hungary, and withdrew all American troops from Europe.

Washington Conference (1921-1922). Although the United States thus refused to join the European "Peace of Paris," she took an active part in the post-war settlement by calling a conference of great powers at Washington to consider arms limitation and discuss matters of mutual concern. An agreement on naval armaments was reached fixing the future strength of the navies of Great Britain, the United States, Japan, France, and Italy according to the ratio 5:5:3:1.75:1.75 respectively. No agreement was reached regarding land or air armaments, but some conventions were adopted condemning the use in war of poison gas and other unpopular devices. A series of treaties was signed covering relations of the powers in the Far East. Japan returned Kiao-Chau to China and sold her interest in the Shantung railway; Great Britain gave up Wei-Hei-Wei; France arranged to withdraw from Kwang-Chow-Wan. The powers agreed to respect the independence of China and not to seek special privileges there but to maintain the "open-door" policy. In the Four-Power Treaty, France, Great Britain, Japan, and the United States promised not to molest each other's possessions in the Far East. Disputes were to be settled by arbitration.

CHAPTER XVIII.

THE INTERLUDE BETWEEN WARS
1918-1939

World War I brought to an end the autocratic Romanov dynasty in Russia, and the resulting revolution enabled that country to carry on an economic, social, and political experiment which was unique in history.

The March Revolution (1917). During the early defeats in the World War, Nicholas II (1894-1917) did not alter his policies but continued to ignore the demands of the political parties and the submerged nationalities. Naturally, popular discontent increased. The decrees of Nicholas dissolved the Duma and commanded the workingmen to cease striking. The Duma refused to dissolve, the workingmen continued to strike, and, with the help of the military garrison, a workingmen's council (soviet) was established at Petrograd. Nicholas II abdicated in favor of his brother, but the Grand Duke Michael did not attempt to carry on the Romanov dynasty because he knew it was hopeless. A provisional government, predominantly bourgeois, was established with Prince George Lvov as President. A program of liberal reform was planned, and a constituent assembly was to be elected to draw up a constitution.

The November Revolution (1917). The attempt of the middle class to establish a democratic government was hampered by (1) the numerous national groups within the country, (2) the lack of any popular enthusiasm for an orderly democracy, and (3) the proletariat which desired economic and social reform. Soviets were formed, discipline in the army became lax, and the Bolshevists demanded the consummation of a peace with Germany. The aggressive Milyukóv, as Minister of Foreign Affairs, desired to continue the War, but as the Soviets increased in power, they forced him to resign. With the help of Socialists, Alexander Kerensky tried to guide the Provisional Government, but the opposition of the Constitutional Democrats, Bolshevists, and reactionaries was too great. The Bolshevists increased in power and numbers. In November, the "Red Guards" (Bolshevists) overthrew Kerensky's provisional government and gained control of the National Congress of Soviets. The political revolution of March was superseded by the economic and social revolution of November.

Bolshevist Russia (1918-1924). Under the leadership of Nicholai Lenin (Vladimir Ulyanov) and Leon Trotsky (Leon Bronstein), the Bolshevist program was carried forward. The objectives were (1) to arrange a peace with the Central Powers, (2) to make the proletariat supreme, (3) to foster economic and social reforms, (4) to consolidate Russia, and (5) to spread communism throughout the world.

Treaty of Brest-Litovsk (1918). The humiliating **Treaty** of Brest-Litovsk was signed because it was impossible for the Bolshevists to carry out their program while still at war. Even though they lost about one-fourth of their land, the terms were beneficial, for Russia was now more homogeneous.

The Proletariat's Dictatorship. The election of a majority of Social Revolutionary delegates to the National Constituent Assembly was distasteful to Lenin and Trotsky. They caused the assembly to be dissolved, and a new body was substituted which was pro-Bolshevist. The Soviet Constitution (1918) gave the franchise to the workers, revolutionary soldiers, and sailors, and denied this privilege to the clergy, nobility, and most of the middle class. A Central Executive

Committee which was responsible to the National Congress made laws and appointed ministers (People's Commissioners). The supremacy of the proletariat was strengthened by organizing an army of the laboring classes and by establishing a judicial system, which would be of service in curbing the anti-Bolshevists. One of these courts was responsible for the condemnation and execution of the Tsar and his family (July 1918).

ECONOMIC REFORMS.   Lenin and his followers had a difficult time during the first four years of governmental control of land and industry due to the ignorance of the people, the opposition of the anti-Bolshevists, and the unstable conditions throughout Europe. To overcome this opposition, Lenin instituted a "New Economic Policy" (NEP) in 1921, which was a combination of state socialism and private capitalism. The NEP was supplanted in 1928 by the "Five Year Plan." The new plan provided for the industrialization of all Russia by 1933. A second "Five Year Plan" was started in 1933, which aimed to increase the production of consumers' goods industries. Non-aggression pacts were arranged in 1934 to continue for a ten-year period. Agricultural pursuits have been speeded by establishing state farms and introducing efficient implements.

SOCIAL REFORMS.   The Bolshevists introduced radical reforms which made Russia a socialistic state. Private ownership of capital property was abolished, and the state took over the control of land and industry. The control of all education was in the hands of the Soviet government. All religion was discouraged, and by 1933 over 70,000 churches had been closed. A philosophy of life which centers around communism was substituted. These changes have been brought about in spite of the fact that the Bolshevists make up less than 2 per cent of the total population of Russia.

BOLSHEVISTS IN CONTROL.   The activities of the advocates of the new social order aroused fear, and caused various governments to array themselves against Russia. From the Treaty of Brest-Litovsk to the collapse of the Central Powers, Germany interfered effectively in Russia. The Allies also opposed Bolshevism during 1918-1919 and encouraged anti-Bolshevist activities. They subsidized and supplied the "White" armies that were supporting the counter-revolutionary government of Admiral Kolchak (provisionally set up at Omsk, Siberia in November 1918). After considerable fighting the Red Army under Trotsky succeeded in forcing foreign and "White" armies from European Russia (1920). Thousands of anti-Bolshevists were ordered shot by the "Cheka" (Supreme Extraordinary Commission to Combat Counter-Revolution and Speculation) which was organized by Dzerzhinisky (1917-1922). Lenin abolished the Cheka but found it necessary to organize a large group of secret police (OGPU) to root out opponents. The Bolshevists were successful in suppressing opposition from within and without.

BOLSHEVISTS ATTEMPT TO REVOLUTIONIZE THE WORLD. Not content with their success in Russia, the Bolshevists' agents sought to overthrow capitalism in other countries. They were able to regain control of the Ukraine, but in other countries the Communists were not strong enough to affect the old order.

FOREIGN POLICY. The original plan to foster world revolution and overthrow capitalism was temporarily abandoned in order to gain foreign financial aid, machinery, and experts to help lessen the industrial and commercial crisis at home. A series of treaties, supplanting the Treaty of Brest-Litovsk, recognized the independence of Finland, Esthonia, Latvia, Lithuania, and Poland. At the Genoa Conference (1922) between Russia and her creditors, the Soviet representatives refused to recognize foreign debts of the Tsarist regime, public or private, on the basis set forth by the Allies. For a while, the European powers refused to have anything to do with Russia, but in 1922, Germany signed the Treaty of Rapallo which granted *de jure* recognition to the Soviet Union.

Union of the Soviet Socialist Republics under Stalin (1924-1939). After the death of Lenin, Joseph Stalin (Joseph Visserionovich Dzhugashvili), son of a Georgian shoemaker, became the leader of the Communists and the dominant force in the Soviet government.

OPPOSITION TO STALIN. Among the men who aspired to succeed Lenin were Leon Trotsky, first commissar for foreign affairs; Zinoviev, organizer and head of the Third Internationale; Dzerzhinsky, former head of the Cheka; Rykov, Lenin's secretary; Kamenev, vice-president of the Union Council of People's Commissars; and Bukharin, a good publicity agent for Communism. At first Zinoviev and Kamenev joined Stalin to oust Trotsky. Later Zinoviev joined with Trotsky in criticising Stalin because of his compromises with capitalism and his decision to postpone indefinitely plans seeking the overthrow of capitalism outside of Russia.

DOMESTIC PROGRAM OF STALIN. The first "Five Year Plan" established distributive and productive schedules which aimed to industrialize the U. S. S. R. by 1933. A second "Five Year Plan" (1933-1938) sought to raise the general standard of living and to increase the production of the consumers' goods industries. Educational opportunities were expanded and compulsory school regulations made more stringent. Rigid supervision and control of the schools were exercised by the Commissariat. A new constitution, with provision for civil and political rights, was adopted in December 1936. Meanwhile, a group of prominent "Old Bolsheviks" were tried, found guilty, and shot for participation in a so-called Trotsky counter-revolution plot. Zinoviev and Kamenev were among those convicted.

FOREIGN AFFAIRS (1924-1938). Stalin set about to restore the Soviet Union to the family of nations by a cooperative foreign policy. By 1932 nearly all countries except the United States had followed Germany's lead and completed agreements for *de jure* recognition. Finally, the negotiations between Maxim Litvinov and President Roosevelt resulted in the recognition of the U. S. S. R. by the United States (1933). Non-aggression pacts to continue for a ten-year period were arranged with several countries (1934). The admission of Russia to the League of Nations (1934) was the high spot of Maxim Litvinov's foreign policy. The Soviet Union and France later entered into a mutual military assistance pact (1936). This agreement was one of the pretexts used by Hitler for remilitarization of the Rhine. Russian relations with all countries, except Germany and Japan, improved steadily during the years 1935-1938. At the end of 1938, however, as a result of the Czechoslovakian crisis and the Conference of Munich (see Chapter XIX) Soviet Russia was again diplomatically isolated.

STALIN AS DICTATOR. Stalin continued to strengthen his position as dictator by stifling all opposition. After he gained control of the Communist party, the leaders of the opposition, including Trotsky, were exiled. His policy was to gain security through coöperation with the capitalistic countries and to make the USSR a self-sufficient socialistic state.

GERMANY (1918-1939)

The history of Germany during this period fell into two divisions: the first part found the Republic in the control of Friedrich Ebert and Paul von Hindenburg; the latter under the dictatorship of Adolf Hitler.

Creation of the German Republic (1919). The flight and abdication of the Kaiser in November 1918 resulted in a contest for control between a coalition Socialist group and the Communists. A threatened coup d'état by the Communists was prevented by the Socialists who succeeded in gaining enough support to lay the foundation for a democratic government. The Weimar Constitution (1919) provided for a federal republic with such democratic provision as universal suffrage, the initiative, referendum, recall, a bill of rights, and proportional representation. Friedrich Ebert was the first president (1919-1925) and was succeeded by Paul von Hindenburg, the Kaiser's Field Marshal (1925-1934).

Progress During First Years of Republic. The first four years of the German Republic witnessed a desperate struggle against the economic anarchy that followed the losses of the World War and the imposition of the Treaty of Versailles. The low point was reached when French armies invaded the Ruhr in an attempt to enforce reparations payment. Then came a turn for the better. The foreign affairs were ably handled by Dr. Gustav Stresemann (1923-1929). He was instrumental in gaining the evacuation of the Ruhr, the signing of favorable trade agreements with Belgium, France, and Great Britain, the adoption of the Locarno Treaty (1925), and Germany's admission to the League of Nations (1926). After a financial crisis, and with the aid of a foreign loan which was granted upon Germany's acceptance of the Dawes Plan (1925), currency was stabilized and international credit established. As economic conditions improved, the new government became more secure.

Rise of Adolf Hitler and the National Socialist Party. An economic relapse, which was part of the world depression, began in 1929; and the resulting political instability made possible the rise of the National Socialist party (Nazis) under the leadership of Adolf Hitler. In the second presidential election of 1932, Hitler obtained over 13,000,000 votes against von Hindenburg's 19,000,000. Cabinets under the leadership of Dr. Heinrich Brüning and General Kurt von Schleicher failed to gain the support of the Nazis in the Reichstag. Finally, upon an invitation from President von Hindenburg, Hitler accepted the chancellorship. A new election was immediately called and resulted in a majority support in the Reichstag (1933). An act was next passed which set aside the Weimar Constitution and conferred dictatorial powers upon Hitler for four years.

The Hitler Dictatorship (1933-1939). In spite of the opposition created by the anti-Semitic campaign and the antagonism of the Protestant and Catholic groups, the Nazis immediately undertook a program of domestic and foreign rehabilitation. The failure of the Powers to grant Germany the right to rearm led to her withdrawal from the Disarmament Conference and the League of Nations. A ten-year non-aggression pact was signed with Poland. To consolidate further his control, Hitler had nearly one hundred leading opponents massacred in a "blood purge" (1934). The death of von Hindenburg (1934) made it possible for Hitler to take over the powers of the presidency. He did not assume the title. The Nazi policies were further entrenched by creating a type of "totalitarian" state. During the three years, 1935-1938, Hitler repeatedly brought Europe to the brink of another world war. The first episode was his decision to "scrap" the Versailles Treaty and develop an army in excess of 100,000 men (1935). Then he violated the Locarno Treaty by marching troops into the demilitarized Rhineland area (1936). In 1938 his seizure of Austria and the dismemberment of Czechoslovakia put an end to the position of inferiority that Germany had occupied, and began a period of German dominance of Europe.

GREAT BRITAIN (1918-1939)

The relation of Great Britain to the various parts of her Empire was modified as a result of the development of democracy after World War I. The self-governing communities of the British Empire are now considered as of equal status in the British Commonwealth of Nations.

Post War Conditions in Great Britain (1918-1939). Great Britain emerged from the World War as the most important maritime and industrial power in Europe. Both her domestic and foreign policies were aimed at retaining this position.

Democracy was still further encouraged by the Fisher Education Act (1918), which set up a progressive program of education; the Electoral Reform Act (1918), which extended suffrage and redistributed the electoral districts; and the so-called Flapper Act (1928), which extended the vote to all women over twenty-one.

Several cabinet changes occurred during this period. Labor formed its first cabinet in 1924 with Ramsay MacDonald as Prime Minister. After a period of control by the Conservatives (1924-1929), MacDonald's party formed a new cabinet. Abnormal conditions, brought on by the depression, were responsible for the creation of a coalition cabinet. This party was in control until the general election of 1935 returned Stanley Baldwin and the Conservatives to power. Great Britain ceased to be a free trade country when Parliament passed the first tariff (1932). The death of King George V brought the bachelor Prince of Wales to the throne as Edward VIII (January 1936). Later in the year, the British Commonwealth of Nations was rocked by the constitutional issue involved in Edward's decision to marry Mrs. Wallis Simpson, twice-divorced American. Rather than give up the woman of his love, Edward abdicated and went into voluntary exile. The Duke of York succeeded him as George VI (December, 1936). In 1937 Baldwin resigned as Prime Minister and was succeeded by Neville Chamberlain. Chamberlain's ministry was marked by unstable international conditions which culminated in war (see Chapter XIX). To cope with the new situation created by the rise of rearmed Germany, Britain embarked on a great armament program involving an expenditure of $7,500,000,000. Economic conditions improved steadily and a balanced budget was realized after 1936.

During the period between wars, Great Britain participated in and sponsored many meetings with the countries of the world to help maintain the *status quo*, to preserve peace through collective security, and to foster a harmonious spirit within the British Commonwealth of Nations.

EIRE (1918-1939). The Sinn Fein Movement, under the leadership of Eamon De Valera and Arthur Griffith, gained momentum during World War I as a result of the Dublin Rebellion (1916). The Sinn Feiners elected to the British Parliament (1918) set up a separate Parliament at Dublin, and elected Eamon De Valera president. The resulting conflict between the Irish Republicans and the British Government was not settled by Lloyd George's Home Rule Bill (1920). Negotiations in 1921 ended with the creation of the Irish Free State with a self-governing status. The six Protestant Counties of Ulster voted to stay out of the Free State. In spite of De Valera's opposition, the treaty was ratified and Arthur Griffith was made president. Griffith did not live long. His successor, William Cosgrave, was able to defeat the Republicans in the election of 1922 and to formulate a constitution acceptable to Great Britain (1922). The Irish Free State was admitted to the League of Nations in 1923. In the elections of 1932, De Valera's party defeated Cosgrave. De Valera's platform aimed to do away with the oath of allegiance to the King which is required of all members of the Irish Dail, to unite northern and southern Ireland, to abolish the payment of land annuities to Great Britain, to change name to Eire, and to suspend the Public Safety Act. As a result of De Valera's policies, Great Britain retaliated by denying the Irish Free State trade privileges. The Anglo-Irish Trade Pact (1936) was an admission by De Valera that the Irish Free State had failed to establish an economic self-sufficient state.

However, after Edward's abdication, the Dail Eireann passed acts abolishing the office of Governor-General and the oath of allegiance to the king. The new constitution (1937) provided even greater independence for Eire. Douglas Hyde became President and De Valera remained as Prime Minister. When World War II broke out Eire remained neutral. Sporadic outbursts by the I. R. A. were offset by De Valera's policy of peaceable demands for greater freedom from Great Britain.

India (1920-1939). The passage of the Government of India Act (1920), which enlarged the native control of local government but left the ultimate power in Britain's hands, did not satisfy the Indians. The leader of civil disobedience in India was Mohandas K. Gandhi, who urged the natives to oppose the British with passive non-cooperation. Gandhi's boycott of British goods increased distress, and an Anglo-Indian Conference met in London (1930-1931), which formulated a program for eventually granting self-government to India similar to the other dominions. The Second India Round-Table Conference (1931), which was attended by Gandhi and other Indian representatives, adjourned without settling the status of India. Upon returning to India, Gandhi started a new campaign of civil disobedience and was imprisoned (1932). A Third Round-Table Conference (1932) drew up a compromise constitution which provided for partial self-government for India. This constitution was finally ratified by the British Parliament in 1935. It finally went into effect in April 1937. Although India was to come to the support of Great Britain in World War II, yet agitation for greater independence continued with Gandhi's passive resistance campaign threatened by those favoring more active opposition.

Egypt (1919-1939). The nationalist insurrection (1919) resulted in the recognition of Egypt as an independent state under Great Britain's supervision, with the former Sultan as King Fuad I (1922). A British Commissioner was appointed to watch over the British interests. The Nationalists (Wafd), under Zaghful as Prime Minister, opposed both Great Britain and King Fuad. After the death of Zaghful (1927), King Fuad was able to gain power at the expense of the cabinet under Yehia Pasha. The cabinet of Tewfik Nissim Pasha (1934-1936) was more satisfactory to both the Egyptians and Great Britain. During 1936 student riots and a consolidation of the nationalist groups caused the British concern. The whole situation was further complicated by the death of King Fuad I (1936). His sixteen-year-old son succeeded to the throne as Farouk I. Constitutional liberties were restored and an all-Wafd Cabinet got control and urged Britain to complete the proposed treaty. The resulting Anglo-Egyptian Pact (1936) was a compromise treaty which eased the tension.

Palestine (1918-1939). Great Britain was given a mandate over Palestine as a result of the Treaty of Lausanne. In 1930 the Jews and Arabs began fighting for the control of the "Wailing Wall." Upon Great Britain's request, a commission was appointed by the Council of the League, which investigated and reported in favor of the Arabs. New rioting by the Arabs broke out in October, 1933; it was caused primarily by the British immigration and land policy in Palestine. The influx of many Jewish immigrants, especially from Germany, resulted in rioting between the Jews and Arabs (1934-1938). An attempt at self-government was made by establishing an elective Legislative Council (1937). But disorders in Palestine continued.

ITALY (1918-1939)

Italy emerged from World War I not only as a unified state but also as an imperialistic power. Internal disorder was fomented by the Socialists, who favored a social revolution, and by the Fascists, who wished to maintain the existing conditions. Failing to suppress the Socialists lawfully, the Fascists gained power through a coup d'état in 1922. Benito Mussolini, leader of the Fascists, proceeded to gain control of the Italian government and to set up a dictatorship.

Internal Consolidation (1922-1939). Political control made it possible for Mussolini to organize industry and place it in the hands of the state. In 1934 a corporate state was set up which aimed to establish a balance between private initiative and social needs. A National Council of Corporation was substituted for the Chamber of Deputies. A *Sixty Year Plan* was contemplated which intended to give Italy first place in the economic world. As a result of an electoral law (1928), Mussolini made it possible for the Fascists to remain in power indefinitely. The Roman Question dating back to 1870 was settled in 1929: (1) the Vatican City was recognized as an independent state, (2) the Catholic religion was accepted as the Italian state religion, and (3) the Pope recognized the kingdom of Italy and accepted 1,750,000,000 lira for the territory which was taken from him in 1870.

Italo-Ethiopian War (1935-1936). Mussolini's imperialistic designs in Africa were furthered as a result of an Italo-French Accord (1935) which gave Italy territory south of Libya, territory along the coast of Eritrea, and the island of Doumerrah. A dispute over the boundary of Abyssinia and the Italian Somaliland was trumped up as an excuse for Italy to mass troops on the border for the conquest of the last remaining independent kingdom in Africa. Haile Selassie, the Ethiopian ruler, appealed to the League of Nations for help. The League condemned Italy's aggression and imposed economic and financial sanctions against her. The failure of the League to include sanctions on oil was a severe blow to Ethiopia. Despite the handicaps, Mussolini's soldiers conquered Ethiopia in a war lasting seven months (October 1935-May 1936). The flight of Haile Selassie and the capture of the capital city, Addis Ababa, resulted in the proclamation of a new Roman Empire by Mussolini on May 9, 1936. During the next year, Mussolini's foreign policy aimed to pacify the European opponents of his conquests. (See Chapter XIX).

FRANCE (1918-1939)

The prestige of France at home and abroad was greatly increased after 1918. Financial disturbances resulted in the depreciation of the franc (1924). A Coalition Ministry (1926) introduced new taxes and helped to stabilize the franc (1928). Proportional representation was abolished (1927). The foreign affairs of France were ably managed by Aristide Briand (1862-1932). The decision of the World Court that the German-Austrian Customs Union (1931) was in conflict with previous treaties was pleasing to the French, who regarded the proposed union as a threat to their security. Franco-American relations, although occasionally strained by what the French regarded as unreasonableness on the war debts, were usually friendly, and there was much popular applause for Lindbergh's flight (1927) and Laval's visit to the United States (1931). A reciprocal trade agreement with the United States was announced in May 1936. President Paul Doumer was assassinated by a fanatic in May 1932. A joint session of the Chamber of Deputies and Senate elected Albert Lebrun to succeed him. A French Colonial Conference was called in May 1933 to lay the foundation for economic recovery. The failure of several cabinets to balance the French budget and the Stavisky pawn-shop scandal resulted in the creation of a national Ministry with former President Gaston Doumergue as Premier (February 1934). The new government was given limited dictatorial powers. However, in November, the National Union Cabinet fell after a vote on the budget, and Pierre-Etienne Flandin became Premier. Elections in 1936 returned a large number of deputies of the left wing (Popular Front). Leon Blum became France's first socialist premier. With a Popular .Front cabinet, Blum sponsored social legislation which greatly reduced the number of strikes. Croix de Feu, a fascist organization, was dissolved; the franc was revalued; a vigorous rearmament program was sponsored; and mutual assistance pacts with Russia and Great Britain were strengthened. But the position of France as the dominating continental power was destroyed in 1938 by the victory of Hitler in the Czechoslovakian crisis (see Chapter XIX).

SPAIN (1918-1939)

The failure of the Spanish army in Morocco and the existence of political dissension made possible a military directorate with General Primo de Rivera (1923) at the head. In 1925 the French and Spanish joined to quell a native uprising in Morocco. The economic disturbances in Spain in 1930-1931 resulted in increased sentiment for a republic, and as a result of the election of 1931, King Alfonso XIII left the country and sought refuge in France. A provisional government was set up with Niceto Alcala Zamora as President. The Republicans had forced the last Hapsburg from power in a "glorious revolution." The Constitution (1931) provided for a president (one six-year term), a unicameral legislature elected by universal suffrage, and a parliamentary system of government, similar to the British. The Catholic Church was separated from the State (1931), and the property of the Jesuits was confiscated (1932). Catalonia was given limited autonomy. Political unrest which had been simmering for five years was brought to the boiling-point by the elections in 1936, which gave the left wing (Popular Front) a large majority in the Cortes. President Zamora was forced out of office, and Premier Manuel Azaña became president. The assassination of a leader of the Right, Jose Calvo Sotelo (July 1936) hastened the beginning of a bloody civil war. The rebels (Rightists) had the support of most of the Spanish army, which had joined General Francisco Franco after he gained control over Spanish Morocco. Neutrality pacts did not stop Italy and Germany from aiding the rebels with troops and supplies. Russia and France supported the loyalists (see Chapter XIX). As the loyalists formed the officially recognized government of Spain, they were entitled, under international law, to purchase supplies in foreign countries. Finally the Loyalists capitulated and Franco became to all intents and purposes a fascist dictator (1939). He started to rebuild Spain after the ravages of three years of a bloody civil war.

OTHER COUNTRIES (1918-1939)

The countries of the Little Entente (Czechoslovakia, Yugoslavia, and Rumania) all adopted constitutions which provided for a democratic government. Czechoslovakia was consolidated economically and politically through the efforts of Dr. Eduard Beneš, foreign minister, and Thomas Masaryk, President (1920-1936). Upon the resignation of Masaryk, Beneš was elected President. Czechoslovakia was the only central European country that clung fast during the whole post-war era to the democratic tradition in which it was founded. Its destruction as an independent country in 1938-1939 was for this reason a doubly poignant tragedy. The internal strife of Rumania weakened that country. Upon the death of Ferdinand I, the boy Michael I became king, as his father Carol had renounced his own claim to the throne. Carol returned to Rumania in 1931, however, and was recognized as

King Carol II by Parliament. The dictatorship which King Alexander had set up in Yugoslavia (1929) continued in spite of a new Constitution (1931). While on a good-will tour, Alexander was assassinated at Marseilles by a Croatian terrorist (1934). Alexander's eleven-year-old son became King Peter II under a regency headed by Prince Paul. In February 1933 the members of the Little Entente signed a pact which provided for a closer union. Although Poland was nominally a republic, it was actually a dictatorship under the rule of Marshal Josef Pilsudski (1926-1935). In spite of opposition to his candidacy, President Ignace Moscicki was reëlected through the efforts of Pilsudski (1933). (For conquest of Poland see Chapter XX.)

Greece became a republic in 1924. Under Premier Venizelos (1928-1932), economic and diplomatic progress was made. A conflict which developed between anti- and pro-Venizelist groups finally ended in a revolution (1935). Premier Tsaldoris' forces were successful in crushing the rebels, who under Venizelos had attempted to establish themselves on the island of Crete. The royalist faction under General Kondylis gained control, and as a result of a plebiscite the former king, George II, was recalled. Of the many monarchs deposed after the World War, George II was the first to regain his crown. Kemal Ataturk[1] was practically a dictator in Turkey. He separated the church and state, abolished the fez, adopted the Latin alphabet, and fostered education. The position of women under the republic has been one of gradual emancipation. The privilege to vote in state as well as municipal elections was given to them (1934). Upon the death of Kemal Ataturk (1938), General Ismet Inonu was elected president by the National Assembly. Inonu had been Kemal's Premier and right hand man. Turkey was being westernized. A Balkan Four-Power Pact signed by Greece, Rumania, Turkey, and Yugoslavia guaranteed the security of their frontiers (1934). Their independence threatened by World War II, the members of the Balkan Entente met in February 1940 and agreed to remain neutral in spite of diplomatic pressure from both Germany and Great Britain and France. Albania and Bulgaria

---

[1] Name taken by Mustapha Kemal after passage of law requiring all persons to assume family names by January 1, 1935.

did not sign the pact. Bulgaria followed the lead of many other states and created a dictatorship with the executive authority as the supreme arbiter.. An attempted coup and rebellion by the military leaders was thwarted by King Boris III, making his dictatorship more secure (April 1935).

THE GERMAN REPARATIONS PROBLEM

Dawes Plan (1924). The inability of Germany to meet her obligations (1923) led France to seize the important industrial area of the Ruhr. The failure of the mark, due to inflation, resulted in the calling of a committee of experts to formulate a plan for dealing with reparations. The resulting Dawes Plan, which was accepted by the powers, provided that Germany must pay specified sums for an unlimited time, and that the mark would be stabilized by a foreign loan of $200,000,000. France evacuated the Ruhr (1925) as a result of this settlement.

Young Plan (1929). The Young Plan set the amount which Germany must pay as $8,800,000,000. As Germany was given fifty-eight years to pay, the principal plus the interest would amount to over 27 billion dollars. Confident that Germany would meet these payments, the Allies withdrew their troops from the Rhineland (1930). A Bank of International Settlement was established in Switzerland.

The Moratorium (1931). The world-wide financial and economic disorders which began in 1929 disturbed the expert calculations of the Young Plan, and by June 1931, Germany faced a complete financial collapse. President Hoover's recommendation for a moratorium of one year met with the approval of all the creditor nations except France. France yielded after forcing Germany to pay that part of her debt which was not subject to postponement, and then allowing the Bank of International Settlement to lend it back to Germany with assured security.

Lausanne Reparations Treaty (July 1932). The Lausanne Reparations Treaty provided that Germany must pay only $714,000,000 as a final settlement for reparations. This settlement was dependent upon a reduction in the war debt owed to the United States. The United States refused reduction. The ultimate result was that Germany made no payments after the Hoover moratorium. With the rise of the Nazi dictatorship all hope of getting further payments evaporated.

The United States and the War Debts. Congress supported the Hoover moratorium but warned the President that it was opposed to further extension or reduction of the war debt. The request of the debtor nations for a consideration of the question in December 1932 was denied, and Great Britain, Italy, Czechoslovakia, Finland, Latvia, and Lithuania made the payment. The French Chamber voted not to pay the December debt installment and forced Prime Minister Herriot's resignation. The other defaulting countries were Belgium, Hungary, Estonia, and Poland. The continuance of token payments by some, and the defaulting by other countries led the United States Congress to pass the Johnson Act which made it illegal to lend money to the defaulting nations (1934). Finland was the only country which continued to meet its obligations in full.

FAILURE OF THE QUEST FOR SECURITY (1918-1939)

After 1918 numerous international conferences were held seeking to stabilize international relations, provide for armament limitation, and bring about permanent security.

The Locarno Conference. The Locarno Conference, (1925) which was attended by the leading states of Europe, arranged several treaties in which the various powers agreed to maintain their existing boundaries and never to go to war with each other in violation of these treaties. Briand of France and Stresemann of Germany were the leaders.

The Kellogg-Briand or Paris Pact. The Paris Peace Pact (1928) through which the principal states of the world "renounce war as an instrument of national policy," was signed by sixty-two nations. This treaty (1928) for the outlawry of war was made possible through the efforts of Briand and Kellogg, the American Secretary of State. In practice the treaty turned out to be only a pious gesture.

Naval Pacts. The naval conferences of 1922, 1927, 1930, and 1936 brought the powers together for the purpose of decreasing navies. The agreements made at the London Conference (1930) between Great Britain, Japan, and the United

States were not renewed in 1936 because of Japan's withdrawal from that Conference when she was refused parity. However, the United States and Great Britain signed an agreement pledging parity (1936).

The Geneva Conference. The Geneva Conference on Disarmament (1932-1934) was unsuccessful in its attempt to limit armaments, and after nearly three years, it ceased to function.

Rearmament (1933-1939). The failure of the nations to arrive at a satisfactory method of disarming and Germany's withdrawal from the Conference led to competitive building of army, air, and naval forces by the world powers until the expenditures were much greater than they were in 1914.

POLITICAL AND ECONOMIC CONDITIONS (1929-1939)

Political Instability (1929-1939). Throughout Europe, cabinet changes were more frequent than usual. The coalition cabinet in Great Britain (1929-1935) was replaced with a government organized by the Conservatives; the national ministry in France had several successors, the last of which was primarily a Centrist cabinet; Hitler and the Nazis established a dictatorship in Republican Germany; Italy proclaimed the existence of a Roman Empire; and even in the United States a new experiment in government took place under President Roosevelt and his New Dealers. Throughout the rest of the world, similar changes occurred.

Economic Unrest (1929-1939). Exports of the leading countries decreased considerably during the period. Production decreased materially. In April, 1933, the United States went off the Gold Standard, and Congress passed a farm-relief-inflation act (May, 1933). Direct government aid was resorted to in many countries as a means of reducing the millions of unemployed. In spite of increased taxes, most countries were unsuccessful in balancing their budgets.

Attempts to Combat Depression. The political leaders recognized that the depression was world-wide in scope. In 1933, President Roosevelt invited representatives of foreign countries to come to a World Economic Conference at Washington. Tariff, currency, and trade were discussed, but the

conference adjourned without reaching an agreement. During
the five years, 1933-1938, many countries signed non-aggression pacts, favored-nation treaties, and reciprocal trade agreements in hopes of alleviating the economic hardships. But the
fundamental problem of how to put to efficient use the enormous technological resources of the modern world remained
unsolved.

SOCIAL AND CULTURAL MOVEMENTS

Social. The political revolutions were all tinged with
social characteristics. Legislation of a social nature was passed
in most countries, and labor increased in importance. Labor
organizations grew. The nationalization of land in Russia and
Spain helped the peasants to become a land-owning group. The
new tendency toward economic coöperation, as opposed to the
old doctrine of economic individualism, perhaps pointed the
way to the proper solution of the economic and social problem,
but the excesses of such collectivist movements as fascism and
communism increased class strife and led to dangerous international tensions (see Chapter XIX). The perfection of a host
of inventions and their application to everyday life revolutionized
society.

Religious. During World War I, the religious groups
worked together, but after the armistice they tended to break
away from each other. The Mohammedans consolidated,
under a caliph (analogous to the Pope) at Constantinople as
head of all Moslems. The caliphate was later abolished by
Kemal Ataturk, the first president of the Turkish republic
(1923) The Protestant sects were split by two great schools
of thought—Fundamentalists and Modernists. The Catholic
Church emerged from the World War strengthened. But the
rise of the Nazis in Germany led to a recrudescence of religious persecution, which at the end of 1938 had developed
into a virtual war on the Catholic Church. The Jews, also,
were persecuted as they had not been since the Middle Ages.

Cultural. Popular education received an added impetus
as a result of World War I. Art, literature, and science all
felt the influence of the new age. A new group of men of
letters appeared whose philosophy was of a radical type.

CHAPTER XIX.

THE NEW EUROPE
1935-1939

In many respects the years 1935-1939 appeared to mark a great turning-point in European and world history. The post-war era of reconstruction dominated by the "Peace of Paris" came definitely to an end. A new era marked by the greatest conflict of ideology since the French Revolution, by a fundamental realignment of historical forces, by renewed international tension, and by the development of revolutionary techniques in diplomacy had seemingly begun. The background of this contemporary period had been the world economic depression which no government had been able to control, and which had made men all over the world responsive to revolutionary ideas. In international politics the dominating event had been the military resurgence of Germany under Adolf Hitler and the Nazi Party. In 1933 Germany was disarmed, economically prostrate, and without influence in world affairs. France was not only the leading nation on the European continent but enjoyed a power and influence unknown since the days of Napoleon. In 1938 a rearmed and aggressive Germany took the leadership away from France with dramatic suddenness and stood able to impose her will on all the smaller countries of Europe. The Conference of Munich, September 29, 1938, marked the formal passing of French leadership into the hands of Germany. The event had long been prepared, yet so great was the previous prestige and power of France and so apparently hopeless the military and economic position of Germany, that few observers imagined that a complete shift in the balance of power within such a short time was possible. The failure of Hitler to keep his Munich pledge, the consummation of the Russo-German mutual assistance pact, and Germany's invasion of Poland precipitated a new world war between the Axis partners on the one hand and Great Britain and her Allies on the other. Thus, the course of history was changed radically by the political, economic, and ideological forces at work during the 1930's.

THE CONTEMPORARY CONFLICT OF IDEOLOGIES

Conflict of ideologies—philosophies of society—is nothing new in the world. We have seen how the whole history of Europe in the nineteenth century was permeated by the struggle of liberalism and conservatism. We have seen how subsects and offshoots of liberalism, e. g., nationalism, economic laissez faire, democracy, romanticism, have frequently found themselves in conflict with each other, and have made strange alliances, sometimes temporary, sometimes permanent, with the sub-sects and offshoots of conservatism. By the beginning of the twentieth century this interplay and exchange of ideals between the old, orthodox liberalism and the old, orthodox reaction had so realigned the various disputing sects that it was no longer possible to recognize the original philosophies of the contending parties. Politics became less and less a matter of principles and basic social ideas and more and more a matter of the personalities of particular politicians and the immediate issues. At the close of World War I, however, the Russian Revolution turned loose in the world, as a serious political and social force, a new theory of society—revolutionary socialism or communism. In the first few years of the establishment of the Soviet Union the governments of Western Europe and the United States tried to find ways to prevent the spread of the Russian idea—they instituted vigorous "red hunts," refused to recognize the Soviet Union, and even sent armies to Russia to crush the revolution by force.

As the economic ills that attended the ending of the war began to lift, the danger of Communist revolution became more remote, and for a period of about ten years (1922-1932) there was less discussion in Europe of the "red menace." In Italy, however, under the leadership of Benito Mussolini, a new movement called fascism had arisen. The relation of this movement to Russian communism was not understood or was largely overlooked during the first years of its development, and it was not until a largely identical movement had arisen in Germany under Adolf Hitler that the idea became widely diffused that fascism and communism were the ideological antitheses of each other—that fascism represented the "reaction of the right" to the communistic "revolution of the left." The coming of the world economic depression of the 1930's stimulated economic and social thinking and served to crystallize various parties and programs favoring social change and to accentuate the "right" and "left" division between fascism and communism. A new world conflict of ideology was in progress, comparable to the conflicts that followed the Protestant Revolt and the French Revolution. For an understanding of contemporary history, therefore, it is necessary to examine in some detail the character of fascism and communism as they appeared in the modern world.

Fascism. As developed first by Benito Mussolini in Italy and later by the German Nazis under Hitler, fascism as a form of political, social, and economic organization was characterized by six leading features.

PERSONAL DICTATORSHIP. Never in history had such great powers been concentrated in the hands of single individuals as those wielded by Mussolini and Hitler. Some of the absolute despotisms of the past had claimed in theory the powers of the modern fascist leaders, but never before had the means of enforcement been so great, the numbers of men controlled so large, or the fields of life supervised so extensive.

INTENSE NATIONALISM. In both Italy and Germany fascism was to capitalize on the deep-rooted human emotion of patriotism and was to develop a militant, aggressive, and intolerant nationalism. This intensification of the national spirit was much like that which appears in other nations only in times of foreign war or grave national crisis. Indeed, the Fascist nations felt that the present was just such a time of crisis, and this feeling called into play all the noble and self-sacrificing, as well as the ugly and ferocious, qualities of deep patriotism.

FORCIBLE SUPPRESSION OF DISSENT. In the Fascist countries all the engines of former despotisms, as well as some new ones to fit the times, were set in motion to suppress internal opposition. Censorship of the press, exclusion of foreign news and propaganda, police espionage, and the severe treatment of political offenders were developed to a point that would have seemed incredible to Metternich, Napoleon III, or even to the Russian masters of suppression at the end of the nineteenth century. The censorship extended far beyond the mere stifling of dissident political opinion; it involved a thoroughgoing government surveillance over the whole literary, scholarly, and artistic life of the nation. Libraries were purged; editions of well-known books were adulterated; free inquiry in the social sciences largely ceased; impartial scholars either were driven from the country, were confined in jails, or were compelled to make themselves the mouthpieces of official views.

ACTIVE LARGE-SCALE PROPAGANDA. One of the features distinguishing fascism from former absolute governments was its active cultivation, on an immense scale, of a religion of loyalty toward the state and toward the leader. In this, as in its militant nationalism, fascism resembled the government of Napoleon I rather than the passive despotism of Metternich. But Napoleon could never have imagined the resources that the Industrial and Scientific Revolution would put at the disposal of the modern propagandist. In Germany, especially, the technique of mass propaganda was developed to an astonishing pitch. Every possible avenue was exploited—radio, motion pictures, press, patriotic organizations, art, education, even music. By these means fascism became a dynamic and expanding force. Its problem was no longer that of keeping down discontent within its own ranks but rather that of safely disposing of its superabundant energy.

EXPANSION OF THE FIELD OF GOVERNMENT. Along with the shibboleths of democracy and intellectual liberty, fascism entirely discarded the popular nineteenth century theory that government should confine its activities to a narrow and well-defined field. Fascism represented a thorough management and disciplining of the life of the nation, a complete absorption of the individual by the state. Although private ownership of property still prevailed, the government rigidly supervised business and industrial activity; and "private enterprise," in the sense understood in democratic countries, hardly existed. Relations between employer and employee were subject to close control. On the one hand, labor was not free to organize and bargain collectively, and on the other hand capitalists were not free to lay off men, reduce wages, or otherwise manage their properties as they saw fit. Everything was subordinated to the needs of the state, and the individual had no rights that the state was bound to respect. One side of fascist control was thus this miliary discipline of the entire people; another side was the paternalism with which the Fascist states assumed responsibility for the personal welfare of the mass of the citizens. If in no democratic country did the individual sacrifice so much to the state, in no democratic country was the individual guaranteed, in return, a condition of tolerable, if low-leveled, economic security.

RACIAL INTOLERANCE. In Germany particularly, but during 1938 also in Italy, fascism was characterized by savage outbreaks of anti-Semitic intolerance. In the official ideology of German fascism, anti-Semitism was associated with a dogma of race purity (Aryanism). Anti-Semitism in Germany was no new thing; long before the advent of fascism it had been one of the ugliest features of German life, and one of Germany's greatest scholars, notably Heinrich von Treitschke, had in the past shocked non-German intellectuals by his willingness to rationalize and justify a movement rooted in medieval superstition and appealing to the basest passions of human nature. But fascism intensified and glorified racial intolerance; it drove such men as Albert Einstein and Sigmund Freud out of their native countries; in pursuance of an official policy, it reduced to destitution a whole population. No other phase of the Fascist program evoked so much indignation in non-Fascist countries; no phase involved so complete a repudiation of the ideas of "enlightenment" that had seemingly been growing in European civilization since the end of the seventeenth century.

Communism. To many persons in democratic countries the second great socio-economic system of our time, communism, contains more essential similarities to than differences from its avowed enemy, fascism. The elements of personal dictatorship, forcible suppression of dissent, active state propaganda, and expansion of the field of government are part and parcel of communism as it is actually practiced in the Soviet Union no less than of fascism in Germany and Italy. There is the same suppression of individual rights in the name of the needs of the commonwealth, the same open and militant repudiation of the liberal ideas of the eighteenth and nineteenth centuries, and the same cultivation of an official religion of the state. Yet communism and fascism found themselves irreconcilable enemies; fascistic theorists talked of waging war against world communism as the most destructive enemy of modern civilization, while to Communists, fascism represented the quintessence of human iniquity. There were not wanting observers who said that in this bitter antagonism we were dealing with a phenomenon akin to the fierce doctrinal strife of religion in earlier times when Arians and Trinitarians fought to the death over the iota in *homoiousion,* or when Catholics and Protestants devastated Europe in the Thirty Years' War. It is true that both communism and fascism had in them elements of religious fervor and religious fanaticism, and their mutual antagonism was an antagonism of ideology rather than an antagonism of practice. This ideological conflict was still present in spite of the Russo-German mutual assistance pact of August, 1939, which was generally viewed as a temporary pact of convenience born of skepticism of British diplomatic sincerity. Nevertheless, the differences between fascism and communism were probably, even in the year 1939, more important than their similarities, and there were strong reasons for believing that these differences would become greater with the passage of time. We may conveniently examine these differences in central philosophies, in the aims for which the respective dictatorships were professedly established, and in the historical traditions that formed their cultural nourishment, by considering the Fascist and Communist attitudes toward the national state, toward capitalism, and toward imperialism.

ATTITUDE TOWARD THE NATIONAL STATE.   Fascism, as we have seen, was intensely national and preached national solidarity and national aggressiveness; communism is international and preaches the solidarity of the working-class throughout the world. Communists regard the exaggerated nationalism of fascism as a smoke-screen thrown up by the privileged bourgeoisie to confuse the minds and destroy the *esprit de corps* of the working-class. The ultimate aim of communism is the disappearance of the national state in the classless society of the future—in the words of Friedrich Engels, Marx's co-worker, the state "withers away." The fact that the state has as yet in Soviet Russia shown no sign of "withering away" as predicted has led many democratic critics to assert that communism will be just as unsuccessful in establishing social equality—a society in which all men shall "give according to capacity and receive according to need"—as were the French radicals of 1793. These critics assert that the leaders of Soviet Russia will not, having tasted the intoxication of absolute power, voluntarily give up their dictatorial control; the whole argument of Marx himself that an entrenched privileged class can only be dispossessed by violent revolution is applied to the new class of government officials. Can we expect these men to abdicate their vested interests any more gracefully than did the bourgeoisie before them or than did the hereditary aristocracy before the bourgeoisie? Nevertheless the Communists have never modified their central doctrine that they aim at a classless, non-coercive society in which the state as a "special repressive force" will no longer be necessary. The present stage of communist development in Soviet Russia is the stage of the "dictatorship of the proletariat," a painful but necessary prelude to the establishment of the democratic society of the future. Whether such a society can ever come about depends, in the last analysis, upon the kind of being man really is, and the most familiar argument against the possibility of the sort of utopia envisaged by the Communist theorists is the argument that "human nature" will always prevent men from coöperating in the unselfish way in which they must coöperate if theoretical communism is to "work" and not be merely another name for the historically familiar despotism and exploitation of the many by the few. Before the Russian Revolution had produced an actual instance of Communist society on a large scale, the English philosopher Bertrand Russell wrote apprehensively of the danger of tyranny in a communist state and added significantly: "These results are not foreseen by Socialists because they imagine that the Socialist State will be governed by men like those who now advocate it. This is, of course, a delusion. The rulers of the state then will bear as little resemblance to the present Socialists as the dignitaries of the Church after the time of Constantine bore to the Apostles. The men who advocate an unpopular reform are exceptional in disinterestedness and zeal for the public good; but those who hold power after the reform has been carried out are likely to belong, in the main, to the ambitious executive type which has in all ages possessed itself of the government of nations. And this type has never shown itself tolerant of opposition or friendly to freedom."[1] This is the strongest possible statement of the "human nature" argument against the possibility of the ideal society of communism; whether the experience of Soviet Russia will confirm it can hardly be told until the period of the "dictatorship of the proletariat" (really a dictatorship of the Communist party leaders in the name of, and professedly in the interest of, the proletariat) shall have been relaxed, and such relaxation cannot be expected until large numbers of young Russians born subsequent to about 1915 and hence educated in the Communist tradition shall have reached the age of active participation in public affairs. Whatever be the rigors of the current communist dictatorship, the ideal of the eventual "withering away" of the state remains an essential article of Communist faith.

ATTITUDE TOWARD CAPITALISM. In both Italy and Germany, fascism arose as a counter-movement to a threatened Communist revolution. The fascists were supported, both politically and financially, by the classes who dreaded a violent

---

1 From *Proposed Roads to Freedom*, by Bertrand Russell. Used by permission of the publishers, Henry Holt & Co.

dislocation. Fascism was a preservation by force of a totter-ing capitalistic regime and was accepted by the great indus-trialists of both Italy and Germany as an unpleasant medicine, perhaps, but as the only alternative to the still more un-pleasant medicine of revolution and confiscation. The Fascist dictatorships were thus established in the interests of, and to save the skins of, the bourgeoisie. The Communist dictator-ship, on the other hand, was established in the interest of the proletariat with the avowed purpose of destroying the bourgeoisie and every vestige of bourgeois ideology. Hence, in countries that economic discontent and factional strife have brought to the brink of anarchy, e. g., Spain, two parties tend to emerge—a party of the right (Fascist) that wishes to put down discontent and factionalism by force and maintain the existing economic stratification of society, and a party of the left (Communist) that wishes to capitalize the existing dis-content to effect a social revolution.

ATTITUDE TOWARD IMPERIALISM AND WAR. The Soviet Union covers about one-sixth of the land area of the world. Even allowing for the fact that a large part of this domain cannot be agriculturally exploited, it is still true that in ultimate natural resources the Soviet Union is second only to the British Commonwealth among political divisions of the world. This vast and immensely rich area was largely un-developed in 1920, and in spite of the enormous strides to-ward general industrialization that were made under the First and Second Five Year Plans, there remains a tremen-dous potential in the development of industry. The Fascist countries, on the other hand, showed the precise reverse of this general economic picture. Germany, Italy, and Japan (a gov-ernment essentially fascist had developed in Japan) were all highly industrialized countries with very dense populations and a grave insufficiency of natural resources. It thus appears to have been an economic reality rather than a difference be-tween Communist and Fascist ideology that was behind the opposing attitudes of communism and fascism toward aggres-sive imperialism. Nevertheless it is a central doctrine of Marx-ist economics that capitalism tends to degenerate into mon-opoly and imperialism, and Communist theorists have built up a suggestive, if not entirely convincing argument that the mainspring of war and imperialism in the modern world is the internal pressure, generated by the nature of capitalism, to find new regions for exploitation. Fascism was, therefore, to Communist theorists merely the last resort of a desperate and over-ripe capitalism clothed in the trappings of national patriotism and racial brotherhood to deceive the naïve and incorrigibly idealistic masses.

Democracy. A third form of political organization considered by many to be the true antithesis of both fascism and communism is the liberal democracy represented by such governments as France, Great Britain, and the United States. It is extremely difficult to give a satisfactory definition of democracy, since partisans of various socio-economic theories are prone to emphasize different aspects of democracy as it has historically grown up, or to identify democracy with a particular economic creed. Thus it is common, especially in the United States, to identify democracy with economic laissez faire, or with decentralization in government, or with the unlimited right of the majority to rule. Actually socio-political organization is too complex a thing to be reduced in such a fashion to a single principle. But fixing our attention on the leading features that characterize modern democratic states, we may tentatively define a democracy as a government based upon popular sovereignty, operating within a constitutional and legal framework guaranteeing civil liberty, and presiding over a socio-economic system permitting substantial scope for individual economic initiative.

POPULAR SOVEREIGNTY. The ultimate power in a democratic state is the people expressing itself by votes either directly or through elected representatives or executives. It is essential to the democratic idea that the individual voters be subject to no coercion or restraint, and to secure this freedom the secret ballot has been generally adopted as a necessary tool. It is also essential to a fully developed democracy that the right to vote be independent of property or social class. This requirement has been substantially attained in the modern democracies, although traces of the old property qualifications still linger, and in large parts of the United States the right to vote is denied in practice, though not by law, on the ground of race.

CIVIL LIBERTY. In the eighteenth and nineteenth centuries, many critics, confining their attention to the popular sovereignty feature, maintained that democracy meant simply the unrestrained tyranny of the majority, or legalized mob rule. "Your people, Sir," said Alexander Hamilton, "is a great beast." "In a democracy," wrote Edmund Burke, "the majority of the citizens is capable of exercising the most cruel oppression upon the minority . . . . and that oppression . . . . will extend to far greater numbers and will be carried on with much greater fury than can almost ever be apprehended from the domination of a single scepter." "If ever the free institutions of America are destroyed," wrote Alexis de Tocqueville, "that event may be attributed to the omnipotence of the majority which may at some future time urge the minorities to desperation and oblige them to have recourse to physical force. Anarchy will be the result, but it will have been brought about by despotism." Against such degeneration as these critics visualized, democracy has chiefly the weapon of civil liberty, with its legal and constitutional protection of individual rights. Though historically not the creation of democracy, and indeed, as the quotations show, long regarded as incompatible with democracy, civil liberty is today democracy's adopted child, as well as democracy's first line of defence. Perhaps most important of the civil liberties now thought necessary as bulwarks of democracy are freedom of speech, assemblage, and petition, freedom of worship, and freedom of the press. In a special sense these freedoms are safeguards of others. But equally essential to a healthy democracy are the legal rights of the English Common and Roman Civil Laws—the right of an accused person to a fair and public trial by jury, his right to be confronted by the witnesses against him and to know the specific offense with which he is charged and the specific law which he is alleged to have violated. Fundamental also is an effective guarantee of equality of all before the law—that there be no discrimination on the ground of wealth, sex, race, religion, or political opinions. Finally, there must be some constitutional or traditional limitation of the scope of government power preventing it from arbitrarily invading personal liberty. Men must be free to live where they please, to select their own occupations, and to be secure in their homes and personal possessions.

ECONOMIC INDIVIDUALISM. Historically, the growth of both popular sovereignty and civil liberty has been intimately associated with the rise of capitalism, and all modern democracies are essentially capitalistic. To many observers, indeed, the most fundamental of all individual rights is the unlimited right to buy, sell, make contracts, and control property. Such observers tend to identify democracy with economic laissez faire, and look upon any government limitation of property right as an invasion of personal liberty. Complete laissez faire has never existed, although a near approach to it was made in England during the middle decades of the nineteenth century. But all modern governments have found it necessary to regulate economic activity to a greater or less degree, and the increasing complexity of the world economic system makes it certain that such regulation will be required even more in the future. But this does not imply the end of democracy. There is no reason for supposing that important civil liberties really depend for their preservation on unlimited economic individualism. A better case could be made out for the exact contrary—that economic individualism, allowed to develop without limitation, would eventually strangle the very liberties in the name of which it had been permitted. Plutocracy—the dictatorship of money—is as dangerous to democracy as any other form of dictatorship. It is, to be sure, a basic requirement of a liberal democracy that there be a large field of choice of occupation and that there exist wide opportunity for individual initiative. And this requirement seems to demand that the economic system be to a considerable degree capitalistic and competitive, but the superstition of nineteenth century liberalism that all social control of economic activity is destructive of liberty is no longer tenable. The real problem facing modern democracy is not the theoretical problem of whether there should be social control of the economic system, but the practical problem of finding such controls as will enable the system to produce and distribute wealth as efficiently as modern technology makes physically possible. Therefore, democracy must seek social efficiency in order to withstand totalitarian systems which endeavor to destroy it.

UPSURGENCE OF FASCISM (1935-1939)

German Rearmament. The Nazi party under Adolf Hitler obtained dictatorial power in Germany in March, 1933. The first two years of Nazi control were spent in a vigorous campaign to consolidate the party's power and to coördinate all political and economic activity within the country. Having forged the whole nation into an efficient, systematized machine, the Nazis began an immense rearmament program in violation of the Treaty of Versailles. By its complete control of the press and of the activities of foreign correspondents and observers, the government was able to conduct the rearmament under a veil of mystery that minimized the risk of foreign interference. Taking skillful advantage of divided counsels among his opponents and of his own ability to act without allowing any warning of his plans to leak out, Hitler presented Europe with one *fait accompli* after another. Universal military training was reintroduced (1935); the Rhineland was reoccupied and fortified (1936); almost before the other powers realized what had happened, Germany had created a formidable air force; in 1936 Hitler reached an agreement with Great Britain permitting Germany to build a navy up to 35 per cent of Great Britain's strength. During this period of German rearmament, the French government was extremely restless and repeatedly threatened reprisals but did not take a firm stand. The British government pursued a tortuous policy reflecting the division of opinion within the country.

Anthony Eden and Collective Security. During the international crisis of 1935, provoked by Italy's attack on Ethiopia, the British Foreign Secretary, Samuel Hoare, was forced out of office by the public indignation that arose after his attempt to arrange a British-French-Italian deal for the partitioning of Ethiopia (the Hoare-Laval Plan). He was succeeded by Anthony Eden, who was committed to a policy of "collective security," i. e., joint action by the powers of the League of Nations to resist the "aggressor nations" (Italy at that time; later Italy, Germany, and Japan). In pursuance of the policy of collective security, the League of Nations led by Britain voted sanctions against Italy, and a large detachment of the British fleet was sent into the Mediterranean as a threatening gesture. Mussolini refused to be intimidated, and the sanctions were only half-heartedly applied. "Collective security" failed to save Ethiopia.

Rome-Berlin Axis. As a result of the Ethiopian crisis, Germany and Italy formed a common front against the League of Nations. This collaboration was known as the "Rome-Berlin Axis." In 1936-1937 the Rome-Berlin Axis pursued a common policy in support of the Spanish Insurgents led by General Francisco Franco. The League of Nations' attitude toward the Spanish Civil War was one of delay and indecision, chiefly because Britain and France, dominating the League Council, seemed unable to reach a consistent policy. The Spanish War developed into an unofficial small-scale international war—France and the Soviet Union furnished supplies to the Loyalists, while Italy and Germany helped the Insurgents. Great Britain occupied an ambiguous position apparently because the supporters of Eden's policy of collective security, or "standing up to the dictators," were influential in, but unable to control, the British cabinet. In 1937 the new British Prime Minister, Neville Chamberlain, found his own policies more and more in conflict with those of his Foreign Secretary, Eden. Early in 1938 Eden resigned because of his disagreements with Chamberlain.

Neville Chamberlain and Appeasement. The resignation of Eden marked an abandonment of collective security in favor of "appeasement," as the new policy of Chamberlain was called. Appeasement involved an attempt to reach a peaceful understanding with the dictator governments (Germany and Italy) by concession of their demands. Appeasement was supported by the argument that the unrest of Europe was fundamentally caused by the injustices of the "Peace of Paris" and that a lasting settlement could come about only if the great "have-not" nations obtained an equitable share in the world's imperial booty. This "realistic" policy was complicated by the fact that the most pressing demands of the dictator governments required the virtual destruction of the independence of the small states of eastern Europe and of Spain. Hitler's ambitions for Germany were known to include a revival of the old German *Drang nach Osten* —an economic and political hegemony over all central Europe and the Balkans. In the way of this hegemony stood the independence of Austria, and more important, the French system of military alliances centering in Czechoslovakia.

German Seizure of Austria. In March, 1938, Hitler, by a sudden stroke, forced the resignation of the Austrian government under Kurt Schuschnigg and immediately followed this by marching an army into Austria and annexing the country. The move was cleverly timed to coincide with a cabinet crisis in France, which made it impossible for the French to act before it was too late. Indignation was expressed in Great Britain at the brutality of Hitler's methods but no action was taken. Hitler enormously increased his prestige by his success and greatly improved his strategic position for an attack upon Czechoslovakia, his next objective.

Czechoslovakian Crisis. During the summer of 1938 it became clear that Hitler was planning a new coup to get control of Czechoslovakia. Czechoslovakia was allied with both France and the Soviet Union and appeared determined to fight to preserve her independence. From the strategic point of view, Czechoslovakia was the key to the whole Danube valley, and it seemed improbable that France and the Soviet Union, both of whose vital interests were at stake, would permit the Bohemian mountain ranges to fall into German hands. Bismarck's famous remark, "Whoever is master of Bohemia is master of Europe" was as true in 1938 as in the nineteenth century. When, therefore, Hitler, using as a pretext a demand for "self-determination" for the Sudeten German minority in Czechoslovakia, threatened to seize these important strategic and industrial areas, Europe was faced with a genuine crisis. In Hitler's previous steps, nothing absolutely vital had been involved, and although the word "crisis" is commonly used to describe the tension that followed the remilitarization of the Rhineland, the seizure of Austria, and other treaty violations, the attack on Czechoslovakia was the first instance in Hitler's march to power where a German success would make a fundamental change completely upsetting the European balance.

Conference at Munich. In September, 1938, Hitler demanded immediate cession of the predominantly German-speaking areas of Czechoslovakia, threatening war if his demands were refused. For several days a new World War seemed almost inevitable. But Neville Chamberlain, in pursuance of his policy of appeasement, was determined to prevent a general war even at the cost of surrendering Czechoslovakia to Germany. He persuaded the French government, led by Eduard Daladier and Georges Bonnet, to repudiate the

Linguistic Map of the SUCCESSION STATES

French treaty engagement to defend Czechoslovakia. Confronted by the desertion of her allies, Czechoslovakia was compelled to submit. At a conference held at Munich on September 29, attended by the "Big Four" leaders, Hitler, Mussolini, Chamberlain, and Daladier, the details of Czechoslovakia's dismemberment were worked out. German military occupation began October 1. Although the conference met ostensibly to decide the fate of Czechoslovakia, it really decided the fate of all central Europe, started Germany on a road to expansion and power to which no limits could be set, reduced French prestige and influence to its lowest point since 1871, and began a new era of *Machtpolitik* with incalculable consequences for the whole world.

Capitulation of Czechoslovakia.[1] As a result of the Munich agreement, Germany was given Sudetenland (consisting of 10,885 square miles and with a population of 3,595,000). That Hitler would dominate the political and economic activities of the remainder of Czechoslovakia was expected. However, neither France nor Great Britain felt that within six months, Hitler would break his pledge to respect the independence of Czechoslovakia and to make no further territorial demands in continental Europe. Nevertheless, with the same technique which had been successful in the conquest of Austria a year previous — (1) preliminary newspaper and radio propaganda, (2) intimidating conferences with political leaders of territory to be brought under German control, (3) concentration and march of Nazi troops, and (4) triumphal entry into the desired territorial area — Hitler added most of the remainder of Czechoslovakia (Bohemia, Moravia, and Slovakia) to the Third Reich while the French and British confined their protests to a verbal barrage (March, 1939). Hungary stepped in, and after four days of fighting annexed the easternmost part of Czechoslovakia, namely Carpatho-Ukraine. This gave Poland and Hungary a long-sought common frontier. Thus, the twenty-year old buffer republic of central Europe came to a temporary end.

The Fascintern. The Roman-Berlin Axis was reinforced in November, 1936, by an agreement between Germany and Japan for coöperation against Soviet Russia. Late in 1937 Germany, Italy, and Japan formed an alliance avowedly directed against the spread of communism. This pact became known as the "Fascintern" (opposed to the "Comintern" or *Third Communist International*). The term "Fascintern" implied a world Fascist movement directed and supported by the

---

1 Refers to Czechoslovakia after Munich.

three greatFascist powers. Such a movement was being vigorously pushed in many parts of the world by economic pressure, propaganda, espionage, and the direct fomentation of revolution. After the Conference at Munich this fascist international movement became more open and violent and gave grave concern to Great Britain, whose position in the Far East was menaced by the Japanese invasion of South China, while an Italo-German promoted revolt threatened Palestine and Suez; and to the United States, which saw in German agitation in South America a threat to the Monroe Doctrine. But the issues were beclouded by the fact that social and economic class interests cut across national interests, and by the extraordinary complexity of the new diplomacy. To many critics, for example, it appeared that the surrender of the democracies at the Conference of Munich was motivated rather by the fear of Communist revolution than the fear of German military power, and that the true interpretation of the conference was to be found in the isolation of Soviet Russia. Some observers even described the warlike preparations of the great western nations in September, 1938, as essentially "shadow-boxing" intended to prepare public opinion for a shifting of the weight of Britain and France toward the "Fascintern." Whatever was the correct explanation of the epoch-making events of 1938, it was certain that not since the French Revolution had there been in the world such a complex struggle of underground forces or a world situation so baffling to men's power to understand and control.

THE NEW DIPLOMACY

In a speech made early in 1938, United States Secretary of State Cordell Hull denounced the "contagious scourge of treaty-breaking" that seemed to have flared up in the world. He was referring in particular to the "undeclared war" being waged by Japan against China in violation of the Nine Power Pact and the Kellogg-Briand Treaty, and to the unilateral scrapping of the Treaty of Versailles by Hitler. Through the year 1938 the "scourge of treaty-breaking" showed itself indeed contagious. While standards of international morality have never been particularly high, it can be said that never before in modern times have treaties and agreements been so cynically disregarded. It was clear, however, that contempt for treaties was but a single phase of a new spirit in international relations. This new spirit was marked by a complete retreat from the humanitarian idealism and the "code of the gentleman" that characterized nineteenth century life and to a considerable degree softened and civilized even the anarchic relations between states.

Totalitarian War. The rise of the Nazi-Fascist ideology, with its concept of the "totalitarian" state (a state in which all the activities of the citizens are supervised and coördinated) and with its repudiation of humanitarianism has been paralleled by a new theory of "totalitarian" war. By totalitarian war is meant war waged by every conceivable device against entire populations and in no way limited by international conventions or considerations of humanity. Terrible as was the World War of 1914-1918, there can be no doubt that the consciousness of a common humanity between the combatants prevented many excesses. But in "totalitarian" war there are no rules and no restraints. Women and children are as legitimate objects of attack as armed soldiers. Most terrifying of all the possibilities of totalitarian war was that of mass air raids, perhaps not even preceded by a declaration of war, on the centers of civilian population, and the partial destruction by gas, fire, and explosives of such great cities as London, Paris, Berlin, Rome. The menace of air raids hung low over the counsels of European statesmen, and tended to make diplomacy resemble more than ever a conference between men with pistols clapped to each other's heads. An object lesson in what Europe would have to expect in a totalitarian war was provided by the Japanese invasion of China (1937-1938).

Unofficial War. A technique of promoting and subsidizing revolution within an officially friendly state with the intention of creating a situation where active intervention might be safe had been developed to a high degree by the Fascist powers. This was the method used by Mussolini in Spain, by Hitler in Austria and Czechoslovakia, and by Japan in Manchuria. The method is particularly effective when used against a democratic government, as the agitators are able to take advantage of the civil liberties of the democracy to carry on subversive activity. To what extent and by what means such movements can be prevented from endangering a democracy is to-day an unsolved problem. The dilemma is that of repudiating an essential condition of democracy by limiting freedom of speech and assemblage, or of permitting an agitation directed ultimately to the overthrow of the democratic system. The technique of unofficial war has many variants and has become a greatly complicating factor in the new diplomacy. It lends itself to hypocrisy and obscurantism, as when Italian submarines operating in the Mediterranean during the Spanish Civil War were described as "pirates" and ostensibly hunted by Italian as well as British destroyers, or when soldiers ordered to Spain were described as "volunteers," or when Hitler declared it was necessary for Germany to "restore order" in Austria, when it was generally believed that the disorder was of his own making.

Terrorism. The deliberate use of terrorism for political ends was another unpleasant feature of Fascist methods. In Austria and in the Sudeten German region of Czechoslovakia, opponents of the Nazi movement fomented from Germany were dragooned into silence if not active support by threats of imprisonment, torture, and economic ruin. Only the most courageous men could stand up to pressure of this nature. The horrible fate of thousands of political refugees showed only too clearly that the threats were not idle.

Dictator Coöperation. A feature of the new diplomacy, shown up in clear light by the Czechoslovakian Crisis and the events following the Conference of Munich, was the advantage held by the dictator governments in their ability to act in concert without the necessity of persuading cabinets to agree, or of considering the effect upon public opinion of the decisions taken. So well developed was the machinery of propaganda in Germany and Italy that Hitler and Mussolini could create overnight almost any current of public opinion that would serve their turn. Democratic governments, on the other hand, were unable to act with the same swiftness. With them there were parliaments, the press, and cabinets of divided minds. Considerations of this sort were responsible for driving European democracies closer to dictatorial control, and were responsible in some measure for the helplessness of some small democratic countries before the demands of larger dictatorial powers.

War of Nerves. After Munich, most observers realized that Neville Chamberlain's optimistic "peace for our time" had not been assured by appeasing Hitler with the Sudetenland. The Paris-Berlin Peace Pact (December 1938), in which Germany and France each agreed (1) to promote good neighborly relations, (2) to recognize as definite the present frontiers, and (3) to remain in contact on all questions involving third powers which were likely to lead to international difficulties, did not materially ease the tension. In the meantime Italian demands for French territories of Tunisia, Nice, Savoy, Corsica, and Jibuti served to strain French-Italian relations. Although Italy reaffirmed the British-Italian Pact of 1938 during a visit of Prime Minister Chamberlain to Rome, the Rome-Berlin Axis partners maintained outward evidence of unswerving loyalty.

The end of Czechoslovakia was followed by Hitler's acquisition of Memel and by strong pledges by Great Britain and France guaranteeing the independence of Eastern European nations including Poland, Rumania, Turkey, and Greece. The concentration of Nazi soldiers in East Prussia preceded Hitler's demands against Poland for Danzig and for rights in the Polish Corridor. Reaffirmed promises of military aid to Poland by Great Britain did not deter the Fuehrer's actions. Frantically, the European nations rushed their armament programs and feverish steps were taken to build diplomatic fronts. The worst was expected and yet a miracle was sought to avoid the impending crisis.

More fuel was added to the war of nerves with the Italian invasion of Albania, the flight of the royal family, and the subsequent announcement that Victor Emmanuel III of Italy was henceforth King of Albania (April, 1939). The next few weeks found, (1) Germany and Italy signing a new treaty guaranteeing military assistance to each other, (2) peace overtures by the new Pope, Pius XII (former Papal Secretary of State, Eugenio, Cardinal Pacelli), (3) the end of the Spanish Civil War with Generalissimo Francisco Franco established as a Fascist dictator, (4) a change in the type of guarantees demanded by Russia in return for supporting the British so-called "Peace Front," and (5) the resignation of Russian Foreign Commissar M. Litvinov and the appointment of V. Molotov which was detrimental to the peace cause of Great Britain and France.

The diplomatic activity reached a new crisis with the announcement of a Russo-German Pact which was signed in August, 1939. The agreement included a statement of non-aggression against each other and a promise of non-assistance to any third power which might attack either Germany or Russia. Once more Hitler and his aides had accomplished the seemingly impossible. Avowed enemies, naziism and communism had made a strange bargain. The seeds for another world war had been well planted.

CHAPTER XX.

WORLD WAR II, 1939–1945

Germany's invasion of Poland on September 1, 1939, led to a declaration of war by both Great Britain and France two days later. Once more the peace of the entire civilized world was threatened. The past decade had witnessed the conflict between China and Japan, the rise of Germany to a position of European dominance, the Italo-Ethiopian War, and the Spanish Civil War; but in each instance, although the policies of leading countries were affected, the new diplomacy had prevented a general European war. However, in the course of events described as the "war of nerves," diplomacy, though frantic in its efforts, failed. Europe and the world girded for a long war. As the lines were drawn, the neutral nations set in motion machinery to (1) preserve their neutrality, (2) develop forces and materials for national defense, and (3) introduce bases for the restoration of peace. Subsequent events which violated the rights of peace-loving neutrals served only to arouse people all over the world and to develop a recognition of the world-conquering ambitions of the Hitler war machine.

FIRST PHASE OF THE WAR (1939-1941)

The first phase of World War II extended from the invasion of Poland on September 1, 1939, until the repudiation by Germany of the Russo-German non-aggression non-assistance pact and Hitler's invasion of Russia on June 22, 1941. It was a period of Nazi success with one victory following another. One after another the European countries were brought into the conflict until only Sweden, Switzerland, Spain, Portugal, and Turkey remained neutral.

Conquest of Poland (September 1939). The first stage of World War II found Germany invading and conquering Poland in a lightning war (blitzkrieg) of only three weeks. The mechanized units of the Nazi army quickly overran Poland and demoralized the Polish forces. Although Warsaw held out for several days, it finally capitulated when further resistance meant only continual loss of life with eventual defeat. In the later stages of the fighting, Russia invaded the eastern Polish frontier and in a series of military successes routed Polish troops. The failure of the British promises of material aid to mature in time to be of real assistance to the Poles, and the completeness of the German victories resulted in the signing of a peace treaty on September 28. Independent Poland again was temporarily wiped off the European map, with Russia taking all Polish land east of the Bug River and with Germany claiming the rest. A portion of the Polish government and some of the military and naval units fled to England, where they continued the prosecution of the war. German and Russian peace overtures to Great Britain and France on the basis of the new *status quo* fell upon deaf ears.

War on the Western Front. Since the end of World War I, France and Germany had constructed hundreds of miles of fortifications along the Western Front. The French Maginot and the German Siegfried (Limes) lines were elaborate steel and concrete arsenals of defense. Entrenched behind their respective fortifications neither the French nor Germans risked an offensive during the first nine months of the war. Meanwhile the British and French worked feverishly to develop additional equipment for modern mechanized warfare.

Russo-Finnish War. Fresh from military successes in Poland, Russian diplomatic pressure gained desired naval and air bases in Estonia and Latvia, and forced concessions from Lithuania which greatly jeopardized the independence of these three countries. Finland's refusal to grant Russian demands for territory and privileges which would endanger Finnish independence started a new war of nerves in the Scandinavian countries. After a month the Soviet press became more and more strongly anti-Finnish. A reported border incident was used as a pretext for Russian mobilization and invasion of Finland (November, 1939). For 105 days, the Finns, a nation of only 3,000,000 persons, struggled against the power of Russia's 180,000,000 while the world watched and marvelled at the stamina of the Finnish soldiers. Behind their defense fortifications on the Karelian Peninsula (Mannerheim Line), the Finns wreaked havoc upon the invading mechanized units of the Russian army. Meanwhile, the League of Nations met, condemned Russia's action, and voted to expel the USSR from the League and to send assistance to the Finns. The odds were too great and the Finns were forced to accept a humiliating peace treaty (March, 1940). Russia obtained (1) more than 12,000 square miles of Finnish territory on the Karelian Isthmus (including Finnish Mannerheim Line) and in the north, (2) Rybachi Peninsula, (3) a 30-year lease of the important naval air base of Hangoe, and in addition Finland, (4) was to enter into a trade treaty with Russia and (5) construct a railroad which, when linked by one to be built by Russia, would connect with the Swedish port of Tornio.

Capitulation of Denmark and Norway. Rumors of an intended Nazi invasion of Scandinavian countries were climaxed on April 9 with the report that Nazi troops had crossed the Danish frontier. As Denmark was in no position to offer any effective military resistance, the Germans were allowed to occupy the territory without any bloodshed. A protective

custody of Denmark was established by Germany which was
to be in force for the duration of the war. Meanwhile thousands of German troops were landing at Norwegian seaports
and hundreds were flown to strategic air fields. With the aid
of the so-called "fifth column" (in Norway, "Quislings"), the
Nazis established themselves in Norway. King Haakon refused to accept Hitler's protective custody and appealed to
his people to preserve Norway's independence. The Allies
sent assurances of aid, but with the Germans established in
Norway and with effective work by the fifth columnists, the
Allies were unsuccessful in ousting the Germans although
several important conflicts took place both on land and sea.
Finally, greatly outnumbered, the British were forced to withdraw and, with the exception of sporadic raids, to leave the
control of Norway in German hands. King Haakon found
refuge in England. Sweden's neutrality was acknowledged,
if not respected.

**Subjugation of the Netherlands, Belgium, and Luxem-
bourg (1940).** Even while Hitler's forces were completing
the conquest of Norway, the Netherlands, Belgium, and Luxembourg (May 10, 1940) were invaded in another surprise
move by the Germans. Luxembourg was easily and quickly
overrun. From a refuge in England Queen Wilhelmina, Prin-
cess Juliana, her consort Prince Bernhard, and their two children learned of the surrender of Holland on May 14. However, the Dutch possessions pledged coöperation with the Allies in carrying on the war. Meanwhile Brussels, the capital
of Belgium, had fallen before the fierce and amazing onslaught
of the German blitzkrieg. On May 28, King Leopold of the
Belgians issued a cease-firing order and he became a voluntary prisoner of Hitler. The swiftness of the German successes in the Low Countries was a great blow to the defensive plans of the Allies, but great faith was placed in the
ability of the French army to establish a new front to stem
the advance. Meanwhile, the British were successful in evac-
uating thousands of soldiers from the port of Dunkerque, in
France, in one of the truly great feats of the first phase of
the war.

Fall of France (June 1940). The German march continued on through northern France and toward the channel ports — possible jumping off places for the planned invasion of the British Isles. With more than a million men, Hitler launched his attack on France. Outflanking the highly vaunted Maginot Line, the Nazis crossed the Somme, Aisne, and Marne rivers as the French hastily retreated. Since the French were unable to form new defense lines that would hold the German panzer divisions, they retreated and surrendered Paris on June 14, 1940. Three days later the World War I hero of Verdun, aged Marshal Henri Pétain, who had succeeded Premier Reynaud, asked for an armistice. In the historic railroad car in the Forest of Compiègne, the French signed an armistice on June 21 which left Paris and northern France in Germany's hands and provided for the establishment of a government at Vichy under the leadership of Pétain and Pierre Laval. The old republic was superseded by a Fascist state controlled by the Nazis. A separate armistice was signed with Italy, who had declared war on Britain and France on June 10, 1940, just before the expected capitulation of France. Under the leadership of General Charles de Gaulle, a French National Committee (Free French) was organized in London to continue the fight with the assistance of those members of the French army and navy who had fled from France. An attempt by the Free French to gain control of the navy and of African possessions was not successful. Fearful lest the Germans obtain control of the French navy, the British destroyed a large number of French naval vessels at Oran, Algeria.

The German Blitzkrieg. The discussion of the new diplomacy[1] reveals the general pattern for World War II in terms of its methods and scope. As he views the quick successive conquests of Poland, Denmark, Norway, Luxembourg, Holland, Belgium, and France (September, 1939—June, 1940), the student may wish to review specific techniques used by this new "invincible" military machine. Operating on a carefully planned timetable, hundreds of dive bombers attacked the area

---

[1] See pages 242-246.

to be conquered dropping bombs and flying low in order to machine-gun troops and disrupt supply and communication lines. Next, panzer tank divisions attacked in line, side by side, spurting flames and firing automatic guns and small cannons. After that the tanks would begin to break through the enemy's lines, turning and striking the enemy's position from the side or the rear. Then the light infantry would be poured into the breaks in the line which had been created by the tanks. The infantry, however, was equipped with armored cars and trucks. Its job was to take over and consolidate the gains. Often hundreds of troops were dropped behind the lines from airplanes with assignments to interrupt power and communication services and to hold strategic spots. Superiority in the air was basic to this type of warfare. Finally, fifth columnists were utilized to divulge important information and to aid in the actual conquest once the invasion is under way.

Battle for Britain. The unsuccessful attempts of Great Britain to aid her allies in stemming the march of the Nazis caused considerable dissension with Prime Minister Neville Chamberlain's war policy. On the day, May 10, 1940, that the Low Countries were invaded Winston Churchill formed a war cabinet with Anthony Eden as war secretary. The new Prime Minister said, "I have nothing to offer but blood, toil, tears, and sweat, . . . but a faith in ultimate victory." The next year was one of the darkest in the history of the British Empire.

PLANES OVER ENGLAND. After the fall of France, Britain girded herself for the threatened invasion. First it was necessary for Germany to knock out the Royal Air Force, as control of the sky over England was essential. The battle reached its greatest height in September and October and although whole communities were strafed with demolition and incendiary bombings, and although considerable damage was inflicted upon seaports, industrial centers, and London, yet the people devised means of defense which kept casualties to a minimum. Nevertheless, production was curtailed and England called upon the members of the British Commonwealth of Nations and upon the United States to aid her in her fight to save democracy and to crush its enemies by supplying both war and consumption materials. Meanwhile the R.A.F. (Royal Air Force) carried the war to German industrial centers. Concentrated attacks were made upon the channel ports to lessen the possibility of invasion.

WAR ON THE SEA. Great Britain and Germany began a new war on the seas which was similar to that fought in World War I. For her part, Great Britain set about to drive German shipping from the seas and to keep the ocean routes open for transporting supplies to the homeland. During the first phase of World War II the effectiveness of the block-ade was partially offset by (1) the German-Russian Pact, (2) Italy's entrance into the war, (3) the fall of France, and (4) German commandeering of supplies in conquered countries. Submarine and air raids on British and neutral shipping re-sulted in a tremendous loss of merchant and naval equip-ment and supplies. (Nearly one-half million tons of Allied shipping was lost in April, 1940.) Such exploits as (1) sink-ing of the *Athenia,* (2) battle of the *Graf Spee,* (3) *Altmark* incident, (4) battles of Taranto and Sardinia with the Italian fleet, (5) sinking of *H.M.S. Hood* and Nazi *Bismarck,* and (6) aid of the British fleet in the battle for North Africa provided the highlights of the war on the sea.

THE BRITISH LIFE-LINE. On the defensive at home Britain was fearful of thrusts at strategic points on her Mediterranean life-line to the East — Gibraltar, Malta, and Suez. In the fall of 1940, the Italians started an offensive against Egypt, but it was checked at Sidi Barrani in western Egypt. A British counteroffensive resulted in forcing the Italians from eastern Libya and the capture of tens of thousands of soldiers. Since Italy was unable to get reinforcements and supplies to her soldiers in Ethiopia, the control of that country was also threatened. However, with the aid of Nazi reinforcements an-other Axis push was undertaken in April, 1941, which was to force the British out of Libya once more A small garrison retained control of Tobruk with the aid of British naval sup-port. Late in May, the Italians in Ethiopia surrendered and

Haile Selassie, who had the help of the British, was restored to the control of his country, which had been in Italian hands since 1936.

The Greeks' Magnificent Stand. With assurances of aid from Great Britain, Premier Metaxas rejected an Italian ultimatum on October 27, 1940. During the next six months the Greeks surprised the whole world by the valiant stand which they made against the Italians in Albania. Meanwhile, the British rushed reinforcements to Greece. However, with control of Rumania (October, 1940), an Axis pact with Bulgaria (March, 1941), and with Yugoslavia under an army coup (which had repudiated a government pro-Axis pact), Hitler massed his troops in Rumania and made ready to assist his Axis partner. Yugoslavia came to the assistance of Greece, but the Nazi machine quickly conquered Yugoslavia and rolled on into Greece. King George II fled to the island of Crete as the British evacuated thousands of troops. The Germans entered Athens on May 27, 1941. In one of the more spectacular victories of the war, the Nazis invaded the island of Crete by using glider troop planes, and within ten days (June 1, 1941) the Greek royal family and thousands of British soldiers were forced to withdraw.

SECOND PHASE OF THE WAR (1941-1942)

The second phase of the war began with the invasion of Russia by the Nazi troops on June 22, 1941. The German-Russian non-aggression pact of convenience was ended and, under the impression that a quick knock-out blow should be dealt to Russia before the final subjugation of England, Hitler launched his Russian campaign. Since this split with Russia was the turning-point in World War II, it aptly marks the beginning of the second phase.

Russia and the German Pact (1939-1941). The signing of the Russo-German pact in August, 1939, provided Stalin with a kind of neutrality which gave him an opportunity to speed his military preparations against the day when they might be needed. However, once the Germans invaded Poland, Stalin did not hesitate to use his soldiers to gain territory in the subsequent partitioning. Military and naval concessions, and later political ones were obtained from Lithuania, Estonia, and Latvia. Finland's refusal to grant Russia the desired privileges resulted in the Russo-Finnish War (see page 249). The exacting of a humiliating peace treaty upon the Finns was to be instrumental in that nation's war upon Russia after the German invasion of June 22, 1941. In the Balkans, Stalin stepped in, and after only light fighting he gained control of Bessarabia and Bukovina from Rumania. Thus Russian territory was extended south to the delta of the Danube. Treaties of non-aggression were signed with both Turkey and Japan. In April, Joseph Stalin became premier of the Union of Soviet Socialist Republics.

German Advance into Russia. The control of the Balkans by Germany caused Stalin considerable alarm since it made possible a 2,000 mile front from the arctic to the Black Sea for an attack against Russia. Further, the rich grain fields of the Ukraine and supplies of Russian oil were closer than ever to Nazi hands. Maintaining that Russia had violated her pact with Germany, Hitler's forces invaded Russian occupied territories on June 22, 1941. The three main attacks were aimed at (1) Bessarabia, (2) Moscow, and (3) Leningrad. Later a fourth drive was made upon Kiev. Carrying out a policy of "scorched earth" as they retreated, the Russians were forced to fall back before Germans, Hungarians, Rumanians, and Finns. Leningrad and Moscow were both threatened, and Kiev actually fell to the Nazis (September, 1941). Terrific losses in men and materials were reported by both sides.

The Russian Counteroffensive. The inability of Hitler's armies to crush the Russians before winter resulted in a great Russian counteroffensive which began with the recapture of Rostov, so-called key to the Caucasus. With defeat facing him for the first time in a major engagement, and with the knowledge of Napoleon's ignoble retreat from Moscow, Hitler ignored the advice of his generals and assumed command of his armies. Handicapped by cold weather and deep snow, the Nazi panzer divisions bogged down. The Russians fought valiantly and each time the Germans attempted to form new lines, they pushed their offensive. By the first of February, 1942, the Russians had relieved the German pressure on Leningrad, Moscow, and in the Donets Basin. The combination of (1) long German supply lines, (2) strong Red Army, and (3) a particularly severe winter made possible effective penetrations of the Nazi defense lines. However, during the spring and summer of 1942, Hitler's military machine surged forward once more in a drive into the Crimea and the Caucasus which more than offset the Russian gains of the previous winter. Russian counteroffensives were unsuccessful, but the defenses in the Moscow and Leningrad areas continued to hold. Meanwhile, the Nazis overran the Kerch Peninsula, besieged Stalingrad, and threatened the Caucasus oil fields. Sevastopol, last Russian outpost in the Crimea, capitulated (July 2, 1942), and Rostov fell before the end of the month. In September, the Germans broke through the Stalingrad defenses. Repeated demands for a second front to force the Germans to withdraw some of their strength from the Russian theater were not answered by action because it was deemed unwise until additional preparations had been made. Russia's allies did aid her by an ever increasing flow of military equipment and supplies, and by an intensified air war against Axis armament, manufacturing, and shipping centers. Meanwhile the United States and Great Britain exerted considerable pressure upon Finland to come to terms with the Soviet Union, but without success. At the beginning of the second winter offensive, Russia's position was desperate.

The African Theater in the Second Phase (1941-1942). In the fall of 1941, the British started still another offensive against the Axis, not only to recapture Libya, but also to help the Russian campaign by forcing the Axis to keep large air and land forces in Africa. With the best of equipment and with adequate supplies for the first time, the Allied forces started a march across Libya that was to bring them to the Gulf of Sirte (January 20, 1942). The British victory in Libya was obtained through the coöperative effort of land, air, and sea forces of both British and native troops. Another German counteroffensive, however, resulted in the loss of Bengazi as Marshal Erwin Rommel obtained reinforcements and supplies from Axis convoys which had eluded British air and naval units. Once more the seesaw battle for North Africa tipped in favor of the German and Italian Africa Corps. From Bengazi, Marshal Rommel pushed east to Derna, Tobruk, and on into Egypt to within seventy miles of Alexandria before he was halted near El Alamein. It was from this position that the British Eighth Army was to start its offensive in November, 1942, which was to drive the Germans and Italians from the whole of North Africa.

Britain in the Mediterranean. Unsuccessful in her efforts to establish a foothold on the continent in Greece, and skeptical of Turkey's final loyalty, but with a pro-British government established in Iraq (June, 1941), the British with the aid of the Free French invaded Syria by way of northern Palestine and western Iraq. At first the French garrisons offered resistance to the Allies, but finally on July 14, 1941, an armistice, previously authorized by the Vichy government, was concluded. Sporadic raids upon Italian shipping were carried out by the British, and in addition, important industrial and naval centers in Italy were continually bombed.

The Battle of the Atlantic. The second phase of the war was characterized not only by the fighting in Russia, Syria, and Africa, but also, in the continued attempt of Germany to cut off Great Britain's sources of supplies, by intensive air and submarine warfare. This battle became more and more important as the policy of the United States changed from one of neutrality to participation as a "non-shooting" member of the Democratic front. In fact, America became the arsenal for Great Britain. Through a multibillion-dollar Lend-Lease program, the means of financing the supplies for the Allies was provided. The occupation of Greenland and of Iceland by the United States and the subsequent convoying of ships to these points by the United States was of first-rate importance to Great Britain. A tremendous reduction in the amount of shipping tonnage lost by sinkings resulted. Meanwhile, President Roosevelt and Prime Minister Churchill met in the Atlantic on board a British battleship and drew up a statement of peace aims (Atlantic Charter). The attack upon a United States destroyer (*Greer*) by a submarine resulted in President Roosevelt's order to "shoot first." As the control of the Atlantic made possible more and more war machines and increased consumption supplies for the British Isles, the Royal Air Force continued its bombing of Nazi-held industrial and military centers. German attacks upon English centers decreased while Hitler's Russian offensive was under way. After the entry of the United States into the war, more and more material help was immediately available to Great Britain and Russia. During the year the submarine toll of shipping was exceedingly high, but through improved use of air and surface craft, the losses were gradually decreased.

THIRD PHASE OF THE WAR (1941-1942)

The third phase of World War II began with the now famous "Day of Infamy," December 7, 1941, when the Japanese initiated their attacks upon Hawaii, the Philippines, other United States island possessions, Malaya, and Hongkong. It is interesting to note that the third phase of World War II began while the second phase was still in progress. The emphasis was rather upon new alliances and a new major theater of activities than upon a chronological basis. The war now became even more of a world war than World War I. No corner of the globe was free of its potential battlegrounds. As the second phase was for Britain and the Soviet Union primarily a period of (1) military setbacks, (2) defensive strategy, and (3) preparation for a future offensive, so the third phase found the United States, as a shooting partner in the war against Germany, Italy, and Japan, pursuing a course dictated by these same three factors.

Collaboration of the United States with Great Britain. The declarations of war in September, 1939, found a strong neutral sentiment in the United States. But as the fight progressed, it became apparent more and more that the United States could not remain completely aloof. President Roosevelt's policy of coöperation centered around the following five-point program: (1) the development of an effective land, air, and sea force to protect the United States, (2) the reorganization of industry and business on a centralized war economy basis, (3) the further consolidation of Western Hemisphere relations, (4) the establishment of a program of aid to the anti-Axis countries which would make the United States the arsenal for the democratic allies, and (5) the formulation of a plan for a more permanent peace. The first president of the United States to be elected for a third term, Franklin D. Roosevelt was able to continue his policies without interruption as a result of his victory over the Republican aspirant, Wendell L. Willkie, in November, 1940.

Building the Military Front. After the Polish invasion, steps were taken to increase the size of the army, naval, and air forces. For the first time during a period of American peace, a compulsory military training act became a law, and male citizens between twenty-one and thirty-five were required to register for possible military service (Burke-Wadsworth Act). Military camps were established, war industries were organized, and modern techniques were studied. After the Pearl Harbor attack, plans were made for a combined war force of 10,000,000 men by the end of 1943.[1]

Industrial Centralization. The spectre of war resulted in more and more governmental control. Boards were established to make possible an even flow of necessary raw materials for defense industries. Priorities were established to guarantee basic goods. New taxes were introduced and old ones were increased to help pay for the war effort. Finally, in January, 1942, President Roosevelt appointed Donald M. Nelson head of the War Production Board with final authority, a position second only to the President in its potential power over business and industry.

Western Hemisphere Solidarity. One of the most important aspects of President Roosevelt's program was the development of a program of economic coöperation and political collaboration with the other countries of the Americas. Conferences were held in Lima (1938), Panama (1939), Havana (1940), and Rio de Janeiro (1942). These conferences aimed

---

[1] Age limits were established at eighteen to thirty-eight for Selective Service requirements.

to assure the countries concerned that the United States (1) had no imperialist designs, (2) had a sincere desire for "good neighbor" relations, (3) would coöperate to prevent foreign intervention, (4) would provide military assistance if any of the countries were attacked, and (5) would work for better trade relations. Upon acquisition of British naval bases in the Western Hemisphere, the United States made them available to the naval forces of Latin America. Relations steadily improved until at the 1942 conference, the nations accepted an anti-Axis stand recommending a diplomatic break with Germany, Italy, and Japan. By the beginning of February most of the countries had severed relations with the Axis.

Aid for the Allies.   In the earliest days of the war, the United States adopted a policy of "cash and carry" which was definitely beneficial to Great Britain. Later, fifty over-aged American destroyers were traded to Great Britain for leases of strategic British naval and air bases in the Western Hemisphere. In March, 1941, a multibillion-dollar Lend-Lease Act provided for an uninterrupted production of war materials for British use. The occupation of Iceland and Greenland and the establishment of naval patrols released British units for naval convoying in other areas. In the process of aiding Britain it was inevitable that attacks upon American ships would result. An attack upon an American destroyer (*Greer*), as has been said, caused President Roosevelt to issue an order to "shoot first." Incidents in the Atlantic brought the United States closer and closer to a complete break with the Axis, but in the meantime, the situation in the Far East was portentous.

Winning the Peace.   President Roosevelt's program included a recognition of the necessity for winning the peace as well as the war. In mid-August, 1941, Prime Minister Churchill and the President of the United States drew up the aforementioned eight-point statement of peace aims (Atlantic Charter) at a secret meeting held on a British battleship. Later (December, 1941) Prime Minister Churchill visited the United States and Canada. In addition to the formulation of plans for the coördinated prosecution of the war, bases for a just peace were discussed. Exiled governments for the conquered countries were recognized, and their collaboration was solicited. Meanwhile President Roosevelt expressed the hope that the new post war world would be founded upon four basic freedoms — (1) speech and expression, (2) religion, (3) freedom from want, and (4) freedom from fear of aggression.

United States — Japanese Relations. The desire of Japan to dictate a new order in the Far East was bound to conflict with the interests of both Great Britain and the United States. The conquest of Manchuria (1931-1932) and the undeclared Chinese-Japanese War (1937-1945) were mute evidence of Japan's plans. Under strong militarist governmental regimes, the Japanese were successful in getting control of some of the richest Chinese provinces and most of the important cities in the north. Meanwhile, Chiang Kai-shek moved his government from Hankow to Chungking. With meagre war supplies, the Chinese continued the fight against Japan. When Japan's invasion of Manchuria was condemned by the League of Nations, that country resigned. The Berlin-Rome-Tokyo Axis bound together Germany, Italy, and Japan and recognized (1) Japan's interests in China, (2) Italy's control in Ethiopia, and (3) Germany's aggrandizement in Austria and Czechoslovakia. Later, in 1940, the members of the Axis pledged military assistance to each other if the United States entered World War II. On the other hand, Great Britain promised aid to the United States if Japan attacked her. Gradually the United States withdrew its exports of planes, munitions, scrap-iron, and oil to Japan. However, attempts were made to appease Tokyo. After the collapse of France, Japan established a so-called protectorate over French Indochina (1940), and in the following year Thailand (Siam) capitulated to Japanese demands. Thus Japan was in a position to threaten the Dutch East Indies, the British in Malaya, and the Americans in the Philippines. A change in the Japanese cabinet (1941) which resulted in a strong pro-Axis militarist government under Premier Tojo caused considerable concern in the United States and Great Britain. A special Japanese envoy,

Saburo Kurusu, discussed with the United States Department of State plans for a peaceful settlement of differences between the United States and Japan. President Roosevelt even appealed to Emperor Hirohito for the continuance of peaceful relations.

Day of Infamy (December 7, 1941). Even while the conferences between the United States and Japan were under way, the Japanese completed plans for a surprise attack upon both British and American possessions in the Pacific. Several hours after fighting began (December 7, 1941), the Japanese Ambassador and the special envoy, Kurusu, handed Secretary Hull a reply to the American statement for a peaceful solution of relations in the Far East. Without any warning and with coördinated air and naval forces, the raids were carried out against Hawaii, the Philippines, other United States island possessions, Malaya, and Hongkong. The raid on Pearl Harbor, base for the Pacific fleet, was extremely costly to the United States in men and in ships, before the Japanese withdrew. This first Japanese offensive resulted in (1) capture of Guam, Wake, and other United States island possessions, (2) capture of Hongkong, (3) invasion of the Philippines, and (4) the obtaining of a foothold on the Malayan Peninsula.

United States at War. The next day, December 8, 1941, President Roosevelt asked for and received from Congress a declaration of war against Japan. Great Britain also declared war on Japan. When Italy and Germany joined Japan in her war against the United States, Congress declared war on these countries. The attack on Pearl Harbor served to consolidate the American people back of the war effort as nothing else could have done. From all sides opposition to President Roosevelt's program disappeared. Congress quickly approved a $59,000,000,000 budget; the war economy was speeded up as both men and industry were drafted in a victory drive. While continuing her aid to Great Britain and Russia, the United States in coöperation with her Allies mapped out a plan for the prosecution of the war. Twenty-six countries signed the *Pact of the United Nations* on January 2, 1942, in which they pledged a common victory against the Axis. China declared war against the Axis and started a new offensive against Japanese-held territory in an attempt to relieve pressure upon British- and American-held possessions. Although the Japanese were able to obtain Manila, General MacArthur with his American soldiers and his Filipino troops continued to offer resistance (February, 1942). Gradually the British were forced out of the Malayan Peninsula and into the fortress of Singapore, where they girded themselves for a long siege. Without adequate air support and smarting under the naval losses of the first few days of the war in the East, the British and American fleets retired temporarily to await air reinforcements. Meanwhile the Dutch East Indies' navy was having spectacular success in its raids upon Japanese shipping. By the first of February, 1942, the United States was able to coöperate with the Dutch in attacking a large Japanese convoy in the Macassar Strait and to inflict heavy damage. A counterattack on Japanese-held islands was also carried out.

Japanese Successes. During the first three months of their war against the United Nations, the Japanese were unbelievably successful. The important Sumatra oil fields were taken. On February 15, Singapore fell and with it went the control of the best ocean route between the Pacific and Indian Oceans. The stubborn resistance of the Dutch was finally cracked and Java was occupied. In quick succession control over Burma, New Guinea, Andaman Islands, and the Solomons was established. These victories, with earlier pre-Pearl Harbor aggression which had resulted in advance air and other bases in China, Thailand, and French Indochina, placed the Japanese in a position to menace Australia and the strategic island steppingstones along the supply route from the United States. The control of the Philippines passed to the Japanese after a four months' delaying action on the Bataan Peninsula. Corregidor, famed island fortress, held out for another month (May 6, 1942). A spectacular token air raid against Tokyo and Yokohama by American flyers under Colonel Doolittle in April served to demonstrate the potentialities of carrier-based planes.

American Victories at Sea. In two thrusts, one in the area between New Guinea and the Solomons and the other near

Midway, the United States air and naval forces inflicted punishing defeats on the Japanese navy in the battles of Coral Sea (May 7-11, 1942) and of Midway (June 3-4). These battles restored to the United States the balance of sea power in the Pacific, which had been lost as a result of the raid on Pearl Harbor. Furthermore, these battles marked the peak of the enemy offensive. Thus a part of the chain of Allied island bases had been preserved for the next phase of the war in the Pacific. Meanwhile still another enemy fleet made a stab at Dutch Harbor in the Aleutians, but once more the United States naval and air forces made it withdraw from the objective. Landings were completed by this Japanese fleet, under cover of a heavy fog, at Kiska, Attu, and Agattu islands. The psychological value of these bases in the Aleutians was much greater than their strategic potential.

FOURTH PHASE OF THE WAR (1942-1945)

During the three previous phases of the war, the student has watched the progress of the war with most of the offensive tactics determined by the Axis partners. In the first phase, the Nazi blitzkrieg met little opposition from any source; in the second, the Soviet Union was unable to halt the Hitler war machine until winter offered a respite and the recapture of some lost territory, but the Germans rolled on to new gains in the Caucasus in the summer and fall of 1942; and in the third phase, Japan quickly gained control of one million square miles of land, and of 100 million people, and of untold wealth in needed material resources, while the Allies were helpless to prevent this aggression. The fourth phase found the Allies ready to take the offensive, in varying degrees, in Africa, Russia, the Pacific, Burma, and in the air over Western Europe. The opening of the second front in June, 1944, resulted in a series of events which culminated in the unconditional surrender of Germany on May 7, 1945.

War in the Pacific. Before the fall of Bataan, General Douglas MacArthur was ordered to proceed from the Philippines to Australia to assume command of the Southeast Pacific. From this island continent defenses against further Japanese aggression were laid and plans for the kind of offensive that limited equipment, supplies, and men made possible were developed. As a result of her conquests in Oceania, Japan's pressure upon China was temporarily lessened. The loss of the Burma Road made it increasingly difficult to get much needed material aid to the Chinese. However, the Chinese did score a victory in the Kiangsi Province (July, 1942) and in the Rice Bowl Battle (December, 1943), they not only effectively blocked an enemy advance toward Chungking, but they also forced the Japanese to retreat toward their Yangtze River bases. In India, the Allies were fashioning another military force to start a future offensive which was aimed at Burma (1944).

First Steps Back. Although the Allied offensive in the Pacific was impeded by lack of men and equipment, by August, 1942, beachheads were secured on the Guadalcanal and Florida islands and gradually enemy resistance was annihilated (February, 1943). From bases at Gona and Buna on New Guinea, the Japanese threatened the important Port Moresby, but finally the foe was forced to retreat and eastern New Guinea was safely in Allied hands. Through coördinated land, air, and sea operations during 1943, the United Nations continued to make new landings in the Solomons, New Georgia, Gilbert, and New Britain islands while other Japanese-held bases were subjected to heavy air attacks. On several occasions, portions of the enemy fleet were met and defeated. The Aleutians were cleared of the foes in September, 1943, when both Attu and Kiska were once more in American hands. Early in 1944, the Allies were ready to attack the enemy at Rabaul and in the Marshall Island area to develop a pincers on the strong Japanese base at Truk.

Conquest of North Africa. The control of North Africa by the Axis constituted a constant threat to the Suez Canal, and a giant pincers movement was developing through the Middle East to join with German forces proceeding into the Russian Caucasus. Furthermore, there was the danger of German infiltration and control of places like Dakar and western Morocco. In November, 1942, General Bernard Montgomery, who had replaced General Auchinleck, started one of the longest and most spectacular offensives of history, in which he chased Marshal Rommel and his vaunted Africa Corps 1300 miles in thirteen weeks — from El Alamein to the Mareth Line in Tunisia. A few days after Montgomery's Eighth Army started its push, American and British forces landed in western North Africa, quickly captured Casablanca and Oran, and completed negotiations with the French for the establishment of a provisional government. The invasion of unoccupied France by Germany, the scuttling of the French fleet at Toulon, the apparent loyalty of the French in Algeria to Vichy, and the presence in Algeria of Admiral Darlan resulted in a government headed by him with General Giraud as military chief. Six weeks later Darlan was assassinated and control was ultimately divided between General Giraud and General Charles de Gaulle, leader of Free French. Meanwhile the forces of Marshal Rommel were squeezed between the forces in the west and those of Montgomery in the east. The Mareth Line was penetrated, Tunis and Bizerte fell, and by the end of May 1943 the enemy had been cleared from North Africa. The Mediterranean life-line was preserved. Half the potential pincers had been destroyed.

Surrender of Italy. Events moved quickly. Preparatory to the invasion of Italy, the island steppingstones were conquered. Sicily was invaded in July, but before the completion of the conquest, Benito Mussolini was forced to resign (July 25, 1943) and his regime came to an end after twenty-one years. King Victor Emmanuel appointed Marshal Pietro Badoglio in his place. Although, for expediency, Badoglio indicated that the war would go on, yet by early September (effective September 8) he completed plans with the Allies for an armistice and the unconditional surrender of Italy. A large portion of the Italian fleet surrendered to the Allies, some ships were scuttled, and a few fell into German hands. The Germans decided to make a stand south of Rome to impede the march of General Clark's Fifth American Army and Montgomery's Eighth. In a spectacular parachute raid, the Germans succeeded in rescuing Mussolini from his Italian captors. On October 13, Italy declared war upon the Germans and took its place at once on the side of the Allies. Meanwhile, a newly organized French army was also fighting in Italy. By the beginning of 1944 the Allies were making breakthroughs in the German defensive line. Landings were made back of the German lines to facilitate the march to Rome. Enemy withdrawals made possible the occupation of Rome by the Allies in June, 1944. In some of the most bitter fighting of the war, the Americans and British attacked the German defense lines and slowly advanced north of Rome until in April, 1945, they overran the Po Valley and forced an unconditional surrender from the Germans (April 29, 1945). The day before, Benito Mussolini had been executed by a firing squad of Italian partisans.

Russian Theater. Once more the Russians came back with a second winter offensive, which was to break the siege of Stalingrad and start them on a march through which they would regain nearly 200,000 square miles of lost territory. The Caucasus pincers was blunted, also. The superior tactics of the Russians in winter campaigning dealt a serious blow to Hitler's prestige. With more and more equipment and supplies, the Russians were able to start a summer offensive which continued on into the fall of 1943 and which gained momentum as a third great winter campaign (January, 1944). Kiev was recaptured (November 1, 1943) by the Russians who then continued the push. At the start of the third winter campaign the Russians had a strong force ready to proceed from Smolensk toward the Baltic States and Poland, while another awaited favorable conditions to go southeast from the Dnieper toward Rumania. The Russians faced their third winter campaign with confidence, and with renewed faith in Great Britain and the United States as a result of the Moscow and Teheran conferences, although the determination of the Polish border presented a real threat to unity. The campaign found the Reds moving ahead on the whole eastern front. In the north the siege of Leningrad was completely broken and Novgorod was recaptured; in the central sector, advances were made in the Pripet Marshes; and in the south, General Vatutin's forces advanced 150 miles to the west toward Rumania (February, 1944).

Forced to fight on two fronts after D-day, the Germans were unable to stop the Russian advances and German soil was first invaded in East Prussia in August, 1944. Unwilling to withstand the ever-increasing power of the Russian military, Rumania, Finland, and Bulgaria signed armistices with the Allies. A fourth Russian winter offensive resulted in the capture of Warsaw, Budapest, Vienna, and eventually Berlin. The Eastern and Western fronts were joined at Torgau in April, 1945.

Softening the Enemy. The fourth phase of World War II found the Allies in control of the skies, not only over Britain, but also over a large portion of the Continent. A constantly increasing tonnage of bombs (the R.A.F. figures: 1940 — 13,000 tons, 1941 — 31,000 tons, 1942 — 50,000 tons, and in eleven months of 1943 — 150,700 tons) was dropped on German and Axis-controlled cities and military targets with uncanny accuracy as the techniques for low-level daylight precision and high-altitude nighttime bombing were improved. Whole cities were laid waste. Berlin was the special target of a series of devastating air raids as were the strategic cities of Frankfurt, Hamburg, Cologne, Essen, Leipzig, and Hanover. At first the clamor for a second front was ignored, save for commando raids, notably at Dieppe (April, 1942). The time was not ripe for invasion. However, the success of new defensive techniques in the war against wolf-pack submarine raiders in the Atlantic reduced the toll of lost shipping from ten a week (1942) to two a week (1943). Thus the constant flow of supplies for the Allies continued unchecked and made possible the concentration of the various talents of the Allies. Meanwhile, the underground movements in many of Hitler's subjugated countries were gaining strength. With the surrender of Italy, tension mounted in the Balkans, and such guerrilla movements as that of Draja Mihailovich, leader of the Chetniks, and of Druz Tito's (Joseph Broz) partisans in Yugoslavia became more intense. Supplied with arms and other equipment by the Allies, Tito's partisans engaged the Germans in a major battle near Zagreb (December, 1943). The attitude of Spain and Portugal became less and less pro-Nazi.

Arsenal for Democracy. Doubtless the greatest Allied battles in the two years after Pearl Harbor were not fought in the sky, on the sea, or in land engagements. They were fought on the production front. To hold this front was the first assignment for the United States. While an armed force of nearly 11,000,000 (August, 1944) was being developed, the greatest army of production workers of all time met the challenge. Let the figures speak — the number of all types of warplanes increased from 17,700 to 250,000; tonnage of all classes of warships from 2,132,000 to 5,000,000 tons; tonnage of merchant ships built increased from 1,163,000 tons (1941) to 19,000,000 (1943); and armored divisions from four to fifteen. From United States ports, sixty million tons of cargo were shipped to United Nations. On a comparative basis, the United States was producing twice the aircraft volume of Great Britain, Japan, and Germany combined; it was turning out more than six times the tonnage of merchant ships produced by the rest of the world; and its production of tanks and artillery was sufficient to meet any need. At the same time, the food-production index was now one-third greater than it was in 1939.

During the war the Axis tried desperately to offset the remarkable productive powers of the Allies by introducing new techniques and implements for fighting, but the inventive genius of the Allies was equal to the challenge. Improved radar protected convoys from submarines and warned the homeland of prospective air attacks. New antitank guns and shells pierced heavily armored enemy tanks. Flame-throwers flushed Germans and Japanese from foxholes, buildings, and caves. Gasoline-spraying incendiary bombs wreaked havoc upon military targets. Superfortresses with tremendous firing power and bomb-carrying capacity stepped up the air war against Japan's mainland. The Germans launched robot bombs and jet-propelled planes in a final attempt to bring England to her knees; but since the robots could not be controlled accurately, they caused more civilian than military damage. The Japanese introduced bomb-carrying balloons which were released against the West Coast of the United States. They were more successful, however, with their suicide (*kamikaze*) planes which attacked naval units and land installations in the Pacific. Preparatory to D-day thousands of small-type landing crafts were constructed by the Allies to facilitate invasion.

By far the most devastating weapon introduced into the history of warfare was the atomic bomb, first used by the United States against Japan in August, 1945. A single bomb released enough energy to cause as much destruction as 2000 bomb-laden B-29's. This bomb was one of the Allies' most guarded secrets.

Second Front. The stepped-up air war against Germany continued during the first part of 1944 while the general staff under the leadership of General Dwight D. Eisenhower developed final plans for invasion of France. On June 6, 1944, 250,000 men in 4000 ships with an air cover of 11,000 airplanes successfully breached Hitler's Atlantic wall on the coast of Normandy. Dissatisfaction within Germany culminated in an attempt by a military bloc to assassinate Hitler (July 20, 1944).

The German defense lines at Avranches were broken. Paris was liberated in August, and in the following month Germany proper was invaded at Aachen. Except for one last frantic counteroffensive in the battle of the bulge, the Germans were constantly pushed back by the Allies on the Western front. The Saar and Cologne were occupied by March, 1945, and then successful fighting in the Ruhr and at Coblenz and Essen made possible the uniting of the Russian and other Allied forces at Torgau.

Unconditional Surrender of Germany. After the failure of the German counteroffensive in the Ardennes Forest, it was obvious that the Nazis could not hold out much longer. Hungary signed an armistice and declared war on Germany. Turkey, Egypt, and Syria joined the Allies. On May 1, 1945, the Germans announced the death of Adolf Hitler and the appointment of Admiral Karl Doenitz as Fuehrer. The next day Berlin fell to Marshal Georgi Zhukov and his Russian forces. Peace rumors were current everywhere. Finally, after preliminary surrenders of German forces in Italy, Holland, Denmark, and northern Germany, the terms for complete unconditional surrender were arranged on May 7 at the schoolhouse headquarters of General Eisenhower in Rheims, France. After five years, eight months, and seven days, the European phase of World War II ended. With the end of hostilities, how-ever, began one of the most widespread manhunts in history, whose purpose was to capture and bring to justice the "war criminals." Hitler was believed dead although his corpse had not been found. Goebbels and Himmler committed suicide along with hundreds of lesser-known Nazis. The long list of captured included Hermann Goering, Joachim von Ribbentrop, Admiral Karl Doenitz, Hjalmar Schacht, Dr. Alfred Rosen-berg, Vidkun Quisling, and Field Marshals von Runstedt, von Kleist, Sperrle, von Leeb, List, and Weichs. The Allied War Crimes Commission for Russia, Britain, and America established machinery to try these leaders.

The Road Back. The European War had been won. Estimates indicate between 9,000,000 and 10,000,000 dead on all battlefields with a like number permanently disabled and millions of others with lesser wounds. Germany and Russia had the highest losses in manpower. To these must be added the millions of civilian casualties from enemy bombings, mass killings, and the deaths in the concentration camps. The total cost was in excess of a trillion dollars.

The problem of establishing popular governments in the liberated countries was extremely difficult. King Haakon VII, Queen Wilhelmina, and King Christian X were joyously acclaimed by the peoples of Norway, the Netherlands, and Denmark respectively. However, rioting thwarted King Leo-pold's return to Belgium. Uprisings in Greece, Syria, and Lebanon were finally put down. The Polish question with a Russian-favored Lublin government and a London govern-ment recognized by Britain and the United States caused friction among the "Big Three." Marshal Tito's Yugoslav partisans occupied Trieste and withdrew only after the British threatened to use force.

Germany was temporarily partitioned among Russia, France, Britain, and the United States. These countries established military governments over their various regions. A Four-Power Allied council was created to control Berlin. With the end of Nazi domination and of the Gestapo, the ingenuity of the Allied military governments was strained to the utmost. The "horror scenes" from the concentration camps at Dachau,

Belsen, and Buchenwald served to increase hatred toward the Nazis.

While Germany tottered, the Allied world was shocked to learn of the death of President Roosevelt (April 12, 1945) less than three months after the beginning of his fourth term. Immediately after taking the oath of office, the new President, Harry S. Truman, pledged the country to a continuation of the war until the unconditional surrender of the enemies. Although President Truman made various cabinet changes, yet he emphasized his support of such basic Roosevelt policies as the creation of a world security organization, adoption of the Bretton Woods monetary plan, and continuation of the trade agreements. In England, the Labor Party gained a sweeping victory over the Conservatives in the first Parliamentary election in ten years, and Clement R. Attlee replaced Winston Churchill as Prime Minister.

Conferences Between Allied Leaders. With present improved modes of communication and of transportation, it was natural that the number of personal meetings of Allied political and military leaders would be relatively frequent, and the exchange of information speedy and continuous. Even before Pearl Harbor, Roosevelt and Churchill had met in the now historic meeting in the North Atlantic (Atlantic Charter). Immediately after Pearl Harbor, the Prime Minister was at the White House for conferences. In June, 1942, Churchill was again in this country to consult with the President and his aides and to plan for a method of assisting in the North African campaign. The Casablanca meeting (January, 1943), lasting ten days and including top military personnel, planned the invasions of Sicily and of Italy, and helped to engender better feeling between Giraud and De Gaulle. In August, 1943, this time at Quebec, Churchill and Roosevelt met and, among other matters of prosecuting the war, laid plans for the Moscow Conference, which was to result in a clear-cut understanding of the relations of the United States, the Soviet Union, China, and Britain in working for victory and in the peace to follow. The Moscow Pact (November, 1943) shattered any hope the Axis might have had for lack of unity among the Allies. The Pact provided for (1) united action against their respective enemies, (2) joint prosecution of the war, (3) joint enforcement of peace terms, (4) an international organization which would recognize both large and small states and recognize the principle of sovereign equality, (5) joint action to maintain peace and security pending the establishment of a system of general security, (6) use of military forces only to make good the above principles and only after joint consultation, and finally (7) regulation of armaments by the Allies. Then, in December, 1943, two significant conferences were held. At the Cairo Conference, Churchill, Roosevelt, and Chiang Kai-shek met and with their military leaders mapped plans for the prosecution of the war against Japan until her unconditional surrender. In the postwar world Japan would be stripped of her conquests of the last fifty years and China would become the dominant power in the Far East. Later at the Teheran Conference, Churchill, Stalin, and Roosevelt further reaffirmed, in this first personal meeting of the leaders, the principles of the Moscow Pact of 1943 and settled plans for military operations in the east, west, and south. Following the Teheran Conference, a meeting between President Inonu of Turkey and Churchill and Roosevelt at Cairo served to further strengthen the growing bonds between that country and the United Nations.

In February, 1945, Churchill, Roosevelt, and Stalin met at Yalta in the Crimea to develop final plans for the defeat of Germany and her occupation and control after victory. The leaders reaffirmed their common determination to strengthen and maintain their bonds of unity in the peace to come. Discussions included the problems of liberated countries and the Polish and Yugoslav questions. In July, 1945, the "Big Three" —Stalin, Truman, and Churchill (later Attlee)—met at Potsdam and decided procedures for denazifying and demilitarizing Germany and for exacting reparations, and they issued the Allied ultimatum to Japan.

FIFTH PHASE OF THE WAR (1944-1945)

A new phase of World War II was evident as the tempo of the war in the Pacific was stepped up. The capture of Kwajalein (February, 1944), the first Japanese territory to be occupied, ushered in a new aspect which led to Leyte, Luzon, and Manila; to Burma; to Okinawa; and to the Japanese homeland. The fifth phase began before D-day and, continuing after the European victory, extended to the end of the war in the Pacific.

Pacific Strategy. General Douglas MacArthur, Fleet Admiral Chester W. Nimitz, and their staff developed a plan of strategy which resulted in a change from "island-taking" to "island-hopping" which left many small pockets of enemy resistance, but which brought noteworthy victories on land, sea, and in the air.

ISLAND CONQUESTS.   In October, 1944, a coördinated military and naval attack resulted in a surprise landing on Leyte in the Philippines which was followed by other landings on Mindoro and in the Lingayen Gulph — only 107 miles from Manila. In February, 1945, that city was liberated and by July practically all organized resistance had ceased. Meanwhile, the marines captured Iwo Jima and Okinawa, a Japanese island fortress less than 400 miles from the Japanese homeland. The occupation of these islands helped to shorten the war.

ON THE MAINLAND. As the Americans came closer and closer to Japan, the pressure upon China was relaxed. With the benefit of additional supplies and equipment, the Chinese forced the Japs to withdraw from their forward bases. Gradually the Chinese and their Allies regained control of Burma, including the Burma Road and the port of Rangoon. A Japanese withdrawal in South China (Kwangsi Province) meant Japan's loss of a corridor which had been used to supply her forces. In June, 1945, Borneo was invaded by Australian veterans of the North African Campaign. Early resistance was light and within two weeks the Australians were in control of the valuable oil fields.

CLEARING THE SEA LANES. Earlier successes of the naval units were followed by a series of engagements which practically reduced the Japanese navy to a task force. An attempt to head off the American invasion of the Philippines was particularly costly to the Japanese navy. Meanwhile submarines were taking their toll of enemy shipping and of naval craft. Most invasions of Japanese territory were preceded by terrific air and naval bombardment.

AIR WAR IN THE PACIFIC. With bases on Guam, Saipan, and Tinian, giant B-29 superfortresses carried the bombing to the Japanese homeland. In three months of concentrated attack, Tokyo was reported 46 per cent destroyed and military targets in Nagoya, Kobe, and Yokohama were practically wiped out. Systematic bombings preceded invasion efforts and were instrumental in the successes in the Philippines, Iwo Jima, Okinawa, and Borneo. In the air, the Americans completely outclassed the Japanese who were unable to break up the "air umbrella" which supported land operations. As the war continued to go against the Japanese, a new Premier, Admiral Baron Kantaro Suzuki, succeeded General Kuniaki Koiso. Premier Suzuki developed a plan of defense against the impending invasion of the homeland and stepped up the use of suicide planes.

Last Steps Back to Tokyo (July-September, 1945). Beginning with the Potsdam ultimatum, which ordered Japan to surrender or face complete annihilation, a series of significant events brought an early end to the war. On August 6 the first atomic bomb devastated the important Japanese base at Hiroshima. On August 8 Russia, fulfilling a previous agreement, declared war upon Japan, and a Soviet army of more than one million men crossed the Manchurian border. Simultaneously the American and British Third Fleet swung into action against the Japanese homeland and the second atomic bomb destroyed a third of the teeming war city of Nagasaki. By August 10 Japan had begun negotiations for surrender, and on September 2 (V-J day) surrender was formally proclaimed.

Significant Dates

Charter for the United
    Nations 1945
Nuremberg Trials . . 1945-1946
State of Israel Established . 1948
Federal Republic of Germany 1949
Korean Conflict . . . 1950-1953
Austrian Peace Treaty . . . 1955

CHAPTER XXI.

THE PEACE AND
THE UNITED NATIONS

For eighteen years after the surrender of the Japanese there was an absence of major military warfare. The peace, however, had not been completely won and a large number of significant problems remained to be solved. Chief among these problems were (1) the development of patterns for the peace treaties, (2) the universal acceptance of the principles of the United Nations, (3) the solution of the problem of international use and control of atomic energy, (4) the establishment of stable governments in many countries, (5) the re-establishment of world trade, and (6) the rehabilitation of citizens in famine-stricken countries.

BACKGROUND FOR PEACE NEGOTIATIONS

The establishment of the peace treaties was complicated by the inability of the victors to work together in peace as they had in war. Furthermore, a shift in the balance of power among the "Big Five" (United States, Russia, Great Britain, France, and China) affected the problem of occupation and control of the defeated nations. China, weakened by years of fighting Japan, was beset by civil war between the Nationalists and the Communists. In

France, the war and the German occupation had taken a toll which delayed both political and economic recovery. The irony of Great Britain's plight was that she began to lose that which she had entered the war to protect, namely her empire. Only Russia and the United States, with opposing political ideologies, emerged more powerful. Against this background the victors sought formulas for peace.

Military Occupation of Germany and Japan. Even before the defeat of Germany, a plan for her temporary partition had been drawn up. Soon after Germany's capitulation, the United States, Great Britain, Russia, and France each occupied their assigned areas, the city of Berlin being controlled by a Four-Power Allied Council. The four powers issued regulations and set up controls aimed at denazifying Germany. East Prussia was separated from Germany, with the Soviets obtaining the northern part and with the rest going to Poland. Substantial reparations in the form of machinery, minerals, ships, and production equipment were exacted from the eastern occupied areas. It was hoped that without a military force or tools for heavy manufacturing, and with production decentralized and limited to peaceful domestic goods, Germany's aggressive potential would be effectively controlled.

At Nuremberg a great trial of war criminals took place (November, 1945–September, 1946) under supervision of the United Nations War Crimes Commission. Eleven of the defendants — including Goering, von Ribbentrop, Keitel, and Kaltenbrunner — were sentenced to death by hanging. (Goering eluded the hangman's noose by taking poison.) The trials set an important precedent in international law because individual leaders were held personally responsible for gross crimes, despite their claims that they had acted as obedient servants of the state.

In Japan, General Douglas MacArthur, the Supreme Allied Commander, was in complete charge of the occupation. However, as a result of the Moscow Conference of December, 1945, the determination of questions of policy affecting Far Eastern problems was placed in the hands of a Far Eastern Commission of eleven nations; but the United States, Russia, Great Britain, or China could block a decision by exercising its veto power.

Peace Treaties of 1947. After sixteen months of discussions, peace treaties with Italy, Finland, Hungary, Bulgaria, and Rumania were ready for ratification by the major powers. Some problems, such as free and open navigation on the Danube River, were left for further study.

ITALIAN TREATY. The settlement with Italy resulted in the internationalization of Trieste and its environs as a free city; the loss of Venezia Giulia and some islands to Yugoslavia; the cession of Briga-Tenda and other Alpine border areas to France; and the loss of the Dodecanese Islands to Greece. The treaty included a provision for the disposition of all Italian colonies in Africa within a year. Italy was ordered to pay reparations totaling $360,000,000 to Yugoslavia, Greece, Russia, Ethiopia, and Albania. The combined strength of the Italian army, navy, and air force was limited to 200,000.

BULGARIAN TREATY. Under the treaty provisions, Bulgaria was the only former Axis country to lose no territory. With the exception of Southern Dobruja, which was taken from Rumania and given to Bulgaria, the boundaries of 1941 were re-established. However, $70,000,000 in reparations were assessed in favor of Greece and Yugoslavia. The manpower of the military forces in Bulgaria was set at 63,700.

FINNISH TREATY. Russia obtained the province of Petsamo and its arctic port and the right to build a naval base on the Gulf of Finland at Porkkala Udd (later abandoned). The Finns also ceded Viborg and other areas of southeast Karelia. In addition, they were ordered to pay Russia $300,000,000 in reparations. A military force of about 42,000 was allowed.

HUNGARIAN TREATY. The Big Four returned most of Transylvania to Rumania and gave Czechoslovakia an important bridgehead on the Danube under the terms of this settlement. Hungary's reparations included $200,000,000 to Russia and $50,000,000 each to Czechoslovakia and Yugoslavia. The army and air force were limited to 70,000.

RUMANIAN TREATY. The last of the treaties of 1947 restored Transylvania to Rumania, but Russia took Northern Bukovina and Bessarabia while Southern Dobruja was ceded to Bulgaria. Russia also exacted reparations of $300,000,000. The military strength for Rumania was established at 133,000.

German and Austrian Treaties. Several attempts were made to draft the German and Austrian treaties. A preliminary conference of deputy foreign ministers was held in London to determine questions of procedure. Subsequent meetings of the Big Four Foreign Ministers held in Moscow, London, and Paris ended in failure. The inability of Russia and the other countries to reach basic agreements meant an indefinite delay in writing the final treaties. While Russia set up a Communist-dominated regime in eastern Germany, the Western Powers proceeded to establish a constitutional government in their zones. Free elections were held in 1949 and the new Federal Republic of Germany came into existence. Although unable to obtain a peace treaty or to reunify his country, the first Chancellor, Konrad Adenauer, worked hard, nevertheless, for sovereignty and rearmament. In 1954 agreements were signed by the Western Powers which led to (1) settlement of the Saar question, (2) recognition of the sovereignty of the Federal Republic, (3) acceptance of the military obligations of the Western European Union, and (4) full West German membership in NATO. After his 1957 re-election Adenauer completed a Soviet-West German Trade Pact, providing $750,000,000 in trade and a basis for repatriation of 80,000 Germans held in Russia after World War II.

The Austrian Peace Treaty was ratified by the Western Powers and Russia in 1955. The treaty recognized Austria's sovereignty, prohibited an Anschluss, restored the boundaries of 1938, and provided for the free navigation of the Danube.

Japanese Peace Treaty. As the sole occupation force in Japan, the United States was in a good position to take a firm stand against Soviet attempts to dictate the peace terms. (The USSR had declared war on Japan only two days before the Japanese capitulation.) In 1951 the United States and forty-eight non-Communist states signed a peace treaty with Japan which provided for full Japanese sovereignty in 1952. The USSR finally signed a declaration in 1956 which ended the technical state of war between the two countries.

THE UNITED NATIONS ORGANIZATION

The League of Nations was organized in 1920 as a united effort for world peace; in 1946 it was dissolved, although some of its independent agencies continued. Prior to this time, however, the need for an effective international organization was recognized throughout the world as essential. The first significant step in this direction was taken at the Dumbarton Oaks Conference in 1944, where the United States, the USSR, Great Britain, and China developed a draft for such an organization of nations. The proposed charter was discussed at the Yalta Conference (February, 1945) by President Roosevelt, Prime Minister Churchill, and Premier Stalin, who agreed to call a worldwide conference. On April 25, 1945, the representatives of forty-six nations convened in San Francisco. (Five additional countries later joined the conference.)

Using the Dumbarton Oaks Charter (modified at Yalta to include a veto power) as a basis of discussion, the conferees adopted in late June, 1945, a charter for the United Nations Organization (UN). The Charter contained many of the elements of the League of Nations Covenant, but it also included new provisions, of which the most important was the provision to place armed forces at the disposal of the Security Council.

At Yalta it had been decided that any one of the Big Five could veto the investigation or even the discussion of an issue. Major criticism was leveled, therefore, at the Charter because it gave the Big Five sole responsibility for maintaining the peace, and this entailed a partial disregard of the rights of small countries. At the San Francisco Conference, however, a compromise was effected which allowed discussion of an issue whenever seven of the eleven members of the Security Council requested it.

The Charter for the United Nations Organization was a significant step forward in man's attempt to achieve permanent world peace and security.* The size of the organization grew rapidly, and by mid-1965 there were 114 member states.

General Assembly. Representatives of member states comprise the General Assembly, which has met in New York City in annual or special sessions. Each member state is entitled to one vote. On important issues concerning peace, security, and membership a two-thirds majority is necessary. The Assembly elects the six non-permanent members of the Security Council and establishes committees. Before 1950 the increasing use of the veto power tended to limit the effectiveness of the Security Council; consequently, the General Assembly, which had been created originally as a great world debating organization, adopted a resolution

---

*The preamble states: "WE THE PEOPLES OF THE UNITED NATIONS DETERMINED to save succeeding generations from the scourge of war, which twice in our lifetime has brought untold sorrow to mankind . . . do hereby establish an international organization to be known as the United Nations."

(November, 1950) permitting it to convene in situations threatening the peace and to recommend courses of peaceful action. The effectiveness and importance of the General Assembly were in this way considerably augmented.

Security Council. Under the Charter, the most important function of maintaining the peace was clearly the responsibility of the Security Council. Permanent members of the Council are the United States, Great Britain, the Union of Soviet Socialist Republics, the Republic of China (Nationalist China), and France. Six non-permanent members are elected for two-year terms from the General Assembly. Each member of the Council is entitled to one representative with one vote. However, all decisions of the Security Council with the exception of procedural matters require an affirmative vote of seven members, including all of the five permanent representatives. The Council has the power to call upon the members of the UN for "air, naval or land forces" to maintain or restore order. Action by the Council is hampered by the requirement of unanimous consent of the permanent members. This power of the so-called veto practically negated the effectiveness of the Council and threatened to wreck the UN until the authority of the General Assembly was increased.

The Secretariat. This body consists of a Secretary-General (appointed by the General Assembly) and his staff who carry out the directives of the UN agencies. The Secretary-General is charged with the responsibility of bringing to the attention of the Security Council situations which threaten the peace. Every effort is made to assist the Secretary-General to operate as a neutral without responsibility or obligation to any member. Trygve Lie of Norway (1946–1953), Dag Hammarskjöld of Sweden (1953–1961), and U Thant of Burma (1961–) were the first three Secretaries-General.

The Economic and Social Council. Consisting of eighteen elected members who serve for three years, this Council initiates and makes studies and reports on international matters in economic, social, cultural, educational, and health areas. The Council has appointed a dozen or more commissions and committees—including the Commission on Human Rights, Social Commission, Economic Commission for Europe, and Employment Commission. Specialized agencies of the UN such as the United Nations Educational, Scientific and Cultural Organization (UNESCO), the World Health Organization (WHO), the Food and Agriculture Organization (FAO), the United Nations Relief and Rehabilitation Administration (UNRRA), and the World Bank are under the jurisdiction of the Economic and Social Council.

The International Trusteeship Council. Through this body the UN established a method for administering and supervising territories which were placed under its control. Such trusteeships are held during interim periods while the people move progressively toward stable self-government and improved economic and social conditions.

The International Court of Justice. This court, which had been established originally in 1922 as the Permanent Court of International Justice at The Hague in Holland under the Covenant of the League of Nations, is the principal judicial organ for the UN. The services of the Court are available to the Security Council, the General Assembly, any of the special agencies of the UN, or any member state. Members are not required, however, to bring their legal problems to the Court but may use other tribunals. Fifteen justices constitute the panel of judges.

The International Labor Organization (ILO). This organization was also an associated agency of the League of Nations. The ILO strives to improve working conditions throughout the world and has established an international labor code. Through its International Institute of Social Studies and its relations with other UN agencies, the ILO provides member nations with valuable research studies.

UNITED NATIONS IN ACTION

When the United Nations General Assembly met in London in January, 1946, fifty-one nations were represented. Paul Henri Spaak of Belgium was named the first president. Elected as the first non-permanent members of the Security Council were Egypt, Mexico, the Netherlands, Australia, Brazil, and Poland. In February, 1946, the General Assembly decided that permanent headquarters should be established in the United States and accepted an offer to locate in New York City. The UN succeeded in settling many disputes, but the use of the veto in the Security Council and other stumbling blocks to coöperative action prevented the solution of many international problems.

Iranian Dispute.   The basis of this dispute was the failure of the USSR to withdraw all troops from Iran by March 2, 1946, in keeping with the tripartite treaty (Great Britain, United States, and Russia). While the Security Council was hearing both sides of the issue, the Russian troops were withdrawn, thus ending the dispute.

Spanish Question.   In April, 1946, Poland brought to the Security Council's attention the alleged menace that Franco's Spain constituted to world peace. After the Council failed to act, the question was deliberated by the General Assembly which recommended that member nations withdraw all diplomats from Spain and that Spain's participation in UN activities be barred. In 1949 and again in 1950, the resolution, which had been ineffective, was reconsidered. Eventually, in 1955, Spain was admitted as a member of the UN with full privileges.

Establishment of Israel.   Unable to find a satisfactory solution for the future of Palestine through negotiations with the Arabs and the Jews, Great Britain referred this problem to the United Nations (1946). The General Assembly voted to partition Palestine into a Zionist state and an Arab state, and when the British mandate ended in 1948, the Jews proclaimed the new state of Israel, which was immediately recognized by the United States and fourteen other countries.

Police Action in Korea.   After World War II, Korea was divided at the thirty-eighth parallel of latitude with the USSR dominating the northern portion and with the United States occupying the southern area. Suddenly, in June, 1950, North Korean Communist forces invaded South Korea. Because the Russian representative was absent from the Security Council, there was no veto by that body over the proposal to send aid to the South Koreans. The UN troops, predominantly Americans under the command of General Douglas MacArthur, were pushed back. Seoul, the capital of South Korea, fell to the invaders but the tide of conflict changed in October, 1950, when UN reënforcements arrived. Meanwhile, the UN General Assembly approved a resolution (with only Communist nations opposed) calling for a united Korea. In November, 1950, the intervention of Chinese Communist forces prevented a clear-cut UN victory, and the war became stalemated. Efforts to achieve a truce were ineffectual until an armistice was signed in 1953, but the realization of the recommended solution (a free and independent Korea, agreed upon by Roosevelt and Churchill at Cairo in 1943) did not materialize.

Other Disputes involving the UN. In a dispute between India and Pakistan, an armistice was arranged which prevented a possible war. Over a period of several years the UN was also moderately successful in keeping fighting between the Dutch and the Indonesians somewhat limited.

There were, however, many instances where the UN was most ineffective. In Hungary, Soviet interference was condemned by the General Assembly, but the efforts of the Hungarians to gain their right to freedom and self-determination were not supported (1956). With the backing of both the United States and Russia, the UN did bring the fighting between Egypt and Great Britain, France, and Israel to an end, but subsequent Egyptian violations of treaty rights were not dealt with effectively.

Atomic Energy Control. After the destruction of Hiroshima and Nagasaki, control of the atomic bomb was considered of utmost importance. The UN General Assembly created the Atomic Energy Commission to make proposals for (1) international exchange of scientific information, (2) control of atomic energy, (3) elimination of the atomic bomb from national armaments, and (4) development of a system of international safeguards. The United States proposed a plan (Baruch Plan) for atomic control by an International Atomic Development Authority in the UN. The USSR then proposed the elimination and destruction of all nuclear weapons and objected to the system of inspections called for by the Plan. Basic disagreement on this problem of inspections stymied the matter and was the crux of subsequent disunity with the Soviets in disarmament negotiations.

Meanwhile, research with atomic weapons went forward, as hydrogen bombs of at least fifty megaton force were exploded in tests. The USSR, Great Britain, and France all exploded atomic weapons during the next decade. (In 1956 eighty-two nations signed the charter of the Atoms for Peace Organization to direct research in atomic energy to peaceful ends.) Knowing that the effects of nuclear fall-out could be dangerous, both the United States and the USSR put forward proposals to ban testing of atomic bombs—in the meantime observing a tacit moratorium on nuclear testing. However, when the USSR resumed testing in 1961, the United States followed suit.

Attempts at Disarmament. The UN General Assembly passed a disarmament resolution (1948) recommending to the Security Council the prohibition of atomic weapons and other instruments of mass destruction, the reduction of standard armaments, and the establishment of safeguards. Further, the Assembly urged coöperation with the Atomic Energy Commission, consideration of an international police force, and the withdrawal of troops from occupied territory. After 1948 there were many meetings, including a seventeen-nation conference in Geneva in 1962. However, the shadow of the cold war was present and various proposals came to naught. Little was accomplished to implement Article 26 of the UN Charter, which provided for a system of armament controls.

The United Nations Today. From the beginning it was apparent that the UN had its weakness (as had all previous supragoverning bodies), and much business was conducted outside the organization by member countries. Throughout the world a whole series of regional organizations and special commitments bound nations to each other militarily, politically, economically, and socially. However, the UN continued to provide a forum where both East and West, neutral and aligned, and large and small nations could be heard. Its pressure upon world opinion was tremendous, and it made noteworthy contributions in non-political fields through its many commissions and committees. Some of the member states have on occasion misused the UN forum in order to increase tension by means of threats and false propaganda; but on the whole the organization has helped to prevent a third world war from erupting as a result of regional disputes.

Significant Dates

Republics of India and Paki-
stan Established 1950
Battle of Dienbienphu . . . 1954
Republic of Indonesia . . . 1954
Suez Canal Crisis . . 1956-1957
Republic of Congo Established 1960
Algerian Independence . . . 1962

CHAPTER XXII.

DECLINE OF COLONIALISM

The expansion of trade and commerce during the nineteenth century served to encourage and perpetuate colonial control of areas throughout the world by colonialist powers. However, the effects of two world wars, an increased enlightenment of peoples, a growing demand for more and more self-government, and the heavy financial burden of maintaining overseas possessions resulted in the complete independence of many new states and the changed status of others.

EUROPE AND AFRICA

By 1912, the whole African continent, except Abyssinia and Liberia, had been appropriated by the European powers. Great Britain, France, Italy, and Germany took most of the continent, but smaller shares were claimed by Portugal, Belgium, and Spain. Fifty years later most of Africa's 240,000,000 people had gained their independence from European countries.

In most of the new states heterogeneity of language and religion, the widespread prevalence of illiteracy, the shortage of skilled workers in the professions and the vocations, the lack of machines, the inadequacy of financial resources, and the presence of widespread poverty with its accompanying poor health conditions resulted in political, economic, and social instability. The countries of western Europe, the United States, and the USSR poured vast sums of money into the continent in an effort to ameliorate the situation and in the hope that the political direction of the countries would be influenced thereby. For the most part the African states tended to seek and accept assistance from both the West and the Communists without commitments to either bloc. The newly emerging states developed agreements for working together. The Union of African and Malagasy States represented one such effort on a non-political basis, and the Afro-Asian Conference (1955) was the first intercontinental conference of colored people in history.

Egypt. From the end of World War I to 1956 Egypt sought to increase its independence from British domination. Nationalism manifested itself in anti-British riots, in the deposition of King Farouk, and in the establishment of the Egyptian Republic under General Naguib (1953). A year later General Gamel Abdel Nasser seized control of the government and succeeded in obtaining an agreement for the withdrawal of all British troops by 1956.

Partially as a result of the decision of the United States, Great Britain, and the World Bank not to support construction of the billion dollar Aswan dam project, Nasser seized control (July, 1956) of the Suez Canal and nationalized it in violation of the Convention of 1888. When peace efforts failed to induce Nasser to retreat from his position, Israel, Great Britain, and France, without consultation with other members of the Western bloc, invaded Egypt and were extremely successful militarily (November, 1956). The UN, backed by both the United States and the USSR, condemned the invasion. The condemnation resulted in a cease-fire soon after fighting began, the organization of a UN emergency force to patrol the area, and the withdrawal of British and French troops from Egypt. Israeli soldiers withdrew from the Gaza strip and eastern Sinai Peninsula (1957) expecting that the UN would guarantee freedom of passage to all ships in the Gulf of Aqaba.

Kingdom of Ethiopia (Abyssinia). After the Italians were forced out of Ethopia during World War II, Emperor Haile Selassie I extended limited political and civil rights to the people. A new constitution was adopted in 1955 with provisions for a bicameral legislature, a judicial system and a definition of the powers of the Emperor.

Algeria. Both Morocco and Tunisia had won their independence from France by 1957, but it was not until July, 1962, that Algeria gained such recognition. After World War II the growth of Arab nationalism caused considerable internal strife and forced the French to send increasingly larger military contingents to Algeria. The army fought a series of skirmishes (1954-1960) against a growing nationalist movement (FLN) which began to terrorize the European colonists (*colons*) and their sympathizers. The *colons,* fearful that the government would negotiate with the FLN and disappointed with the failure of France to end the war, established (1958) a Committee of Public Safety supporting the return to power of General Charles de Gaulle. De Gaulle's election, however, did not bring the solution which the *colons* desired. Sporadic outbursts of fighting continued and a revolt, led by four French generals who sought to prevent Algerian independence, was crushed (1961). Finally, the seven years of war came to an end with the recognition (1962) of Algeria as a sovereign state, and with the exodus of tens of thousands of *colons* to southern France.

The Republic of Congo. The Congo's desire for complete self-government led Belgium and Congolese leaders to establish the free and independent Republic of Congo (1960). Efforts to obtain united support for a central government were thwarted by various factions, and one of the dissident areas, the southern province of Katanga, seceded from the Republic. Widespread violence, the strong objection to Belgian troops in the Congo, lack of a stable government, and infiltration efforts by the Communists led to UN intervention and the dispatch of UN troops to the Congo to establish law and stability and to reunite the Republic.

Republic of South Africa. Formerly known as the Union of South Africa, which was established after the British had gained control of the area following the Boer War, the Republic of South Africa is a country rich in resources and controlled by a government dedicated to apartheid policies. When the apartheid program ran afoul of the broader foreign policy of the British Commonwealth of Nations and also of the UN, Prime Minister Hendrik Verwoerd withdrew his country from the Commonwealth (1961) and declared South Africa an independent republic.

Other African Countries. Nigeria and Ghana became independent in 1960, but chose to remain members of the Commonwealth of Nations. The British colony of Kenya hopes to join these countries when its plans for independence by 1964 have been realized. In addition, there are a number of independent countries and colonies—ranging from tiny Gambia with its population of 280,000 to the Sudan with 12,000,000 people. Also, there still remain a score or more of possessions—protectorates, territories, and enclaves—controlled by Great Britain, Spain, Portugal, and France. It is to be expected that the desire of these possessions to join the new Africa will bring increasing pressure to bear upon those European states to grant them self-government.

EUROPE AND THE MIDDLE EAST

The Middle East continued unstable and explosive after World War II, despite efforts to improve the situation. With the gradual withdrawal of Great Britain and France from many of the small countries, nationalist trends arose and became sufficiently strong to prevent other countries from moving in to take over control. The Arab League was formed (1945) in order to promote political and cultural coöperation and to defend the independence of the member states.

Israel. Israel, a new republic established in 1948 after the UN General Assembly approved partition of the British mandate in Palestine, was from the beginning opposed by the Arab League. Border skirmishes with Arab neighbors were frequent, and Israel's involvement in the Suez Canal episode increased the tension between Arabs and Israelis.

Iran (Persia). The final withdrawal of Russian troops from Iran in May, 1946, was most significant in preserving that country's independence. Another crisis occurred when a nationalist leader, Mohammed Mossadegh, proposed to nationalize the British owned Anglo-Iranian Oil Company (1951). Shortly after the bill passed, Mossadegh became Prime Minister. His gradual assumption of dictatorial power, however, led to his downfall, and he was dismissed by the Shah. His successor, Zahedi, concluded new agreements with the oil company which provided that the company remain the property of Iran along with a 50 per cent share of the profits.

Iraq. This nation, formerly known as Mesopotamia, was recognized as an independent kingdom in 1932. Political and economic instability has characterized the country in recent years. In July, 1958, King Faisal was killed in a *coup d'etat* and a new republic under General Abdul Karim el-Kassem was set up. The government pursued a neutralist course until February, 1963, when Kassem was overthrown and executed. Colonel Abdel Arif, the provisional president, immediately sought closer ties with Egypt and joined a new United Arab Republic.

Other Countries. Two French territories, Syria and Lebanon, became independent after World War II when French troops were withdrawn in 1946. The Republic of Syria merged with Egypt and Yemen into a new United Arab Republic (1958) but three years later withdrew and set up an independent government. In April, 1963, however, Syria joined with Egypt and Iraq in a second United Arab Republic. Lebanon, with a large Christian population, continued its pro-Western outlook after acquiring independence. In 1958 efforts of anti-Western groups to undermine the government resulted in President Chamoun inviting the United States to send troops to restore order. This action averted a crisis and preserved Lebanon's independence.

Jordan, which gained its independence in 1946, has been torn by political and economic strife for many years. After King Abdullah Al-Hussein was assassinated in 1951, his eldest son, Talal, ascended the throne. Parliament, however, removed him after a few months for medical reasons, and his son, Hussein I, was crowned. In 1958, after the assassination of King Faisal of Iraq, King Hussein called upon the British for assistance in controlling pro-Nasser and Communist groups that were trying to depose him. The presence of British troops in Jordan eased the situation.

Saudi Arabia, an independent kingdom with rich oil reserves, is a strong member of the Arab League. King Saud (1953-1964) received technical assistance from the United States and Great Britain for the internal development of his country.

Yemen, a democratic monarchy, has had a pattern of internal strife for many years. In 1963, Yemen became a battleground for clashes between Egyptian troops supporting the republicans and Saudi Arabian forces assisting the royalists. An agreement for withdrawal of Egyptian troops in 1965 paved the way for an end to this civil strife.

EUROPE AND THE FAR EAST

The basic urges that led to the formation of nationalist states in Africa produced a similar result in Asia. Certainly, one of the more significant outcomes of World War II was the changed relationships between the colonies and the mother countries. The achievement of solid independence was not obtained merely by the recognition of the sovereignty of a people. In a world dominated by cold war tactics, newly independent nations were potential pawns in the hands of seasoned politicians with a political ideology to export.

India, Pakistan, and Burma. Nationalism in India developed rapidly after 1918 under the leadership of Mohandus K. Gandhi, the father of Indian independence. Rivalry between Hindus and Moslems, however, resulted in bloody rioting and impeded the formation of a single Indian state. Finally, in 1947, the issue was resolved with the establishment of two countries—the predominantly Moslem Pakistan and India, both as Commonwealth members. Burma, which had been administered by the British East India Company, chose to be a completely independent state outside the Commonwealth (1948). Border strife between India and Pakistan erupted into a state of war in 1965.

Indochina. The overseas possessions of France in Indochina were occupied by the Japanese during World War II. Nationalist tendencies were strengthened during this period, but after the war civil strife raged between Communists and anti-Communists. France tried to solve her colonial problems through a French Union which would have given more freedom to the people. Laos, Cambodia, and Cochin China were organized into the Federation of Indochina, but when the French attempted to force Vietnam into the Federation, war broke out between France and Vietnam Communist forces. Northern Indochina was occupied by the Communists after a decisive French defeat at Dienbienphu (1954).

Cambodia declared its independence in 1953 and set up a constitutional form of government. Laos gained recognition as a sovereign state within the French Union and complete independence through the Geneva Agreement (1954).

Vietnam also achieved complete freedom under the Geneva Agreement. The country was divided into two parts with the dividing line on the seventeenth parallel—the pro-Western Republic of Vietnam south of the line, and the pro-Communist Democratic Republic of Vietnam to the north. Violation of the Geneva Agreement by North Vietnam culminated in a war with South Vietnam in which the United States provided massive military and economic assistance (1963-   ).

Republic of Indonesia. After the Japanese military occupation of Indonesia, there followed four years of war before the Dutch capitulated to the desire for independence and recognized the Republic of Indonesia on a partnership basis. This relationship ended in 1954, but West New Guinea was retained as a Dutch possession. It was not until October, 1962, that bitter wrangling and sporadic fighting between Indonesia and the Netherlands ended. The Dutch withdrew from West New Guinea and made way for a UN police force which supervised the orderly transfer of control of the territory to Indonesia in May, 1963.

BRITAIN AND THE COMMONWEALTH

Throughout the world other countries gained more freedom and independence. Great Britain, in particular, experienced the gradual breakup of its empire. Many former colonies, however, retained certain status within the Commonwealth. Of these, we have already mentioned India, Pakistan, Nigeria, and Ghana. In addition, Ceylon, a former British crown colony, became an independent nation within the Commonwealth (1948). The limited constitutional monarchy of the nine Malay states and the former colonies of Malacca and Penang exercised their sovereignty as the Federation of Malaya (1956), but within the Commonwealth. The British crown colony of Cyprus became a republic in 1960 after four years of bloody war which found native Cypriote, Greek, and Turkish groups opposing British control, but it remained within the Commonwealth. And when the West Indies Federation received its freedom in 1962, all except Jamaica voted to retain Commonwealth ties with Great Britain.

Burma, on the other hand, chose to remain outside the Commonwealth. Southern Ireland, which had been an independent state within the Commonwealth, severed all ties with Great Britain in 1949 and dropped the name "Eire." Lastly, the withdrawal of the Union of South Africa in 1961 was another indication of the disintegration of the empire and the weakening of Commonwealth bonds.

CHAPTER XXIII.

CIVILIZATION IN THE TWENTIETH CENTURY

The current century has been one that has witnessed more far-reaching changes in man's economic, scientific, religious, social, and cultural life than ever before. Characterized by a speed of action, man's ways of earning a living and of living together had many compensations, but there were many drawbacks as well.

ESSENTIAL FACTORS IN RECENT ECONOMIC GROWTH

A widespread impact of industrialization was achieved in the twentieth century, with the newer national states of Europe and the United States making the greatest progress. Technical inventions provided the basis for growth of great industries in both hard and soft goods, in synthetic and natural products, in services such as transportation and communication as well as in sources of power like electricity and oil, and in the development of tremendous business and financial organizations.

Man's World of Work. Changed conditions demanded workers with new skills and new abilities, making products that did not exist in 1900. The number of people in agricultural work decreased significantly with the expansion of large-scale farming, improved techniques, and knowledge of crop production.

Economic Imbalance.   In contrast to the rising standards of living in western European countries and the United States, so-called have-not nations were without basic necessities. This economic condition of underprivileged peoples became a major issue as both the West and the Communists, through large loans, sought to raise the standards of living in these countries as well as influence their political thinking.

World Markets.   Attempts to assist the flow of goods from country to country (while protecting basic domestic industries and agricultural products) were made through reciprocal tariff laws. Furthermore, the European Common Market (1958) and other economic blocs sought to facilitate the free movement of products among their members while protecting the economic resources of each from excessive competition.

THE WORLD OF SCIENCE

Fundamental changes affecting the everyday life of peoples everywhere were the product of scientific know-how. Building upon the basic discoveries of an earlier period, the modern scientist (who was supported through large-scale research and development programs of industry, government, and higher education) improved and perfected machines and products while making his own contribution to the world and to knowledge. A different kind of life developed out of the new scientific and technological advances. High speed transportation, improved media for communication, and a concentration of population in urban and suburban centers changed the daily routine of life, while new drugs and improved techniques for the treatment of disease prolonged it. At the same time, science produced a devastating power to destroy life and to wipe out civilization by means of a long-range air striking force: guided missles and rockets with atomic and hydrogen warheads.

Physical Sciences.   It was in the field of physics that the most spectacular progress was made. Roentgen's discovery of the X ray (1895), Planck's issuance of the quantum theory (1900), and Rutherford's modern conception of radioactivity (1904), along with Albert Einstein's theory of relativity provided a basis for a new understanding of the composition of matter. These findings eventually led to the discovery of the neutron by Chadwick

(1932) and the explosion of the first atomic bomb in 1945 with the force of 20,000 tons of TNT. A more powerful hydrogen bomb was created in 1952 and the Russians exploded one of these bombs with the force of 50 million tons of TNT (1961). With the development of powerful rocket engines, earth satellites traveling 18,000 miles an hour were placed in orbit (the first *sputnik,* by Russia in 1957), and manned space flights were successfully executed by the Soviets (April, 1961) and later by the Americans (February, 1962). With vast stores of knowledge about astronomy, mathematics, engineering, chemistry, and the biological sciences, the USSR and the United States rushed programs to place a man on the moon by 1970. Meanwhile, atomic energy was being adapted to produce electrical power and to provide fuel for all types of engines for use in peaceful pursuits.

In chemistry there were many practical applications of a wealth of new knowledge about matter. Synthetic materials were substituted for such natural products as cotton, silk, and rubber. Nations that had long been dependent upon others to supply critical needs gained a new independence through substituting synthetics. Chemotherapy became increasingly important in the treatment of infection as more and more chemical compounds with therapeutic qualities were developed.

Biological Sciences. Man's constant quest for increased understanding and his persistent questioning of previously accepted conclusions led to new concepts about Darwinism as supplementary scientific data were applied to man's nature and his heredity. From the work in the laboratories came new ideas about mutations in hereditary characteristics of plants and animals as well as increased knowledge of cell physiology. Progress achieved in one science opened new areas of research in related fields such as mathematics, engineering, psychology, sociology, medicine, agronomy, and nutrition.

Medicine. Significant progress in medicine and surgery—with emphasis upon drugs (such as the new antibiotics and vaccines), vitamins, and hormones, and with reliance upon elaborate machinery and equipment for X rays and for open heart and brain surgery—meant the saving of thousands of lives. In countries of western Europe, Canada, and the United States dread diseases such as tuberculosis, poliomyelitis, yellow fever, smallpox, and pneumonia were practically eliminated as major health problems.

(But cancer and cardiac diseases continued to be a major cause of death, even though medical research gave top priority to finding cures.)

Advances in knowledge about the causes of disease (especially the discovery of viruses), along with the research of scientists in embryology, cytology, and bacteriology, have increased the life expectancy of man by many years over that of the nineteenth century. To names of earlier contributors to medical knowledge like Edward Jenner (vaccination), Joseph Lister (antiseptic surgery), and Louis Pasteur (sterilization) must be added twentieth-century names of Sir Frederick Banting (insulin), Dr. Gerhard Domagk (sulpha drugs), and Dr. Jonas Salk (polio vaccine) for their contributions in the prevention and cure of diseases. Meanwhile, there are many areas in the world where the benefits of the new medicine and surgical techniques have been unavailable and the potential for a longer and more healthful living has not been realized.

Applied Science. The new knowledge about man and his world, obtained through scientific study and research, opened new vistas for adaptation to everyday living. Progress in engineering ushered in an era of automation that materially changed man's ways of production and his methods of doing business. So-called electronic brains (computers) supplied answers to all kinds of problems—from determining one's bank balance to providing fantastic information about the cosmos. In 1962 the satellite Telstar inaugurated a whole new area in communication with its transmission of telephone messages and television programs between Europe and the United States.

Philosophy. The emphasis on a more scientific world continued the trend away from the Neo-Scholasticism and metaphysics of earlier periods. Greater emphasis was placed upon an empiricism that stressed sensory experience as the only source of knowledge and upon the pragmatism of William James, Bertrand Russell, and John Dewey which held that the truth of all concepts is determined by practical results.

After World War II, Jean Paul Sartre's school of existentialism, which viewed man as an individual in a purposeless universe who is required to exercise his free will against a hostile environment, gained widespread support. On the other hand there were leading philosophers such as Alfred North Whitehead and, in his later years, Karl Barth who fled from the scientific and materialistic to seek answers through reliance upon the humility of man and faith in God.

CONTEMPORARY RELIGIOUS TRENDS

The religious trends of the twentieth century were characterized by three periods. The first period witnessed an adjustment in the last part of the earlier century to changes necessitated by the separation of church and state in several countries. The second period was dominated by the confusion and the frustrations of religion as it confronted science, technology, and public education. Finally, the third period saw an increased compatibility between religion and those concepts in philosophy and psychology which attempted to assist in man's quest for spiritual comfort.

Church and State. In spite of the influence of the church upon government, education, and the daily lives of the people, the process of separation of the religious from the secular during the first half of the twentieth century continued. Certain Communist countries outlawed the Catholic Church, but by 1960 there was increasing evidence of religious tolerance in some iron curtain countries. Elsewhere, there was a generally harmonious relationship between church and state.

Religion and Science. There were many elements in industrial societies, which emphasized science, technology and urban living, that were bound to have a negative effect on the individual's religious life. The dogma of Christianity and other religions seemed to be in conflict with many scientific findings. Atheism and agnosticism had more and more followers. New religious sects and denominations advocating more liberal interpretations of the spiritual gained adherents, but religious leaders clung fast to their dogma, the church organization, and its methods, and this served to widen the gap between religion and science.

Religion and Modern Society. Eventually many churchmen made adjustments to the new society without sacrificing basic tenets. Among the Protestants, in particular, neoorthodox beliefs gained adherents. Pope John XXIII, who had succeeded Pius XII in 1958, called the first Ecumenical Council in nearly a century (1962) to review many of the basic practices of the Catholic Church.

One effect of the two world wars was to lessen the real or imagined conflict between sciences, technology, and secular education on the one hand and religion on the other. Renewed interest and support of the church approached a kind of renaissance. Meanwhile, a trend to consolidate religious denominations, especially among Protestants, continued.

RECENT SOCIAL CHANGES

The truly dynamic society of the twentieth century with its pattern of flexibility and mobility was decidedly different from its earlier counterpart. The growth of great urban and suburban population centers had many advantages, but there were disadvantages. Society became more and more interdependent, and periods of peace and war, of prosperity and depression, and of plenty and famine produced instability and insecurity.

Social Legislation. Laws providing for compensation during unemployment, pensions after retirement, security in old age, and assistance for medical and health care were passed in many countries. In some states efforts were made to meet some of these needs through private insurance programs as a partial means of stemming the tide toward socialism.

Modern Living. As more and more women became part of the labor market, their political and social rights were more universally recognized, especially in western Europe. Some of the customs and requirements of centuries were abandoned or modified. Continued growth of the middle class was in evidence after 1900 and it became inevitable that, as the economic and social status of the population improved, minority groups would demand more rights and privileges.

Education. As the world became more interdependent and as society became more complex, education at all levels became popular. Gradually illiteracy was reduced. New courses were added to the curriculum in both the natural and social sciences.

To a greater extent than ever before, Communist governments used education as a means of promoting their own ideologies and providing a basis for supporting their own policies. By controlling the contents of textbooks, especially in such fields as religion, government, history, philosophy, and sociology, a government could wield tremendous influence. On the other hand, mass media for communication—such as the printed word, radio, television, and a literate people—provided the basis for a new dignity of man, but in too many places, especially Communist-dominated areas, the individual was completely subservient to the demands of the state.

ART, LITERATURE, AND MUSIC

The art, music, and literature of the twentieth century found its themes in the past, the present, and the future. As had been true in every modern age, the fine arts were tremendously influenced by the great masters of earlier periods, but the shackles of tradition were cast off more quickly and completely than ever before.

Modern Art. The trend in art was to reveal the moods of the times—both materialistic and psychical, optimistic and pessimistic, and believable and illusional.

The Impressionist school of Edouard Manet, Claude Monet, Camille Pissarro, and Auguste Renoir and the Post-Impressionists Paul Cézanne and Vincent van Gogh were followed by the new Expressionism typified by the paintings of the Swiss Paul Klee and the Germans Max Beckmann and Franz Marc, the Surrealism of the Spaniards Salvador Dali and Joan Miró, the Cubism of Pablo Picasso (which culminated in his great work "Guernica," 1937), and Nonobjective painting—the completely abstract works of Wassily Kandinsky, Kasimir Malevich, and Piet Mondrian.

In sculpture, the realism and expressionism of Auguste Rodin continued into the twentieth century; however, by mid-century, the abstract influence of Ivan Mestrovic became predominant.

The New Architecture. The influence of modern society upon architecture is found in the contemporary house, apartment building, church, school, factory, skyscraper, or public building. With the use of old and new materials (such as steel, concrete, aluminum, chromium, and glass) and with new techniques (such as slab construction, window-wall treatment, air-conditioning, and automatic high-speed elevators) the new architecture stressed designs that were less ornate and were governed by function. The Austrian Otto Wagner, the German Walter Gropius, the Swiss Le Corbusier, the Finn Eliel Saarinen, and the Italian Pier Luigi Nervi made notable contributions to modern architecture.

Literature in the Twentieth Century. Many of the writers of the present period were influenced by the social and political trends of a society that had made significant material progress; yet they were disillusioned by two major world wars and man's inability to cope with many of his social problems. Other writers used the new science of psychology—Freud and Jung—with its emphasis on mental processes and inner feelings for their themes. Although prevented by the limitations of language from going to the extremes (as had been done in painting and to a lesser degree in music), writers made efforts to deviate from the traditional through writings such as those of the Imagists—an outgrowth of the symbolist school of the nineteenth century.

Among the leading novelists and dramatists who represent the spirit of the times are: Franz Kafka (Czech); John Galsworthy, George Bernard Shaw, D. H. Lawrence, T. S. Eliot (English); André Gide, Marcel Proust, Albert Camus (French); Hermann Hesse, Ranier Maria Rilke, Thomas Mann, Bertolt Brecht (German); James Joyce and W. B. Yeats (Irish); Maxim Gorky, Boris Pasternak, Ilya Ehrenburg (Russian); and Friedrich Dürrenmatt (Swiss). From the pens of a host of writers came thousands of novels, dramas, and poems which found an increasing market in practically every country of the world, popularized by the introduction of the "paperback" book.

Today's Music. While the romantic music of great composers such as Robert Schumann, Felix Mendelssohn, Frédéric Chopin, and Franz Liszt, the music dramas of Richard Wagner, and the nationalistic works of Giuseppe Verdi, Anton Dvořák, Edvard Grieg, Rimsky-Korsakov, and Claude Debussy were played and enjoyed by millions, the twentieth century sought, nevertheless, its own musical interpretations and techniques in the schools of atonality and polytonality. Arnold Schönberg fostered the atonality approach which rejected traditional tonality and employed a twelve-note system. Polytonality, as interpreted by Igor Stravinsky, made use of several keys simultaneously, utilizing acoustic properties which strike the ear most effectively instead of appealing to the emotions. Outstanding contemporary composers who have also strongly influenced modern techniques are Paul Hindemith, Serge Prokofiev, and Béla Bartók. Folklore music continued to have an important place in most countries, and jazz and swing music became more and more popular.

CHAPTER XXIV.

· CONTEMPORARY EUROPE

Postwar Europe turned out to be much different from the one which had been anticipated in 1939. The great losses and shifts of population, the destruction of entire cities, and the want of necessities for daily living were almost unimaginable. Two powerful victors, representing two conflicting political ideologies, emerged to rebuild and reshape the battleground. The United States assumed the leadership of the West, and in a new role became heir to the responsibility of protecting the rights of free people to determine and maintain their sovereignty unimpeded by foreign intervention. The USSR, on the other hand, extended her form of communism to those Eastern countries which she had "liberated" and attempted to manipulate them through economic and political control. Struggling to define their domestic and foreign policies in a changed world, many countries thus found their policies being determined, and in some cases decided, by others.

RECONSTRUCTION AND DEFENSE

One of the more significant outcomes of World War II was the effort to restore economic capability to the countries of Europe and to give assistance to some of the "have-not" nations. It was apparent that economic aid would be a most important factor in influencing political policies and support. The very nature of the postwar world thus tended to bring nations closer together politically. Such early coöperative ventures were the Western European Union (1948) and the Council of Europe (1949). Out of these beginnings came arrangements for defense agreements—the North Atlantic Treaty Organization and other media for unified actions.

Marshall Plan. The temporary program known as the United Nations Relief and Rehabilitation Administration (UNRAA, organized in 1943) provided a first step in the rebuilding of Europe, but it was succeeded by the Marshall Plan (1947) when it became obvious that reconstruction required a long range coördinated and integrated program. The Plan (also known as the European Recovery Program), financed by the United States, succeeded in hastening the return of sound economies to many countries of western Europe. The USSR and her satellites did not participate in the Plan because of an unwillingness to accept the conditions for aid which required some form of inspection within the recipient countries. Russian efforts to sabotage the entire program were unsuccessful.

Other Economic Programs. From these earlier efforts in assisting countries came programs from both the East and the West that poured billions of dollars into undeveloped nations everywhere. The Western countries, convinced that economic aid was an important means of containing communism, thus laid the foundation for coöperation among nations of the free world and provided a basis for establishing NATO and the Common Market.

North Atlantic Treaty Organization (1949). Out of the Brussels Treaty of 1948, which provided for collective security and pledged armed assistance to any member attacked, came the North Atlantic Treaty Organization (NATO). The original members of NATO were the United States, Canada, Great Britain, France, Italy, Belgium, the Netherlands, Luxembourg, Portugal, Denmark, Norway, and Iceland. Later Turkey, Greece, and West Germany joined. Each member is represented on the NATO Council by its foreign minister. When the ministers are not in session, permanent representatives carry out the Council's work. Progress in organizing an effective military force was slow because most of the nations found their other commitments a tremendous financial burden, especially since they were trying to place their domestic economies on a sound basis. Gradually NATO armed forces were built up and limited nuclear capability was achieved which included missile bases. The military headquarters are in Europe under the command of the Supreme Allied Commander in Europe, General Lyman L. Lemnitzer, who succeeded General Lauris Norstad on November 1, 1962.

The Soviet Bloc and the Warsaw Pact. Russia bound her satellite nations to her with a series of military pacts. She dropped an "iron curtain" between the states in her bloc and the outside world. An effort was made to integrate the national economies into one system, and this relationship, based on military and economic coöperation, was formalized (shortly after West Germany was granted full sovereignty) in the Warsaw Pact of 1955 which bound together the USSR and Albania, Bulgaria, Czechoslovakia, Hungary, Poland, Rumania, and East Germany through a twenty-year mutual defense treaty.

Southeast Asia Treaty Organization (SEATO). In addition to relying on NATO, the United States joined with Australia, France, Great Britain, New Zealand, the Republic of the Philippines, Pakistan, and Thailand in a treaty which provided for mutual assistance in the Pacific area (1954). The Southeast Asia Treaty Organization obtained the enthusiastic support of several Asian countries, such as the Philippines and Thailand, who felt themselves menaced by the resurgence of Japan as well as by Red China.

Central Treaty Organization of the Middle East (CENTO). The United States, Great Britain, Iran, Pakistan, and Turkey are bound together in a series of mutual assistance pacts which is the basis for CENTO (1959). Basically, these agreements carry forward the mutual security pledges of the Baghdad Pact (1955). CENTO emphasizes economic development as well as military coöperation.

GOVERNMENTS OF WESTERN EUROPE

In the immediate aftermath of the war, countries of Western Europe were faced with a gigantic problem of rebuilding their cities and rehabilitating their people. Larger problems loomed as the countries sought ways of stabilizing their economies and planning for a future.

Great Britain. Great Britain emerged at the end of the war victorious but without prestige or resources to meet her empire commitments or to undergird her economy. In the first general elections after the war, the Conservatives were decisively defeated by the Labor party. The Labor Prime Minister, Clement Attlee, intended to continue Churchill's foreign policy, but this proved to be impossible. Loans of large sums of money from the United States, Canada, Australia, and New Zealand did not stabilize the currency or alter the basic financial woes. Attlee's government pushed its program of nationalization of the Bank of England and of the coal mines, but the unfavorable balance continued.

END OF AN EMPIRE. Disintegration of the British empire began in August, 1947, with the establishment of the dominions of Pakistan and India. Resulting events rocked the political and economic foundations of the Commonwealth. As previously noted, many colonies and territories gained their sovereignty either within or outside the pale of the Commonwealth.

POLITICAL AND ECONOMIC TRENDS. The Labor party's program of nationalization continued in the field of public utilities— especially transportation, communications, and the gas and electric industries. A National Insurance Act provided "cradle to the grave" protection and the National Health Service Act (1946) provided medical and dental care for all. Still plagued with financial woes, the British devalued the pound sterling in still another effort to ease the economic crisis (1949).

The Labor party was defeated in the general election of 1951 and Prime Minister Churchill and his Conservatives were returned to office. King George VI died and was succeeded by his daughter as Elizabeth II (1952). Under Churchill a gradual program of de-emphasizing socialization was adopted and stringent steps were taken to improve the economy. When Churchill resigned in 1955, Anthony Eden was named Prime Minister. Economic conditions greatly improved, but foreign policy was clouded with continued defections by British overseas territories. Early in 1957 Eden resigned; he was succeeded by his Chancellor of the Exchequer, Harold Macmillan, who, in a general election in 1960, won a third successive victory for the Conservatives.

Realizing that the economy of Great Britain was inseparable from that of the Common Market countries, Macmillan worked hard to obtain full membership within that group rather than promote the so-called Outer Seven economic bloc. In 1963 these efforts were thwarted by France's opposition. Great Britain immediately returned to the European Free Trade Association as a source for economic coöperation. Prime Minister Macmillan resigned in October, 1963, and was succeeded by Sir Alexander Douglas-Home. A Labor party victory in the 1964 general elections elevated Harold Wilson to Prime Minister.

France. General Charles de Gaulle, who became provisional president in 1944, resigned in 1946 when he was unable to obtain for the Fourth French Republic a constitution which carried stipulations for a strong executive department. As a Marshall Plan recipient, France made considerable progress toward economic rehabilitation. French Foreign Minister Robert Schuman's plan for pooling European coal and steel production became effective in 1953 and provided the basis for France's leadership in the Common Market. A plebescite in the Saar resulted in that area uniting with West Germany politically (1957) and economically (1960).

The establishment of the French Union under the new constitution failed to satisfy the demands of the overseas possessions for increased sovereignty. Forced out of Indochina, France found it also increasingly difficult to retain control in North Africa. Failure to meet the Algerian crisis (1958) brought de Gaulle out of retirement to take over "the powers of the republic" in order to save it. The Fifth French Republic was proclaimed and a new constitution which greatly increased the power of the President and the stability of the cabinet was adopted (September, 1958). Charles de Gaulle became the first President of the Fifth Republic (December, 1958). The conflict with Algeria continued until that country's recognition as a sovereign state (1962). Relations between West Germany and France improved greatly and by 1963 both countries were working together in NATO, the Common Market, and other joint efforts for military and economic security. The French Community, comprising the French Republic, the six African republics which became independent in 1960, and the overseas territories and departments, replaced the French Union of the Fourth Republic.

ELECTION OF 1962. The election of 1962 gave President Charles de Gaulle's Union for a New Republic Party a parliamentary majority and augured well for at least five years of strong political unity. Since the founding of the First French Republic no party had ever had a parliamentary majority. Governments had been dependent upon coalitions of party blocs.

Federal Republic of Germany (West Germany). The Federal Republic of Germany was created out of the British, French, and American zones of Germany in 1949 with Dr. Konrad Adenauer as Chancellor and Theodore Heuss as President. Complete sovereignty was granted in 1955. Despite Western appeals to unify East and West Germany through free elections, the Soviets demanded direct negotiation by West Germany with the USSR-dominated East German government. Threats by the USSR and East Germans to force the West out of West Berlin were met by pledges from Great Britain, France, and the United States to remain in that city until a just and equitable solution could be found to the problem of unification. To stop the flow of tens of thousands of East Germans to West Berlin, a concrete wall twenty-seven miles long was constructed (1961) by East Germany on the sector border, and traffic between the two parts of the city was restricted to official checkpoints.

Meanwhile the Federal Republic of Germany gained acceptance in the West as a member of NATO, the Western European Union, the Common Market, the European Coal and Steel Community, and Euratom (European Community of Atomic Energy). Relations between Germany and France became characterized by more and more coöperation. As a member of NATO, West Germany was rearmed. From 1950 to 1962, West Germany tripled its gross national product in an amazing example of economic recovery. The Saar plebiscite ended French administration of that area. Ludwig Erhard succeeded Adenauer as Chancellor in 1963.

Italy. King Victor Emmanuel III abdicated in favor of his son, but a national plebiscite resulted in the establishment of a republic (1946). Under Premier Alcide de Gasperi, the government waged a successful uphill fight against Communist efforts to obtain control. With the help of the United States, Italy started on the road to economic recovery, greatly assisted by her membership in the European Coal and Steel Community, Euratom, and the Common Market. Italy also belonged to NATO and the Council of Europe. Italy and Yugoslavia accepted a settlement of the Trieste problem which divided the territory into two zones—the northern part going to Italy and the southern section to Yugoslavia. Trieste remained a free port (1954).

Spain and Portugal. The governments of Great Britain, France, and the United States were openly opposed to the Fascist dictator, General Francisco Franco. Diplomatic relations with Spain were severed by many countries, Marshall Plan aid was withheld, and Spain was denied admission to the UN. As the cold war intensified, it became apparent that the Western Powers needed Spain on their side. The United States loaned Spain $62,000,000 to assist her economic development in return for the privilege of building military bases in that country (1952). Two years later this aid had increased to over $225,000,000. Through a comprehensive economic stabilization program, conditions in Spain improved greatly until, in 1962, a degree of prosperity was achieved. Spain was admitted to the UN (1955) and gained membership in the Organization for European Economic Cooperation (1959). She also sought affiliation with the Common Market as an associate member.

Portugal, neutral in World War II, was to all intents a dictatorship under Premier Antonio de Oliveira Salazar who had been in control since 1932. The country favored the West, joined NATO and the UN, and signed agreements with the United States for military bases in the Azores; and when India invaded the Portuguese enclave of Goa (1962), a storm of Western protest was heard in the UN. Opposition to Salazar's autocratic control increased, but efforts at reform were ineffectual.

The Benelux Nations. The Benelux countries of Belgium, the Netherlands, and Luxembourg coöperated with each other after 1947 in an effort to foster economic growth and rehabilitation. These nations worked hard to strengthen the Western European Union, NATO, the UN, and the Common Market. After the establishment of the free and independent Republic of Congo (1960), Belgium turned to the Common Market as a means of

stabilizing her economy and maintaining her position as an export-
ing nation. King Baudouin succeeded his father, who abdicated in
1951.

The loss of Indonesia (1947) and West New Guinea (1962)
were severe blows to the Netherlands, which depended upon trade
to maintain the economy. Queen Juliana became the reigning
sovereign when her mother Wilhelmina abdicated in 1948.

Scandinavia. Norway, Denmark, and Iceland cast their
lots with the West and with NATO. Sweden, on the other hand,
pursued a course of strict neutrality, fearful that she might antag-
onize the USSR. The Scandinavian countries moved more and
more toward a form of socialism as contrasted with the communism
of Soviet-controlled states. During the past decade Norway, Denmark, and Sweden attained a high level of economic prosperity and
political stability. Each of these three countries has a king as the
hereditary head of state.

Austria and Switzerland. Austria became a republic in
1945, but did not regain complete independence until the signing
of the peace treaty in 1955. Efforts of the Communists to win
control were fruitless. Austria is a member of the UN, and
maintains a close relationship with certain economic coöperative
organizations. The government has entered into a mutual assistance security pact wtih the United States.

Switzerland, a federal republic, continued a course of strict
neutrality. As one of the few countries of the world which is not a
member of the UN, Switzerland feels that joining that organization could affect her neutrality adversely. However, Switzerland
became associated with some of the economic and social agencies
of the UN, and with the European Free Trade Association. A national militia is maintained which has a powerful air arm. Switzerland is one of the more prosperous countries of the world.

GOVERNMENTS OF EASTERN EUROPE

The iron curtain countries of Europe, with their Communist
systems, contrast sharply with the democracies of Western Europe.
The efforts of the Soviets to dominate and control their destinies
by treaty, by persuasion, or by force determined the political and
economic characteristics of these countries.

The Union of Soviet Socialist Republics. The USSR emerged from World War II as the strongest power in all Europe. Immediately she took advantage of her new position to dominate the governments of all countries on her borders and to export communism throughout the world.

INTERNATIONAL ACTIVITIES. The USSR was successful in fostering Communist governments in the Balkans—with the exception of Greece and Turkey. In the United Nations Russia used the veto in the Security Council to prevent that body from acting effectively against Communist aggression. When NATO was organized, the USSR lodged a formal protest with the UN stating that it was an aggressive pact and therefore a violation of the Charter. The Western bloc maintained that it was a defensive pact. Meanwhile, a Soviet-China thirty-year mutual assistance treaty was signed by Stalin and the Chinese dictator Mao Tse-tung, which gave Russia a powerful new ally. Through the Warsaw Pact (1955) the members of the Soviet bloc were bound together militarily and economically (1955). Tension between the West and the East increased.

POLITICAL. The USSR, a federation of fifteen republics with a population in excess of 210,000,000, gained considerable territory including Estonia, Latvia, Lithuania, parts of Finland and Poland, and Bessarabia, Ruthenia, and Bukovina. Joseph Stalin ruthlessly stamped out all opposition to his Communist doctrines and fostered and intensified the cold war. When Stalin died in 1953 he was succeeded by Georgi Malenkov. Malenkov was soon replaced by Bulganin; but it was assumed that the real power was held by the Secretary of the Communist Party, Nikita Khrushchev. New friendliness in Russia's attitude toward other nations culminated in a meeting at Geneva (1955) of the heads of the governments of the USSR, the United States, Great Britain, and France. Meanwhile Khrushchev condemned Stalin's "cult of the one man" and substituted the Leninist doctrine of collective leadership. By the end of 1956, the "destalinization" approach had backfired. Strikes in the Ukraine and political unrest in East Germany, Lithuania, and Estonia took place. Poland actually obtained increased political independence as a result of a revolt in Poznan, but efforts by anti-Stalinists to set up a more liberal government in Hungary were crushed ruthlessly by Soviet military forces, indicating to the world that the USSR's aggressive policies had not changed. In 1958 Khrushchev was elected Premier, strengthening thereby his control of Russia. Subsequent events weakened his hold: Yugoslavia's independent communism was denounced by the USSR, but Tito managed to maintain a middle course. In 1962, the forced withdrawal of Russian missles from Cuba, the invasion of India by China against Russian advice, and economic instability within the USSR served to decrease further the prestige of Khrushchev. Aleksei Kosygin as premier and Leonid Brezhnev as first secretary succeeded Khrushchev in 1964.

ECONOMIC AND SOCIAL. The Soviet Communist philosophy was characterized by the complete nationalization of all economic and cultural resources, coupled with a political dictatorship and with the curbing of religious groups. Through a series of five-year plans which impinged upon every aspect of economic life, the USSR moved ahead at a rapid pace in production of coal, steel, and electrical power, in heavy industries, and in transportation and communication. Although agricultural production lagged behind the needs of the country and the collective farm system was not so effective as anticipated, progress was made nevertheless in this area. With emphasis upon heavy industry rather than upon consumer goods the basis for a tremendous supply of military equipment was gained.

In education, efforts were concentrated on the development of scientists and engineers with a goal to exploit the use of atomic energy for nuclear weapons and for a source of industrial power. The launching of heavy earth satellites (1957) and the orbiting of the world by the first man in space, Major Yuri Gagarin on April 12, 1961, opened a new era in man's knowledge of the universe. This technical know-how was applied to rocket missiles and to other military weapons. Meanwhile educational opportunities were greatly increased, especially in basic elementary schooling, the training of technicians and specialists, and the professions.

Yugoslavia. Under Marshal Tito, Yugoslavia broke away from Stalin and Russian Communist influence to establish its own national Communist state. The United States gave aid to Yugoslavia as a potential bulwark against Soviet communism. In 1955 a government mission headed by Bulganin and Khrushchev visited Tito with promises to recognize his independent communism.

Consequently, diplomatic relations were resumed with the USSR and her satellites. However, Tito promised to keep his commitments to the West. Recent efforts by the USSR to have Tito give up his form of communism have been ineffectual, although relations between the two countries have improved. Yugoslavia's claims to Trieste were settled by a treaty with Italy in 1954 in which she was given the southern part of Trieste and access to this free port.

Satellite Countries. Behind the iron curtain are the Soviet satellites of Albania, Bulgaria, Czechoslovakia, East Germany, Hungary, Poland, and Rumania. After World War II, people's republics were established by Communist regimes in Albania, Bulgaria, and Rumania. The Communists seized control of Czechoslovakia in 1948 by forcing President Eduard Beneš to resign and paving the way for the dictatorship of Klement Gottwald, thus ending the only democratic government in central Europe.

The Communist-dominated Committee of National Liberation gained control of Poland (1947) and established a people's republic. Opposition to the oppressive measures of Stalinist extremists became overt in the revolt of the workmen in Poznan (1956). Wladislaw Gomulka was restored to party leadership and Poland became more independent and liberal. In this manner Poland secured a large measure of independence from the USSR, especially in domestic matters.

The People's Republic of Hungary developed out of the Communist take-over in 1947. Attempts by Premier Imre Nagy to pursue a moderate policy were opposed by the extreme Communists and he was forced out of office (1955). Khrushchev's destalinization program was interpreted as favoring a more lenient policy; Nagy was recalled as Premier and widespread demonstrations followed. When the security police fired upon the demonstrators, rioting followed. Efforts by anti-Stalinists to set up an independent government were crushed ruthlessly by Soviet military forces; Premier Nagy was removed (and later executed); and a Soviet-approved Premier, Janos Kadar, took over complete control of the country (1956).

The German Democratic Republic (East Germany) was created (1949) as a Communist-dominated state out of the USSR zone of Germany and its sector of Berlin, with a Soviet-type constitution. Thoroughly ensconced in East Germany, the USSR tried various tactics to make untenable the position of the United States, Great Britain, and France in West Berlin and West Germany.

Finland. The Communists held the balance of power in the postwar government of Finland until 1948 when a non-Communist government was elected. In spite of Soviet pressure Finland managed to maintain its sovereignty. A mutual assistance and friendship pact with the Soviets was effective in keeping Finland out of agreements with the West. Economic conditions improved after the USSR cancelled half of the reparations awarded her (1948).

Greece and Turkey. Communist efforts to seize control in Greece and Turkey were thwarted by the Truman Doctrine and by the changed attitude of Yugoslavia after that country's withdrawal from the Cominform. With Marshall Plan assistance and assurances of support from the West, both Greece and Turkey joined NATO and coöperated in setting up military bases. Both countries made significant economic progress after the war.

ECONOMIC COÖPERATION AND THE COMMON MARKET

The development of strong national states in Europe during the nineteenth century caused not only political rivalry but also stiff economic competition. Trade barriers between various countries had stifled interchange of goods, and efforts to achieve economic coöperation had been most unsuccessful until after World War II. The aftermath of the devastating war pointed out the need for thorough economic coöperation, and such programs as the United Nations Relief and Rehabilitation Administration and the Marshall Plan (European Recovery Program) provided the means for working together to solve economic problems.

Organization for European Economic Recovery. After World War II a permanent body known as the Organization for European Economic Recovery was set up to coördinate the expenditure of various funds available for economic rehabilitation. (In 1961 this body was replaced by the Organization for Economic Cooperation and Development.) By 1951 the industrial production of countries receiving assistance had increased 50 per cent over that of 1947. Continued efforts were made by the members to provide assistance to develop nations and to improve world trade.

UN Agencies for Economic Coöperation. Besides the Economic and Social Council and the International Labor Organization of the UN, one of the most effective organizations to implement economic growth and development was the International Bank for Reconstruction and Development (World Bank), established in 1945. During the first fifteen years of operations it made three hundred loans amounting to nearly $6 billion to fifty-eight countries throughout the world.

The Council of Europe (1949). Ten non-Communist countries (later enlarged to sixteen) of Western Europe participated as members of the Council of Europe. Military discussions were excluded from the deliberations, which were concerned basically with economic, political, and social areas for coöperative action. The Council encouraged the development of new and specialized fields for coöperation.

The Colombo Plan. Established in 1950 under Great Britain's leadership, the Colombo Plan included among its members Great Britain, Canada, Australia, New Zealand, and eventually all the free nations of southeast Asia. The members comprised donor nations and receiver nations. The donor nations pledged themselves to give $2.5 billion over a six-year period and to help raise another $2.5 billion through bank loans and contributions, the money being used to develop resources and food production and to provide a constructive program for the economic rehabilitation of southeast Asia.

European Coal and Steel Community (1953). Efforts toward recovery and integration of the free countries of Western Europe were made in the form of agreements for the production, expansion, and coördination of coal and steel resources. A fifty-year treaty signed by France, Italy, West Germany, Belgium, the Netherlands, and Luxembourg provided for a nine-member board wtih considerable power to adjust production, change tariffs, and establish regulations. The idea for the Coal and Steel Community originated with Jean Monnet, but it has been called the Schuman Plan after Robert Schuman, foreign minister of France, who was responsible for putting forward the proposal for the Community.

European Economic Community (Common Market).
The European Economic Community (Inner Six), an extension
of the European Coal and Steel Community, is an organization
which aims to increase industrial and agricultural production,
eliminate tariff barriers, facilitate the free flow of goods among its
members, and decrease political tensions. Established by the Treaty
of Rome (1957), it hopes to eliminate tariffs among its members
by 1967. The original signatories to EEC were France, Belgium,
West Germany, Italy, the Netherlands, and Luxembourg. Common Market coöperation has contributed to significant increases in
production and to the highest level of prosperity known to the
member states.

Actually, the Common Market represents a third vital economic competitor for the world's markets—in addition to the
United States and the Soviet Union. Although a strong Common
Market is bound to affect adversely certain aspects of the American
economy, yet the policy of the United States is to support and
encourage EEC in the belief that a Europe, economically strong,
is the best deterrent to the Communist bloc. As the Common
Market is expanded to include more and more states, it will be
able to pool a population, resources, and manufacturing potential
that will approach, and in some instances surpass, that possessed
by the great powers today. Economic coöperation and integration
in Western Europe may become significant insofar as it carries
with it the framework for possible political unification.

European Free Trade Association (EFTA). As coöperation among the countries of Europe for military purposes through
NATO increased, it became apparent that political expediency
would dictate the creation of more than one economic bloc. Under
British leadership, the EFTA (Outer Seven) was established
(1960) by Great Britain, Norway, Sweden, Denmark, Austria,
Switzerland, and Portugal. Lacking some of the fundamental
drives (for joint economic action) of the European Common
Market, the Association proved much less effective and for that
reason several members, including Britain, sought affiliation with
the Common Market. However, France's veto (January, 1963)
of Britain's request for entry into the Common Market revived
the EFTA, which reaffirmed its aims and went forward with plans
to reduce tariffs among its members at a rate faster than that of
the EEC.

TWO WORLDS

Although the United Nations had been established for the express purpose of joining all nations into an effective organization for peace and security, including economic stability, it has not fulfilled the aspiration for one world under strong UN leadership. The outstanding fact about the world since 1945 was its division into two hostile camps, each dominated by a major power. Some nations remained neutral, but most of them, willingly or unwillingly, were ranged on the side of the Western Powers or on that of the Communist bloc. Tension between East and West grew steadily in a cold war, as repeated crises brought the world to the brink of yet another hot war. Through a large number of alliances, pacts, and organizations that affected the economic, social, and political policies of the various countries, the forces in support of competing ideologies which divided civilization into two worlds were molded; and these forces were aimed at influencing the course of action of a third bloc—the uncommitted nations.

It is clear that, although man developed weapons with fantastic ability to destroy and confidently plans to place a man on the moon within the next decade, he is, nevertheless, unable to find the key to living at peace with his fellow man on earth.

Chronology of
Significant Dates (1450-1963)*

1450-1559

1450-1455	First printing with movable type (Gutenberg at Mainz).
1453	Capture of Constantinople by Ottoman Turks.
1455-1485	Wars of the Roses (England).
1492	Conquest of Moors completed (Granada, Spain).
1492	Discovery of New World (Christopher Columbus).
1497-1498	Discovery of all-water route to India (Vasco da Gama).
1504	Spanish conquest of Naples.
1508	League of Cambrai (coalition against Venice).
1513	Discovery of Pacific Ocean (Nuñez de Balboa).
1517	Martin Luther denounced abuse of indulgences (95 Theses).
1518-1531	Huldreich Zwingli preached reform doctrines at Geneva.
1519	Disputation at Leipzig (Luther vs. Johann von Eck).
1519-1522	Circumnavigation of globe (Ferdinand Magellan).
1521	Luther excommunicated. Diet of Worms.
1524-1525	Peasants' Revolt crushed in Germany.
1526	Hungarians crushed at Mohacs by Turks.
1527	Sack of Rome by Imperial troops.
1529	Term "Protestants" first used (Diet of Speier).
1529	Peace of Cambrai (Charles V and Francis I).
1530	Definitive Lutheran doctrine set forth (Confession of Augsburg).
1533-1556	Thomas Cranmer Archbishop of Canterbury.
1534	Act of Supremacy made Henry VIII head of English Church.
1534	Order of Jesuits founded (Ignatius Loyola).
1535	*Institutes of the Christian Religion* (John Calvin).
1536-1564	Calvin at Geneva.
1543	*Revolutions of the Celestial Bodies* (Nicolaus Copernicus).
1545-1563	Council of Trent (Catholic Reformation).
1553-1558	Catholic reaction in England under Mary I.
1555	Religious peace of Augsburg. *"Cuius regio, eius religio."*
1555	Abdication of Charles V.
1559	Peace of Cateau-Cambrésis ending half a century of intermittent warfare between France and the Empire.

1559-1598

1559-1572	John Knox preached Calvinism in Scotland.
1566	"League of Beggars" in Netherlands.
1571	Turks defeated at Lepanto (Don John of Austria).
1572	Massacre of St. Bartholomew's Day (Catherine de' Medici; Admiral de Coligny; Huguenots).
1576	Pacification of Ghent.
1579	Union of Utrecht.
1582	Gregorian Calendar.

* Refer to page 323 for dates for Chief European Rulers.

1587   Execution of Mary, Queen of Scots, in England.
1588   Defeat of Spanish Armada by English.
1589   Henry of Navarre (Bourbon) became Henry IV of France.
1598   Edict of Nantes. End of French religious wars.

1598-1648

1600-1610   Financial reforms of Sully.
1600   English East India Company chartered.
1614   Last meeting of Estates General in France previous to Revolution (Marie de' Medici).
1618-1648   Thirty Years' War.
1620   Sailing of *Mayflower*.
1624-1642   Ascendancy of Cardinal Richelieu in France.
1625   Huguenot insurrection in France.
1628   Petition of Right accepted by Charles I of England.
1629   Peace of Lübeck. Edict of Restitution (return of confiscated lands to Catholic Church).
1632   Battle of Lützen. Victory and death of Gustavus Adolphus.
1636   John Hampden refused payment of ship money in England.
1640-1660   Long Parliament in England.
1642-1646   Civil war in England. "Great Rebellion."
1643-1661   Cardinal Mazarin in power in France.
1648   Peace of Westphalia. General settlement of European affairs after Thirty Years' War.

1648-1715

1648-1653   Disturbances of Fronde in France.
1649   Trial and execution of Charles I of England.
1653-1658   Unopposed rule of Oliver Cromwell.
1659   Peace of the Pyrenees (France, Spain). Marriage of Louis XIV with Spanish Infanta. Renunciation of French claims on Spanish crown.
1660   Restoration of monarchy in England (Charles II).
1667-1668   War of Devolution (Louis XIV).
1672-1678   Dutch War (Louis XIV).
1679   Habeas Corpus Act (England).
1685   Revocation of Edict of Nantes. Persecution and emigration of Huguenots.
1686   League of Augsburg formed against Louis XIV.
1687   *Principia* (Isaac Newton).
1688   "Glorious Revolution" in England.
1689   Declaration of Right (Bill of Rights) in England.
1689-1697   War of the League of Augsburg (or Palatinate) (Louis XIV).
1697   Peace of Ryswick.
1700   Death of Charles II of Spain precipitated struggle over partition of Spanish dominions.
1700-1721   Great Northern War (Charles XII, Peter I and allies).
1701   Frederick of Brandenburg assumed title of King of Prussia.
1702-1713   War of Spanish Succession (Grand Alliance, Louis XIV).
1704   Battle of Blenheim (Marlborough and Prince Eugene defeated French).
1707   Act of Union (England, Scotland).
1709   Battle of Poltava (Peter I defeated Charles XII).
1713   Peace of Utrecht-Rastadt. General settlement of War of Spanish Succession.
1715   Death of Louis XIV.

1715-1789

1720	Speculative fever. Mississippi scheme of John Law in France, South Sea Bubble in England.
1748	*Spirit of the Laws* (Montesquieu).
1752	Publication of *Encyclopedia* begun (Diderot).
1756	"Black Hole of Calcutta."
1756-1763	Seven Years' War (England against France, Prussia against Austria, France, and Russia).
1757	Battle of Plassey. Robert Clive master of Bengal.
1757-1761	Ascendancy of William Pitt in England.
1759	Capture of Quebec (Wolfe defeated Montcalm)
1760	End of French power in India.
1761	*The Social Contract* (J. J. Rousseau).
1762	Death of Elizabeth of Russia turned scale of war on continent in favor of Frederick the Great.
1762-1796	Catherine II, the Great, of Russia.
1763	Peace of Paris. Settlement of Seven Years' War.
1765	Stamp Act aroused antagonism in British colonies.
1768	Annexation of Corsica to France.
1768-1774	Russo-Turkish War. Russia obtained footing on Black Sea.
1772	First partition of Poland.
1774-1776	Attempted reforms of Turgot.
1776	American Declaration of Independence.
1776	*Wealth of Nations* (Adam Smith).
1777	Defeat of Burgoyne by Americans at Saratoga.
1778	France joined American colonists against England.
1780	Russia, Denmark, Sweden in Armed Neutrality in English-French war.
1781	Capitulation of Yorktown.
1781	*Compte Rendu* (Jacques Necker).
1783	Peace of Paris. American independence recognized.
1783-1787	Calonne, Minister of Finance in France. Increasing financial difficulties.
1787	French Assembly of Notables refused to accept taxation reform.
1788	Opposition of French parlements. Summoning of Estates General.
1789	Beginning of French Revolution.

1789-1815

1789	Estates General met at Versailles (May 5).
1789	Third Estate formed National Assembly (Mirabeau, Sieyes) (June 20-27).
1789	Revolt of Paris. Storming of Bastille (Camille Desmoulins) (July 12-14).
1789	Abolition of feudal privileges (July-August).
1791	Constitution of 1791. Limited monarchy.
1791	Declaration of Pillnitz (Frederick William II, Leopold III) (August).
1792	Invasion of France stopped at Valmy (Dumouriez, Kellerman), (September 20).
1792-1797	War between France and the First Coalition (April).
1792	National Convention abolished monarchy (September 21).
1792-1793	Trial and execution of Louis XVI.
1793	War declared against Great Britain, Holland, Spain.
1793-1794	Dictatorship of Committee of Public Safety (Danton, Robespierre, St. Just, Couthon).

1793	Second partition of Poland.
1793-1794	Reign of Terror.
1794	Polish revolt crushed (Kosciuszko).
1795	Constitution of the Year III (France).
1795	Beginning of government of Directory (1795-1799).
1795	Final partition of Poland and end of Polish independence.
1796-1797	Bonaparte invaded Italy. Defeat of Austrians.
1797	Reorganization in Italy. Treaty of Campo-Formio.
1798	Establishment of Roman and Helvetic Republics.
1798	Bonaparte's expedition to Egypt. Battle of the Nile (French fleet destroyed by Nelson).
1799-1801	Second Coalition against France.
1799	French defeats on Rhine, in Switzerland, and in Italy.
1799	Coup d'état of 18th Brumaire (Nov. 9). Directory overthrown. Constitution of Year VIII. Bonaparte First Consul.
1799-1804	Consulate in France. Bonaparte practically dictator.
1800	Bonaparte's second Italian campaign (Marengo).
1801	Peace of Lunéville. French frontier extended to Rhine.
1801	Concordat (Pius VII and France).
1802	Peace of Amiens (Great Britain and France).
1803	Renewal of war between Great Britain and France.
1804	Publication of Code Napoleon.
1804	Napoleon proclaimed Emperor of the French.
1805	Third Coalition against France (Great Britain, Russia, Austria, Sweden).
1805	Surrender of Austrian army at Ulm.
1805	Battle of Trafalgar. Nelson destroyed French sea-power.
1805	Battle of Austerlitz. Austria and Russia defeated by Napoleon.
1805	Peace of Pressburg. Napoleon master of Italy.
1806	Confederation of the Rhine set up by Napoleon. Formal end of the Holy Roman Empire.
1806	War declared by Prussia against Napoleon. Battles of Jena and Auerstadt. Humiliation of Prussia.
1806	Berlin Decrees. Beginning of Continental System.
1807	Battle of Friedland. Collapse of resistance to Napoleon by Prussia and Russia.
1807	Peace of Tilsit.
1808-1814	Peninsular War (Spain and Great Britain against Napoleon).
1809	Austrians defeated at Wagram. Peace of Vienna (or Schönbrunn).
1810	Annexation of Holland to France.
1812	Napoleon's invasion of Russia and disastrous retreat from Moscow.
1813	Battle of Leipzig. Napoleon defeated. Allies began invasion of France.
1814	Capture of Paris by Allies. Napoleon abdicated.
1814	Restoration of Bourbons (Louis XVIII).
1814	Congress of Vienna opened (September).
1815	Return of Napoleon from Elba.
1815	The Hundred Days. Napoleon defeated at Waterloo; exiled to St. Helena.
1815	General reorganization of Europe by Congress of Vienna.

1815-1849

1815	Quadruple Alliance to enforce treaty. Holy Alliance (Alexander I of Russia).
1817	Underground liberal movement in Germany. Wartburg Festival.

1818	Congress of Aix-la-Chapelle. Withdrawal of army of occupation from France.
1819	Carlsbad Decrees suppressing liberalism. Reaction in England. "Six Acts."
1820	Liberal uprising in Spain.
1820	Congress of Troppau.
1820	Cato Street Conspiracy in England.
1821	Congress of Laibach.
1821	Liberal uprising in Italy crushed.
1821-1829	Greek War of Independence.
1822	Congress of Verona.
1823	French intervention in Spain to crush liberal revolt.
1823	Monroe Doctrine.
1827	Turkish fleet destroyed by English, French, and Russians at Navarino Bay.
1828-1829	Russo-Turkish War.
1829	Treaty of Adrianople. Greek independence.
1830	July Revolution at Paris. Louis Philippe, King of the French. Charles X deposed.
1830-1832	Revolt in Poland suppressed.
1830-1833	Belgian revolt against Dutch successful.
1832	Reform Bill in England.
1834	German customs union (*Zollverein*).
1838-1848	Chartist agitation in England.
1839-1842	Opium War (Great Britain, China).
1840	Penny post established in England.
1840-1848	Ministry of Guizot in France. Growing discontent.
1845-1846	Famine in Ireland.
1846	Repeal of Corn Laws in England.
1848	*Communist Manifesto* (Karl Marx, Friedrich Engels).
1848	February Revolution in Paris. Second French Republic Revolutionary movements in Milan, Vienna, Berlin.
1848	Metternich resigned.
1848-1849	Austro-Sardinian War (Charles Albert).

1849-1914

1851	Coup d'état of Louis Napoleon.
1854-1856	Crimean War (Great Britain, France, Turkey against Russia).
1856	Treaty of Paris.
1857	Sepoy Rebellion in India.
1858	Plombières Agreement (Cavour, Napoleon III).
1859	War of France and Sardinia against Austria. Battles of Magenta and Solferino. Withdrawal of Napoleon III (Truce of Villafranca).
1859	*Origin of Species* (Charles Darwin).
1860	Tuscany, Parma, and Modena join Sardinia.
1860	Expedition of Garibaldi to Sicily.
1861	Victor Emmanuel II king of Italy. All Italian peninsula except Venice and Rome united.
1861	Emancipation of serfs in Russia.
1861-1867	French intervention in Mexico.
1861-1890	Prince Bismarck leader in Prussia and German Empire.
1864	Austro-German seizure of Schleswig-Holstein.
1866	Seven Weeks' War (Prussia, Austria). Battle of Sadowa (Königgratz). Italy annexed Venetia.

1867	Second Reform Bill in England (urban workingmen enfranchised).
1867	Federal union of Dominion of Canada.
1867	Ausgleich (Austria-Hungary).
1867	First volume *Das Kapital* (Karl Marx).
1870	Doctrine of Papal Infallibility.
1870-1871	Franco-German War. Battle of Sedan. Abdication of Napoleon III. Third French Republic.
1870-1871	Annexation of Rome to Kingdom of Italy.
1871	United German Empire.
1871	Treaty of Frankfurt.
1871	Uprising of Paris Commune crushed.
1872	Ballot Act in England.
1873	May Laws against Catholics in Germany.
1873-1875	Civil disorder in Spain.
1875	Great Britain acquired control of Suez Canal.
1875	Constitutional Laws of Third French Republic.
1876	Revolts in Balkans against Turks. Bulgarian massacres.
1877-1878	Russo-Turkish War.
1878	Congress of Berlin. Settlement of Eastern affairs. Austrian administration of Bosnia-Herzegovina.
1879-1887	Jules Grévy, President of French Republic. End of serious monarchist effort.
1881	Alexander II of Russia assassinated (Nihilists, Terrorists).
1883	Triple Alliance formed (Germany, Austria, Italy).
1886	First Home Rule Bill defeated (Gladstone).
1887-1889	Boulangist agitation in France.
1890	Resignation of Bismarck.
1891	Anti-Semitic pogroms (Russia).
1891	Encyclical *Rerum Novarum* (Leo XIII).
1891-1902	Trans-Siberian Railway.
1892	Dual Alliance (France, Russia). Strengthened 1894.
1894-1899	Dreyfus Case.
1894-1896	Armenian massacres.
1895	Jameson Raid (South Africa).
1896-1899	Cretan revolt. Turco-Greek War.
1898	Large scale naval program in Germany.
1898	Fashoda Incident (France, Great Britain).
1898	Spanish-American War.
1899	First Hague Conference.
1899-1902	South African (Boer) War.
1904-1905	Russo-Japanese War.
1904	Rupture between French government and Vatican.
1904	Anglo-French Entente Cordiale.
1905	Revolution in Russia. Duma conceded.
1905	First Moroccan Crisis.
1905	Separation of Sweden and Norway.
1906	Conference of Algeciras (Moroccan question).
1907	Anglo-Russian agreement. Foundation of Triple Entente.
1907	Second Hague Conference.
1907	Encyclical *Pascendi* condemning modernism.
1908	Annexation of Bosnia-Herzegovina by Austria.
1911	Parliament Act in Great Britain.
1911	Agadir Incident.
1911-1912	Turco-Italian War.
1912	Failure of Haldane Mission (Naval reduction).
1912	Anglo-French Entente strengthened.
1913	Balkan Wars. Military preparedness fever.

1914-1958

1914	Outbreak of World War. Battle of the Marne.
1915	Russian defeats in East. Failure of Dardenelles campaign.
1916	Struggle for Verdun. Somme offensive by British.
1916	Rumania enters war.
1917	United States enters war.
1918	Treaty of Brest-Litovsk. Final German effort in West.
1918	Armistice signed.
1919	German Republic.
1919	Peace of Paris. League of Nations.
1921-1922	Washington Conference. 5:5:3 naval ratio agreed upon.
1922	Fascist coup places Mussolini in power in Italy.
1923	French occupation of Ruhr. German financial collapse.
1923	Corfu Incident.
1924	Dawes Reparations Plan.
1924	Death of Lenin precipitates struggle for power in Soviet Union.
1925	Locarno Treaties.
1926	Admission of Germany to League of Nations.
1928	Five Year Plan begun in Soviet Union.
1929	Lateran Treaty solves "Roman Question."
1929	Young Plan for settlement of reparations.
1929	Collapse of stock prices, beginning of world depression.
1930	Evacuation of Rhineland.
1931	Republic in Spain.
1932	Conference of Lausanne.
1933	Nazi dictatorship in Germany (Adolf Hitler).
1934	"Blood Purge" in Germany.
1934	Attempted Nazi coup in Austria. Assassination of Premier **Dollfuss**.
1935-1936	Italo-Ethiopian War. Sanctions voted by League of Nations.
1936	Remilitarization of Rhineland.
1936	Outbreak of Spanish Civil War (Francisco Franco).
1937	Japan begins conquest of China.
1938	Germany annexes Austria.
1938	Czechoslovakian Crisis., Conference of Munich.
1939	German Russian Mutual Assistance Pact.
1939	Britain and France declared war on Germany.
1939-1940	Russo-Finnish War.
1940	German conquest of Denmark, Norway, Luxembourg, Holland, and Belgium.
1940	Italy declared war on France and Great Britain.
1940	Fall of France.
1941	German invasion of Russia.
1941	Japanese raid on Pearl Harbor.
1941	United States declared war on Japan, Germany, and Italy.
1945	Surrender of Germany.
1945	First atomic bomb used. Surrender of Japan.
1946	United Nations convenes. UN Disarmament Resolution.
1948	Communists seized control of Czechoslovakia.
1949	North Atlantic Pact.
1950	Korean Crisis.
1955	German sovereignty.
1956-1957	Suez Canal Crisis.
1958	European Common Market.
1961	Russia's Gagarin first man in space.
1961	Berlin Wall.
1962	Algerian independence.
1963	France vetoes Britain's application for membership in the Common Market.

Chief European Rulers
Since 1500

Albania
1478-1913,	Part of Turkey
1913-1914,	William of Wied, prince
1918-1927,	Republic
1928-1939,	Zog I
1939-1943,	Part of Italy
1943-1945,	Provisional Government
1945- ,	Republic

Premier:
1945-1954,	Enver Hoxha
1954- ,	Mehmet Shehu

Austria
1493-1519,	Maximilian I
1519-1520,	Charles I (V as Holy Roman Emperor)
1520-1564,	Ferdinand I
1564-1576,	Maximilian II
1576-1612,	Rudolph V (II as Holy Roman Emperor)
1612-1619,	Matthias
1619-1637,	Ferdinand II
1637-1657,	Ferdinand III
1658-1705,	Leopold I
1705-1711,	Joseph I
1711-1740,	Charles II (VI as Holy Roman Emperor, III of Hungary)
1740-1780,	Maria Theresa
1780-1790,	Joseph II
1790-1792,	Leopold II
1792-1835,	Francis I (II as Holy Roman Emperor)
1835-1848,	Ferdinand I (IV of Hungary)
1848-1916,	Francis Joseph
1916-1918,	Charles I (IV of Hungary)
1918-1938,	Republic
1938-1945,	Annexed to Germany
1945- ,	Republic

President:
1945-1950,	Dr. Karl Renner
1951-1957,	Theodore Koernor
1957- ,	Adolf Schaerf

Belgium
1516-1713,	Part of Spanish Monarchy
1713-1797,	Part of Austrian Monarchy
1797-1815,	Part of France
1815-1830,	Part of Netherlands (Holland)
1831-1865,	Leopold I
1865-1909,	Leopold II
1909-1934,	Albert
1934-1944,	Leopold III
1944-1950,	Prince Charles (Regent)
1951- ,	Baudouin I

Bulgaria
1393-1878,	Part of Turkey
1879-1886,	Alexander, prince
1887-1908,	Ferdinand I, prince
1908-1918,	Ferdinand I, king
1918-1943,	Boris III
1943-1946,	Regency
1946- ,	Republic

Courland
See Latvia

Croatia
1102-1918,	Part of Hungary
1918- ,	Part of Yugoslavia

Czechoslovakia
1471-1516,	Ladislaus II
1516-1526,	Louis
1918	Part of Austria - Hungary
1918-1939,	Republic
1939-1945,	Annexed to Germany
1945- ,	Republic

Presidents
1920-1936,	Thomas Masaryk
1936-1948,	Dr. Emil Benes
1948-1952,	Klement Gottwald
1952-1957,	Antonin Zapotocky
1957- ,	Antonin Novotny

Denmark
1481-1513,	John
1513-1523,	Christian II
1523-1533,	Frederick I
1533-1559,	Christian III
1559-1588,	Frederick II
1588-1648,	Christian IV

1648-1670,	Frederick III
1670-1699,	Christian V
1699-1730,	Frederick IV
1730-1746,	Christian VI
1746-1766,	Frederick V
1766-1808,	Christian VII
1808-1839,	Frederick VI
1839-1848,	Christian VIII
1848-1863,	Frederick VII
1863-1906,	Christian IX
1906-1912,	Frederick VIII
1912-1947,	Christian X
1947- ,	Frederick IX

Estonia

1346-1561,	Part of Estates of Teutonic Knights
1561-1721,	Part of Swedish Monarchy
1721-1917,	Part of Russian Empire
1918-1940,	Republic
1940- ,	Republic of U.S.S.R.

Finland

1290-1809,	Part of Swedish Monarchy
1809-1917,	Part of Russian Empire
1919- ,	Republic

France

1461-1483,	Louis XI
1483-1498,	Charles VIII
1498-1515,	Louis XII
1515-1547,	Francis I
1547-1559,	Henry II
1559-1560,	Francis II
1560-1574,	Charles IX
1574-1589,	Henry III
1589-1610,	Henry IV
1610-1643,	Louis XIII
1643-1715,	Louis XIV
1715-1774,	Louis XV
1774-1792,	Louis XVI
1792-1804,	First Republic
1804-1814,	Napoleon I, emperor
1814-1824,	Louis XVIII
1824-1830,	Charles X
1830-1848,	Louis Philippe
1848-1852,	Second Republic
1852-1870,	Napoleon III, emperor
1870-1940,	Third Republic
1940-1945,	Vichy Government
1945-1958,	Fourth Republic
1958- ,	Fifth Republic

Presidents:

1871-1873,	Adolph Thiers
1873-1879,	Marshall MacMahon
1879-1887,	Jules Grévy
1887-1894,	F. Sadi Carnot
1894-1895,	Casimir-Périer
1895-1899,	Félix Faure
1899-1906,	Émile Loubet
1906-1913,	Armand Fallières
1913-1920,	Raymond Poincaré
1920-1921,	Paul Deschanel
1921-1924,	Alexandre Millerand
1924-1931,	Gaston Doumergue
1931-1932,	Paul Doumer
1932-1940,	Albert Lebrun

Vichy Dictators:

1940-1942,	Marshal Pétain
1942-1945,	Pierre Laval (Dictator)

Presidents:

1945	Charles de Gaulle
1946	Felix Gouin
1946-1947,	George Bidault
1947-1954,	Vincent Auriol
1954-1958,	René Coty
1958- ,	Charles de Gaulle

Germany

Up to 1806,	Part of Holy Roman Empire
1815-1866,	Part of Germanic Confederation
1871-1888,	William I
1888	Frederick III
1888-1918,	William II
1918-1934,	Weimar Republic
1934-1945,	Nazi Dictatorship

Presidents, Weimar Republic:

1919-1925,	Friedrich Ebert
1925-1934,	Paul von Hindenburg

Fuehrer:

1934-1945,	Adolf Hitler

Federal Republic of Germany

Presidents:

1949-1959,	Theodore Heuss
1959- ,	Heinrich Luebke

Chancellors:

1949-1963,	Konrad Adenauer
1963-1966,	Ludwig Erhard
1966- ,	Kurt Kiesinger

German Democratic Republic

President:

1949-1960,	Wilhelm Pieck

Chancellor:

1949-1960,	Otto Grotewohl

Dictator:

1960- ,	Walter Ulbricht

Great Britain
Sovereigns of England, 1485-1707
1485-1509, Henry VII
1509-1547, Henry VIII
1547-1553, Edward VI
1553-1558, Mary I
1558-1603, Elizabeth I
1603-1625, James I (VI of Scotland)
1625-1649, Charles I
1649-1660, Republic (Oliver Cromwell)
1660-1685, Charles II
1685-1688, James II (VII of Scotland)
1689-1694, William III and Mary II
1694-1702, William III
1702-1714, Anne (Queen of Great Britain after 1707)

Sovereigns of Great Britain, 1707-1801
1707-1714, Anne
1714-1727, George I
1727-1760, George II
1760-1820, George III, (King of Great Britain and Ireland after 1800)

Sovereigns of Scotland, 1488-1707
1488-1513, James IV
1513-1542, James V
1542-1567, Mary
1567-1625, James VI (I of England, 1603-1625)
1603-1707, Successions as in England

Sovereigns of the United Kingdom of Great Britain and Ireland 1801—
1801-1820, George III
1820-1830, George IV
1830-1837, William IV
1837-1901, Victoria
1901-1910, Edward VII
1910-1936, George V
1936, Edward VIII (abdicated)
1936-1952, George VI
1952- , Elizabeth II

Prime Ministers of Great Britain since 1868:
1868-1874, William E. Gladstone
1874-1880, Benjamin Disraeli
1880-1885, William E. Gladstone
1885-1886, Marquess of Salisbury
1886, William E. Gladstone
1886-1892, Marquess of Salisbury
1892-1894, William E. Gladstone
1894-1895, Earl of Roseberry
1895-1902, Marquess of Salisbury
1902-1905, Arthur J. Balfour
1906-1908, Sir Henry Campbell-Bannerman
1908-1916, Herbert H. Asquith
1916-1922, David Lloyd George
1922-1923, Andrew Bonar Law
1923, Stanley Baldwin
1924, J. Ramsey MacDonald
1924-1929, Stanley Baldwin
1929-1935, J. Ramsey MacDonald
1935-1937, Stanley Baldwin
1937-1940, Neville Chamberlain
1940-1945, Winston Churchill
1945-1951, Clement Attlee
1951-1955, Winston Churchill
1955-1957, Anthony Eden
1957-1963, Harold Macmillan
1963-1964, Alex. Douglas-Home
1964- , Harold Wilson

Greece
1453-1829, Part of Turkey
1829-1832, Republic
1832-1862, Otto I
1863-1913, George I
1913-1917, Constantine I
1917-1920, Alexander I
1920-1922, Constantine I (restored)
1922-1924, George II
1924-1935, Republic
1935-1941, George II (restored)
1941-1944, German Occupation
1944-1946, Archbishop Samaskino (Regent)
1946-1947, George II (restored for second time)
1947-1964, Paul
1964- , Constantine II

Holland
See Netherlands

Holy Roman Empire
1493-1519, Maximilian I
1519-1558, Charles V
1558-1564, Ferdinand I
1564-1576, Maximilian II
1576-1612, Rudolph II
1612-1619, Matthias
1619-1637, Ferdinand II
1637-1657, Ferdinand III
1658-1705, Leopold I

1705-1711,	Joseph I
1711-1740,	Charles VI
1742-1745,	Charles VII
1745-1765,	Francis I
1765-1790,	Joseph II
1790-1792,	Leopold II
1792-1806,	Francis II (after 1804 Francis I, Emperor of Austria)

Hungary

1490-1516,	Ladislaus II
1516-1526,	Louis II
1526-1918,	Part of Austrian Monarchy
1918-1920,	**Republic**
1920-1946,	Kingdom
1946- ,	Republic

Regent:

1920-1944,	Admiral Horthy

President:

1946-1948,	Zoldan Tildy
1948-1952,	Arpad Szakasits
1952- ,	Istvan Dobi

Ireland (Eire, 1937-1949)

1922-1937,	**Self-governing Dominion of British Empire**
1937- ,	**Republic**

Presidents:

1938-1945,	Douglas Hyde
1945-1959,	Sean T. O'Kelly
1959- ,	Eamon de Valera

Italy

Kings of Sardinia

1720-1730,	Victor Amadeus II
1730-1773,	Charles Emmanuel III
1773-1796,	Victor Amadeus III
1796-1802,	Charles Emmanuel IV
1802-1821,	Victor Emmanuel I
1821-1831,	Charles Felix
1831-1849,	Charles Albert
1849-1878,	Victor Emmanuel II (King of Italy after 1861)

Kings of Italy

1861-1878,	Victor Emmanuel II
1878-1900,	Humbert
1900-1946,	Victor Emmanuel III (abdicated)
1946- ,	Republic

Dictator:

1922-1943.	Benito Mussolini

Presidents.

1946-1948,	Enrico de Nicola
1948-1955,	Luigi Einaudi
1955-1962,	Giovanni Gronchi
1962- ,	Antonio Segni

Latvia

1237-1549,	Part of Estates of Teutonic Knights
1549-1629,	Part of Polish Monarchy
1629-1721,	Part of Swedish Monarchy
1721-1917,	Part of Russian Empire
1918-1940,	Republic
1940- ,	Constituent Republic of U.S.S.R.

Lithuania

1501-1793,	Independent Part of Polish Monarchy
1793-1917,	Part of Russian Empire
1918-1940,	Republic
1940- ,	Constituent Republic of U. S. S. R.

Montenegro

1696-1735,	Danilo, prince-bishop
1735-1782,	Sava and Vasilije
1782-1830,	Peter I
1830-1851,	Peter II
1851-1860,	Danilo I, prince
1860-1910,	Nicholas I, prince
1910-1918,	Nicholas I, king
1918- ,	Part of Yugoslavia

Netherlands

1516-1581,	Part of Spanish Monarchy
1581-1584,	William the Silent, stadholder
1584-1625,	Maurice
1625-1647,	Frederick Henry
1647-1650,	William II
1650-1672,	John De Witt, grand pensionary
1672-1702,	William III, stadholder (King of England and Scotland 1689-1702)
1711-1747,	William IV, nominal stadholder
1747-1751,	William IV, hereditary stadholder
1751-1795,	William V
1795-1806,	Republic
1806-1810,	Louis Bonaparte, king

1810-1813,	Part of France
1813-1840,	William I, king
1840-1849,	William II
1849-1890,	William III
1890-1948,	Wilhelmina
1948- ,	Juliana

Norway

1397-1814,	Part of Danish Monarchy
1814-1905,	Part of Swedish Monarchy
1905-1957,	Haakon VIII
1957- ,	Olav V

Poland

1492-1501,	John I Albert
1501-1506,	Alexander I
1506-1548,	Sigismund I
1548-1572,	Sigismund II
1573-1574,	Henry of Valois (Henry III of France)
1575-1586,	Stephen Báthory
1587-1632,	Sigismund III Vasa
1632-1648,	Ladislaus IV
1648-1668,	John II Casimir
1669-1673,	Michael Wisniowiecki
1674-1696,	John III Sobieski
1697-1704,	Augustus II
1704-1709,	Stanislaus Leszczynski
1709-1733,	Augustus II
1733-1734,	Stanislaus Leszczynski
1734-1763,	Augustus III
1764-1795,	Stanislaus II Poniatowski
1795-1918,	Partitioned among Russia, Prussia, and Austria
1918-1939,	Republic
1939-1945,	Partitioned by Germany and Russia
1945-1946,	Provisional Government
1947- ,	Republic

Popes, The

1492-1503,	Alexander VI
1503	Pius III
1503-1513,	Julius II
1513-1521,	Leo X
1522-1523,	Adrian VI
1523-1534,	Clement VII
1534-1549,	Paul III
1550-1555,	Julius III
1555	Marcellus II
1555-1559,	Paul IV
1559-1565,	Pius IV
1566-1572,	Pius V

1572-1585,	Gregory XIII
1585-1590,	Sixtus V
1590	Urban VII
1590-1591,	Gregory XIV
1591	Innocent IX
1592-1605,	Clement VIII
1605	Leo XI
1605-1621,	Paul V
1621-1623,	Gregory XV
1623-1644,	Urban VIII
1644-1655,	Innocent X
1655-1667,	Alexander VII
1667-1669,	Clement IX
1670-1676,	Clement X
1676-1689,	Innocent XI
1689-1691,	Alexander VIII
1691-1700,	Innocent XII
1700-1721,	Clement XI
1721-1724,	Innocent XIII
1724-1730,	Benedict XIII
1730-1740,	Clement XII
1740-1758,	Benedict XIV
1758-1769,	Clement XIII
1769-1774,	Clement XIV
1775-1799,	Pius VI
1800-1823,	Pius VII
1823-1829,	Leo XII
1829-1830,	Pius VIII
1831-1846,	Gregory XVI
1846-1878,	Pius IX
1878-1903,	Leo XIII
1903-1914,	Pius X
1914-1922,	Benedict XV
1922-1939,	Pius XI
1939-1958,	Pius XII
1958-1963,	John XXIII
1963- ,	Paul VI

Portugal

1495-1521,	Emmanuel (Manoel) I
1521-1557,	John III
1557-1578,	Sebastian
1578-1580,	Henry
1580-1640,	Part of Spanish Monarchy
1640-1656,	John IV
1656-1667,	Alfonso VI
1667-1706,	Pedro II
1706-1750,	John V
1750-1777,	Joseph
1777-1786,	Maria I and Pedro III
1786-1816,	Maria I
1816-1826,	John VI
1826	Pedro IV
1826-1828,	Maria II
1828-1834,	Miguel

1834-1853,   Maria II
1853-1861,   Pedro V
1861-1889,   Louis I
1889-1908,   Charles I
1908-1910,   Manoel II
1910-   ,   Republic

Prussia
Electors of Brandenburg
1499-1535,   Joachim I
1535-1571,   Joachim II
1571-1598,   John George
1598-1608,   Joachim Frederick
1608-1619,   John Sigismund
1619-1640,   George William
1640-1688,   Frederick William
1688-1701,   Frederick III (as Frederick I, King of Prussia, 1701-1713)

Kings of Prussia
1701-1713,   Frederick I
1713-1740,   Frederick William I
1740-1786,   Frederick II
1786-1797,   Frederick William II
1797-1840,   Frederick William III
1840-1861,   Frederick William IV
1861-1888,   William I (German Emperor, 1871-1888)
After 1871 part of German Empire

Rumania
1500-1856,   Part of Turkey
1861-1866,   Alexander John Cuza, prince
1866-1881,   Carol I, prince
1881-1914,   Carol I, king
1914-1927,   Ferdinand I
1927-1930,   Michael
1930-1940,   Carol II
1940-1947,   Michael (abdicated)
1948-   ,   Republic

Russia
1462-1505,   Ivan III
1505-1533,   Basil IV
1533-1584,   Ivan IV
1584-1598,   Theodore
1598-1605,   Boris Godunov
1613-1645,   Michael Romanov
1645-1676,   Alexius
1676-1682,   Theodore II
1682-1689,   Ivan V and Peter I
1689-1725,   Peter I
1725-1727,   Catherine I

1727-1730,   Peter II
1730-1740,   Anna
1740-1741,   Ivan VI
1741-1762,   Elizabeth
1762   ,   Peter III
1762-1796,   Catherine II
1796-1801,   Paul
1801-1825,   Alexander I
1825-1855,   Nicholas I
1855-1881,   Alexander II
1881-1894,   Alexander III
1894-1917,   Nicholas II
1917-1923,   Republic
1923-   ,   Union of Soviet Socialist Republics

Dictators (Communist):
1917-1924,   Nicholas Lenin
1924-1953,   Joseph V. Stalin
1953-1955,   Georgi Malenkov
1955-1958,   Nikolai A. Bulganin
1958-1964,   Nikita S. Khrushchev
1964-   ,   Aleksei Kosygin

Scotland
See Great Britain

Serbia
1459-1830,   Part of Turkey
1804-1813,   Karageorge, prince
1817-1839,   Milosh
1839   ,   Milan
1839-1842,   Michael
1842-1858,   Alexander
1858-1860,   Milosh
1860-1868,   Michael
1868-1882,   Milan, prince
1882-1889,   Milan, king
1889-1903,   Alexander
1903-1921,   Peter
1918-   ,   Part of Yugoslavia

Slavonia
See Croatia

Slovakia
See Czechoslovakia

Sloveniva (Carniola, etc.)
1300-1809,   Part of Austrian Monarchy
1809-1813,   Part of French Empire
1813-1918,   Part of Austrian Monarchy
1918-   ,   Part of Yugoslavia

Spain
1479-1504,   Ferdinand and Isabella
1504-1506,   Ferdinand and Philip I

1506-1516,	Ferdinand and Charles I
1516-1556,	Charles I (V of Holy Roman Empire)
1556-1598,	Philip II
1598-1621,	Philip III
1621-1665,	Philip IV
1665-1700,	Charles II
1700-1746,	Philip V
1746-1759,	Ferdinand VI
1759-1788,	Charles III
1788-1808,	Charles IV
1808-1813,	Joseph Bonaparte
1813-1833,	Ferdinand VII
1833-1868,	Isabella II
1870-1873,	Amadeo of Savoy
1873-1875,	Republic
1875-1885,	Alphonso XII
1886-1931,	Alphonso XIII
1931-1939,	Republic

Presidents.

1931-1936,	Niceto Zamora
1936-1939,	Manuel Azâna

Dictators:

1939-	Francisco Franco

Sweden

1397-1523,	Part of Danish Monarchy
1523-1560,	Gustavus I Vasa
1560-1568,	Eric XIV
1568-1592,	John III
1592-1604,	Sigismund
1604-1611,	Charles IX
1611-1632,	Gustavus II Adolphus
1632-1654,	Christina
1654-1660,	Charles X
1660-1697,	Charles XI
1697-1718,	Charles XII
1718-1720,	Ulrica Eleonora
1720-1751,	Frederick I
1751-1771,	Adolphus Frederick
1771-1792,	Gustavus III
1792-1809,	Gustavus IV
1809-1818,	Charles XIII
1818-1844,	Charles XIV
1844-1859,	Oscar I
1859-1872,	Charles XV
1872-1907,	Oscar II
1907-1950,	Gustavus V
1950-	Gustavus VI

Turkey

1451-1481,	Mohammed II
1481-1512,	Bayezid II
1512-1520,	Selim I
1520-1566,	Suleiman II
1566-1574,	Selim II
1574-1595,	Murad III
1595-1603,	Mohammed III
1603-1617,	Ahmed I
1617-1618,	Mustapha I
1618-1623,	Othman II
1623-1640,	Murad IV
1640-1648,	Ibrahim
1648-1687,	Mohammed IV
1687-1691,	Suleiman III
1691-1695,	Ahmed II
1695-1703,	Mustapha II
1703-1730,	Ahmed III
1730-1754,	Mahmud I
1754-1757,	Othman III
1757-1773,	Mustapha III
1773-1789,	Abdul Hamid I
1789-1807,	Selim III
1807-1808,	Mustapha IV
1808-1839,	Mahmud II
1839-1861,	Abdul Medjid
1861-1876,	Abdul Aziz
1876	Murad V
1876-1909,	Abdul Hamid II
1909-1918,	Mohammed V
1918-1922,	Mohammed VI
1923-	Republic

Presidents

1923-1938,	Kamal Ataturk
1938-1950,	General Ismet Inonu
1950-1960,	Celal Bayar
1960-	General Cemal Gursel

Union of Soviet Socialist Republics
See Russia

Yugoslavia (State of Serbs, Croats, and Slovenes)

1918-1921,	Peter I King of Serbia, 1903-1918)
1921-1934,	Alexander I
1934-1946,	Peter II (Regency Council)
1946-	Federated Republic

Dictator:

1946-	Marshall Tito (Joseph Broz)

Bibliography

Abbott, W. C., *Expansion of Europe* (1938)

Adams, G. B., *Constitutional History of England*, Rev. by Schuyler (1934)

Albrecht-Carrié, R., *A Diplomatic History of Europe Since the Congress of Vienna* (1958)

American Historical Association, *A Guide to Historical Literature* (1961)

Andersson, Ingvar, *A History of Sweden* (1956)

Artz, F. B., *Reaction and Revolution: 1815-1832* (1935)

Ashton, T. S., *The Industrial Revolution, 1760-1830* (1952)

Aydelette, W. O., *Bismarck and British Colonial Policy* (1937)

Baring, Maurice, *The Russian People* (1911)

Bassett, J. S., *The League of Nations* (1928)

Benns, F. L., *Europe Since 1914*, 8th ed. (1954)

Bernal, J. D., *Science in History* (1954)

Black, C. E., and Helmreich, E. C., *Twentieth Century Europe, A History* (1959)

Bowle, John, *Western Political Thought* (Barnes & Noble, 1961)

Brogan, D. W., *The French Nation from Napoleon to Pétain* (1957)

Bryce, James, *Modern Democracies,* 2 vols. (1921)

The New Cambridge Modern History (1958)

Carr, E. H., *A History of Soviet Russia,* 4 vols. (1950-1954)

Chapman, C. E., *History of Spain* (1918)

Churchill, W. S., *The Second World War,* 6 vols. (1948-1953)

Clough, S. B., *The Economic Development of Western Civilization* (1959)

——, and Cole, C. W., *Economic History of Europe,* 3rd ed. (1952)

Cole, G. D. H. (with Raymond Postgate), *The British Common People, 1746-1946* (1961)

Cruttwell, C. R. M. F., *History of the Great War, 1914-1918,* 2nd ed. (1936)

Curtis, Edmund, *History of Ireland,* 6th ed. (Barnes & Noble, 1950)

Dampier, W. C., *History of Science,* 4th ed. (1949)

Easton, Stewart C., *Brief History of the Western World* (Barnes & Noble, (1962)

Ergang, Robert, *Europe in Our Time,* 3rd ed. (1958)

Fay, S. B., *Origins of the World War* (1941)

Florinsky, M. I., *Russia: A History and Interpretation* (1953)

Gillespie, J. E., *Europe in Perspective, 1815 to the Present* (1948)

Grant, A. J., and Temperley, H. W. V., *Europe in the 19th and 20th Centuries,* 6th ed. (1952)

Halévy, Elie, *A History of the English People in the Nineteenth Century,* 6 vols. (Barnes & Noble)

Hasluck, E. L., *Foreign Affairs, 1919-1937* (1938)

Hayes, C. J. H., *A Political and Cultural History of Modern Europe,* Vol. II (1939)

Hobson, J. A., *Evolution of Modern Capitalism,* 4th ed. (1949)
Holborn, Hajo, *A History of Modern Germany* (1959)

Kirchner, Walther, *History of Russia,* 3rd ed. (Barnes & Noble, 1963)
———, *Western Civilization Since 1500* (Barnes & Noble, 1958)

Landman, J. Henry (with Herbert Wender), *World Since 1914,* 10th ed.
  rev. (Barnes & Noble, 1961)
Langsam, W. C., *The World Since 1914,* 7th ed. (1954)
Larsen, Karen, *A History of Norway* (1958)
Laski, A. J., *The Communist Manifesto, A Socialist Landmark* (1948)
Lenard, Phillip, *Great Men of Science* (1933)
Littlefield, Henry W., *History of Europe, 1500-1848,* 5th ed. repr. (Barnes &
  Noble, 1963)
Lukacs, J. A., *The Great Powers and Eastern Europe* (1954)
Lunt, W. E., *History of England,* 4th ed. (1957)

Mantoux, Paul, *Industrial Revolution in the Eighteenth Century* (1937)
Marriott, J. A. R., *England Since Waterloo,* 15th ed. (Barnes & Noble, 1954)
———, *A History of Europe: 1815-1939,* 5th ed. (Barnes & Noble, 1948)
———, *Modern England: 1815-1939,* 5th ed. (Barnes & Noble, 1948)
———, *A Short History of France* (1944)
Marx, Karl (with Friedrich Engels and Nicolas Lenin), *The Essential Left*
  (Barnes & Noble, 1961)
Mason, S. F., *Main Currents of Scientific Thought* (1953)

Ogg, F. A., and Zink, Harold, *Modern Foreign Governments* (1953)

Pares, Bernard, *History of Russia,* 5th ed. (1953)
Pickles, Dorothy, *France: The Fourth Republic,* 2nd ed. (1958)

Seignobos, Charles, *Evolution of the French People* (1949)
Shepherd, W. R., *Historical Atlas,* 8th ed. (Barnes & Noble, 1959)
Slosson, P., *Europe Since 1815* (1954)
Sontag, R. J., *European Diplomatic History, 1871-1932* (1933)
Swain, J. W., *Harper History of Civilization,* Vol. II (1958)

Toynbee, A. J., *A Study of History,* 2 vols. (1947-1957)
Trevelyan, G. M., *British History in the Nineteenth Century and After,* 2nd
  ed. (1937)
———, *History of England,* 3rd ed. (1945)
Trevelyan, J. P., *A Short History of the Italian People,* 4th ed. (1956)

Valentin, Veit, *The German People* (1946)
Von Rauch, George, *A History of Soviet Russia* (1957)

Wagner, D. O., ed. *Social Reformers* (1934)
Webb, Sidney, and Beatrice, *The History of Trade Unionism* (1920)
Wolff, R. L., *The Balkans in Our Time* (1956)

Index

Abd-el-Kader, 126
Abdul Hamid II, 128
Abyssinia, 148; see also Ethiopia
Adenauer, Konrad, 279, 306
Adowa, battle of, 112
Adrianople, Treaty of, 23
"Adullamites," 78
Aehrenthal, Alois von, 169
Africa, partition of, 144-149; World War II, 256-257, 265-266; (1945 ff.), 286-289
Afro-Asian Conference (1955), 287
Agadir Incident, 146, 169-170
Aix-la-Chapelle, Congress of, 16
Albania, invaded by Italy, 245; (1945 ff.), 278
Alexander I, Russia, 15, 16, 21
Alexander II, Russia, 115, 116
Alexander III, Russia, 116, 118
Alexander I, Serbia and Yugoslavia, 127, 220
Algeciras, Conference of, 146, 168
Algeria, 126, 288; see also Africa
Allenby, General, 182
Alliance system, 159-173
Alphonso XII, Spain, 108
Alphonso XIII, Spain, 108-109, 218
Alsace-Lorraine, 56, 166
Amadeo of Savoy, 107-108
Anarchism, 71-72, 164-165
Anglo-Iranian Oil Company, 289
Angoulême, Duke of, 17, 18
Arab League, 289, 291
Arif, General A., 290
Arkwright, Richard, 4
Armistice, 183
Arriaga, Manoel, 110
Article 26 (of the UN Charter), 285
Ashley, Lord, 28
Asquith, Herbert, 79, 82
Aswan dam, 287
Ataturk; see Kemal Pasha
Athenia, 253
Atlantic Charter, 258, 260, 272
Atomic bomb, 270, 284, 295
Atomic Energy Commission, 284, 285
Atomic energy control, 284-285
Atoms for Peace Organization, 285
Attlee, Clement R., 272, 304
Auchinleck, C. J. E., 265
Auriol, Vincent, 291
Ausgleich, 52, 131
Australasia, 151
Australia, World War II, 263, 264
Austria, postwar, 193; seized by Hitler, 239; (1945 ff.), 278-279, 308
Austria-Hungary, 131-132, 167, 186; postwar breakup, 184-185; revolution of 1848, 35-37
Austro-Sardinia War (1859), 43
Azaña, M., 219

Badoglio, Pietro, 266
Baudouin I, Belgium, 308
Baghdad Pact, 303
Bakewell, Robert, 4
Bakunin, Mikhail, 71, 116
Baldwin, Stanley, 213
Balkan revolts, 123-125
Balkan Wars, 128-130, 170, 255
Ballot Act, 78
Bank of International Settlement, 221
Banting, Frederick, 296
Barth, Karl, 297
Bartók, Béla, 300
Baruch Plan, 284
Beckmann, Max, 299

Belgian Congo, 145
Belgium, 110-111; independence of, 24; neutrality of, 29, 172-173; World War II, 250, 271
Bell, Alexander Graham, 5
Beneš, Eduard, 185, 219, 311
Benelux countries, 307-308
Bentham, Jeremy, 21
Berchtold, Count, 171
Berlin (1945 ff.), 311
Berlin, Conference of, (1884-1885), 146
Berlin, Congress of, 124
Berlin-to-Baghdad Railway, 130
Bessarabia, 127, 278
Bethmann-Hollweg, Chancellor, 105-106, 171, 173, 186
Bismarck, 253
Bismarck, Otto von, 48-57, 98, 99, 100-104, 159, 165, 239
Blanc, Louis, 12, 32, 68
Blitzkrieg, 251-252
Blocs in French Chamber, 89
Blum, Leon, 218
Boer War, 76, 151, 160-161
Boers, 145, 151
Bohemian revolt (1848), 35-36
Bolsheviki, 207-211
Bonnet, Georges, 240
Boris III, Bulgaria, 184, 220
Bosnia-Herzegovina, 124, 169
Botha, Louis, 151
Boulanger Episode, 94
Bourgeoisie, 9-10, 14-15, 18, 25, 30, 88, 139; and Communism, 231, 232-233; and Socialism, 61, 70, 99
Boxer Rebellion, 139
Brandenburg, Count, 35
Brecht, Bertolt, 300
Brest-Litovsk, Treaty of, 182, 207
Brezhnev, L., 310
Briand, Aristide, 95, 217
Bright, John, 9, 75
British East India Company; see East India Company
British Empire, 150-155, 213-216, 292
British-Italian Pact (1938), 245
British North American Act, 150
Bucharest, Treaty of (1913), 129
Bukharin, N., 210
Bukovina, 278
Bulganin, Nikolai, 309
Bulgaria, 128, 184, 221, 268, 277, 278
Bülow, Prince von, 105, 161
Bundesrat, 99
Burke, Edmund, 235
Burke-Wadsworth Act, 259
Burma, 291, 292
Burschenschaft, 22
Byron, Lord, 21, 23

Caillaux, Joseph, 170
Cairo Conference, 273, 284
Cambodia, 291
Cambon, Paul, 161, 162
Campbell-Bannerman, Henry, 82
Camus, Albert, 300
Canada, Dominion of, 150-151
Canning, 19, 22-23
Cánovas del Castillo, 108
Cape-to-Cairo Railway, 161
Caprivi, Count, 104-105, 159
Carbonari, 22
Carlos I, Portugal, 109
Carlsbad Decrees, 22
Carlyle, Thomas, 28
Carnegie, Andrew, 156
Carol II, Rumania, 220

332